W9-AXK-686

# THIS
# PLACE
# ON
# EARTH

FROM THE LIBRARY OF
•Emily R. Squires•
FROM THE LIBRARY OF

FROM THE LIBRARY OF

Emily K. Squires

# THIS

HOME

# PLACE

AND THE

# ON

PRACTICE OF

# EARTH

PERMANENCE

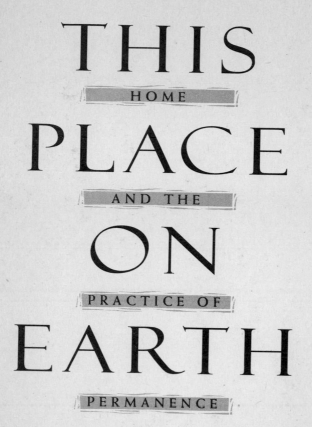

ALAN THEIN DURNING

## SASQUATCH BOOKS
### SEATTLE

Copyright ©1996 by Northwest Environment Watch.
All rights reserved. No portion of this book may be reproduced or utilized in any
form or by any electronic, mechanical, or other means without the prior written
permission of the publisher.
Paperback edition 1997.

Printed in the United States of America.
Distributed in Canada by Raincoast Books Ltd.
01 00 99 98 97   5 4 3 2 1

Cover design: Karen Schober
Cover illustration: Debra A. Hanley
Interior design and composition: Kate Basart
Map: The map of the Pacific Northwest, on page ix, was created by Cynthia Thomas
for Northwest Environment Watch. It appeared in *State of the Northwest*, NEW
*Report No. 1*, by John C. Ryan, copyright 1994 by Northwest Environment Watch.
The map is based partly on Conservation International (CI) and Ecotrust, "Orginal
Distribution of Coastal Temperate Rain Forests of North America," Portland 1991.
Revisions for the NEW publication were based on forest data in CI, Ecotrust, and
Pacific GIS, "Coastal Temperate Rain Forests of North America," Portland, 1995. See
also David D. McCloskey, "Cascadia," Cascadia Institute, Seattle, 1988.

Library of Congress Cataloging in Publication Data
Durning, Alan Thein.
          This place on earth : home and the practice of permanence / Alan Thein
          Durning.
                    p.          cm.
          Includes bibliographical references and index.
          ISBN 1-57061-127-0
          1. Life style—Northwest, Pacific.  2. Simplicity.  3. Home.
          4. Environmental responsibility.  I. Title.
HQ2044.U62N674  1996
306—dc20                              96-20592

Sasquatch Books
615 Second Avenue
Seattle, Washington 98104
(206)467-4300
books@sasquatchbooks.com
http://www.sasquatchbooks.com

Sasquatch Books publishes high-quality adult nonfiction and children's books
related to the Northwest (San Francisco to Alaska). For information about our
books, contact us at the above address, or view our site on the World Wide Web.

# CONTENTS

**NORTHWEST**ENVIRONMENT**WATCH**

*This Place on Earth* is the flagship book of Northwest Environment Watch (NEW), a wholly independent, not-for-profit research center in Seattle, Washington. NEW's mission is to foster an environmentally sound economy and way of life in the Pacific Northwest—the biological region stretching from southeast Alaska to northern California, and from the Pacific to the crest of the Rockies. NEW is predicated on the belief that if we cannot create an environmentally sound economy here, in the greenest part of history's richest civilization, it probably cannot be done. If we can, we will set an example for the world.

Founded by Alan Durning in 1993, NEW serves as a monitor of the region's environmental conditions and a pathfinder for routes toward a lasting economy. Through action-oriented interdisciplinary research, NEW provides citizens, elected officials, educators, and the media with reliable information about what sustainable development is and how to achieve it.

NEW creates the tools for reconciling people and place, economy and ecology. NEW's book series strives to provide both generalists and experts with cutting-edge findings on a wide range of topics, such as the current health of ecosystems, the relationship between cars and cities, the creation of green jobs, getting prices to tell the ecological truths, and the hidden costs of everyday objects. Publications include *Stuff: The Secret Lives of Everyday Things*, by John C. Ryan and Alan Thein Durning; *The Car and the City*, by Alan Thein Durning; *Hazardous Handouts*, by John C. Ryan; and *State of the Northwest*, by John C. Ryan.

Northwest Environment Watch is governed by a seven-member board of directors and is funded by individual member contributions, foundation grants, and publications sales. NEW's work is carried out by a small staff and large corps of volunteers.

Northwest Environment Watch
1402 Third Avenue, Suite 1127
Seattle, Washington 98101-2118
206-447-1880
206-447-2270 (fax)
nwwatch@igc.apc.org
http://www.speakeasy.org/new/

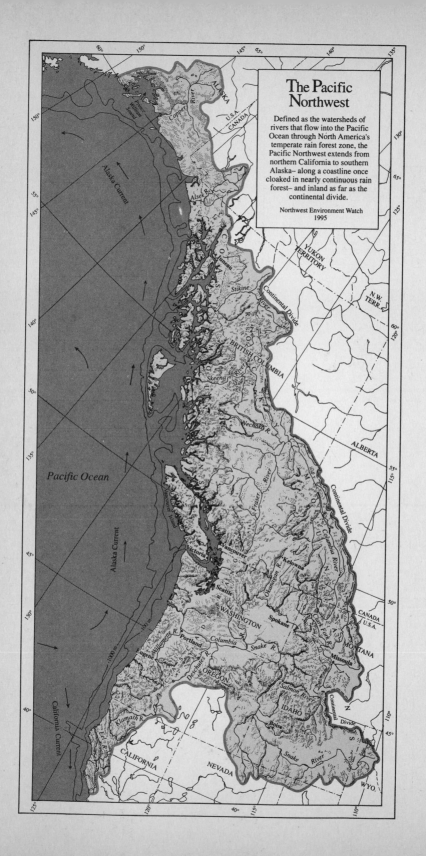

## The Pacific Northwest

Defined as the watersheds of rivers that flow into the Pacific Ocean through North America's temperate rain forest zone, the Pacific Northwest extends from northern California to southern Alaska– along a coastline once cloaked in nearly continuous rain forest– and inland as far as the continental divide.

Northwest Environment Watch
1995

*chapter one*

# PLACE

*August*

**I AM BACK IN SEATTLE.** I am exhausted, lonely, and off-balance—the damp air smells disconcertingly like childhood. At the moment, being here feels like defeat. It reminds me of the times when my brother and sister swam out to the log and I turned tail and crawled onto the beach.

I am haunted by the fear that by coming here I have turned tail on the cause that has occupied my last decade. I tell myself I am changing tactics, but I do not always trust this idea. At a minimum, I cannot fully explain my reasons for being here, nor why I am so determined to stay.

I came here, I suppose, to find out what it means to live responsibly in desperate times. Perhaps I came here in hopes of finding out what *permanence* would look and feel like—and to practice it while we still have the chance. Perhaps I came to confront head-on

1

the pain and paradox of living in an economy that seems to thrive on the death of nature. Maybe I came here in the hope that *place* might be the escape hatch for a fractured society hurtling toward the environmental brink.

All I can say with confidence is that I came here because, a year ago, a grinning barefoot peasant in the Philippines pitied me—the one thing I could not stand — and her pity became like a seed in my shoe. It sprouted, grew into my dreams, and tormented me. It sent me scurrying to the only place that ever felt like home. And it put down a taproot that has now bound me here, in this moss-cloaked neighborhood where everything is smaller than my memories.

Coming home did not come naturally because allegiance to locale is alien to my family. I am from a line that reveres wanderers. My father, second son of a self-taught Irish merchant and a Polish Jew, fled the bigotry of the South at age sixteen and never looked back. My mother is a tenth-generation descendant of Puritans who sailed to Massachusetts from England after the *Mayflower's* voyage. Beginning with the third generation in the New World, the family began moving to a new town with each generation. By the sixth generation, they had crossed the Mississippi. The seventh generation reached the Pacific; the eighth crossed to Asia. The ninth and tenth also kept moving. For two centuries or more, my ancestors died in different states than the ones in which they were born. I grew up hearing the stories of these people—pioneer farmers, merchants, missionaries, military officers, and geographers.

Even the friends my family has attracted have been international vagabonds: my grandmother's guest books, kept since she was first married, record all the places where her many visitors ever lived. Seven ink-filled volumes stand on her shelf, reading like catalogs of exotic ports. I grew up paging through them, dreaming of the places I would one day inscribe in Grandma's book. Recently,

I found an entry in uneven script: "Alan Durning, age 11, world traveler."

The three of us in my litter have collected stamps in our passports the way we used to collect bottle caps. Until recently, it has been uncommon for any two of us to be in the same time zone at once. I have been especially successful at mobility. The longest I have ever lived in the same room is three years; in the same house, six. Most of my life, I have surpassed the national average of moving every fifth year; I have rarely put up more than two consecutive calendars at the same address. Shortly after college, I set up base camp in Washington, D.C., where I joined the staff of a research center charged with monitoring the world's social and ecological health. A few years of seventy-hour weeks later I had been promoted and began hopscotching the globe myself, studying everything from poverty to atmospheric chemistry. It was urgent stuff: documenting injustice, testifying before Congress, jet-setting on behalf of future generations.

Then came the seed. I was in the Philippines interviewing members of remote hill tribes about their land and livelihood. On a sweltering day in the forested terrain of the Banwa'on people, a gap-toothed chief showed me the trees, streams, and farm plots that his tribe had tended for centuries. It was territory, he insisted, they would defend with their lives. As the sun finally slid lower in the sky, he introduced me to a frail old woman who was revered by the others as a traditional priestess. We sat under a sacred tree near her farm and looked out over the Ma'asam River. She asked through an interpreter, "What is your homeland like?"

She looked at me with an expectant smile, but I was speechless. My eyes dropped. Should I tell her about my neighborhood on the edge of Washington, D.C., the one where I then lived with my wife, Amy, and our son, Gary? The one where we could not let Gary play outside our apartment because of the traffic?

She repeated the question, thinking I had not heard. "Tell me about your place." Again, I could not answer. Should I tell her about the neighborhood we had previously fled, the one where the dead bodies of young men kept turning up in the alleys? The one where police helicopters were always shining their spotlights through our windows? The one that had since erupted in riots and suffered the psychotic nonchalance of a serial killer? I said nothing.

The truth was I lacked any connection to my base in Washington, D.C., and for some reason, for the first time, it shamed me. I had breakfasted with senators and shaken hands with presidents, but I was tongue-tied before this barefoot old woman.

"In America," I finally admitted, "we have careers, not places." Looking up, I recognized pity in her eyes.

**PICTURE NORTH AMERICA FROM SPACE.** Look at the upper left and start an imaginary line on the rugged coast of southern Alaska. Climb the ridges that encircle Prince William Sound. Cross the snowy teeth of the Chugach Mountains and descend through kettle-pond country to the feet of the towering Alaska Range. Rise again to the bitter heights and, turning southeast along the crest, clip the corner of the Yukon Territory. Enter British Columbia and veer east through its folding north.

Turn your line south when you reach the Continental Divide in the Rocky Mountains. Follow that divide down the thousand-mile spine of British Columbia, across Montana, along the buttressed ridges of the Idaho border, and into Wyoming as far as Jackson Hole.

There, leave the divide and turn westward toward the coast. Following the swells and benches that limit the Columbia Basin, dip southward into Utah and Nevada, then northward again around the high desert of central Oregon. When you approach the Cascade Mountains, veer southwest through the tangled topography of northern California to the crest of the Coast Range. Just north of San Francisco Bay, descend to the shores of the Pacific.

The line you have drawn is an unfamiliar one. You won't find it on maps by Rand McNally. But it shows a geographical unit more real, in an ecological sense, than any of the lines governments draw. You have drawn a biological region—a *bioregion*. Specifically, you have outlined the watersheds of rivers flowing into the Pacific Ocean through North America's temperate rain forest zone.

Rain forests, the largest outside of the tropics, stretch along the coast from San Francisco Bay to Prince William Sound in a fifteen-hundred-mile belt. Running through this landscape of mammoth evergreens are salmon-filled rivers that rise inland—sometimes hundreds of miles inland—among corrugated ranges and desert plateaus.

The unity of this diverse bioregion is in the movement of its water; every ounce of moisture that the ocean throws into the sky and the sky hurls down on the land inside this region's borders tumbles toward the rain forest coast. If it does not evaporate or get trapped in underground aquifers along the way, the water will reach that dripping shoreline through one of several hundred swift, cold rivers. Most likely, it will travel through the Columbia—the biggest Pacific-bound flow in the Americas—or the Fraser—home to the Earth's greatest populations of migrating salmon.

But water that falls outside the boundaries will never touch the rain forest. It will run off in other directions—into the Yukon River and Bering Sea, into the Mackenzie and Saskatchewan Rivers and the Arctic Ocean, into the Missouri and Mississippi Rivers and the Gulf of Mexico, into the salt pans and dry washes of the land-locked Great Basin, or into the Sacramento River and San Francisco

Bay. It will define other natural places, other units of ecology, but it will not glide through the mossy rot of temperate rain forests.

This place, defined by water running to woodlands, has no perfect name. You could call it the Rain Forest Province, the North Pacific Slope, or—as some do—Cascadia. But it is simpler to press into service a name from common parlance, a name that already denotes the place's economic and demographic center of gravity. It is best to call this place—the part of northwestern North America that is connected to the Pacific through rain forests—the Pacific Northwest.

After all, the human settlement patterns in the Pacific Northwest already give many of its people a cultural sense of kinship that roughly coincides with this natural unity. The place has a densely populated core and a vast, buffering hinterland. Its heart extends along a corridor from Vancouver and Victoria, British Columbia, through Seattle and Tacoma, Washington, to Portland and Eugene, Oregon. If you travel away from this urbanized strip in almost any direction, population diminishes in an unbroken gradient until you have crossed into other bioregions with other human hubs.

For reasons both cultural and ecological, therefore, the Pacific Northwest is one of the Earth's natural places. It exists apart from any government's recognition of it as a single place. It exists in a more fundamental way. It is manifest on the face of the land. It is there. It can be discovered.

Natural units of place such as this have always mattered more to people than has humanity in general or the planet in its entirety. Indeed, history is unequivocal: people will sacrifice for villages, homelands, or nations, even giving their lives. But humans seem unwilling to sacrifice for their planet, despite the fact that it is now suffering proportionately greater losses from social decay and environmental destruction than do most countries at war.

Specialists have known for decades that burgeoning numbers of people and their surging consumption of material resources were making the scale of human impacts on the Earth unsupportable. Homo sapiens has produced far more protoplasm—more mass of living tissue—than any other species in the four-billion-year evolutionary record. Earth's 5.8 billion people and their domesticated animals eat 3 percent of all the plant matter that grows on land each year—the staple of terrestrial food chains. Add the habitats burned, paved, plowed, grazed, cut down, or otherwise turned to human ends and the figure rises to 39 percent. Humans appropriate two-fifths of all plant matter that grows on land each year, a state of affairs that cannot last. This extreme disruption of ecosystems will end. The question is whether people will end it voluntarily and creatively, or whether nature will end it for them, savagely and catastrophically.

Humanity's failure to act in defense of the Earth is conventionally explained as a problem of knowledge: not enough people yet understand the dangers or know what to do about them. An alternative explanation is that this failure reflects a fundamental problem of motivation. People know enough, but they do not care enough. They do not care enough because they do not identify themselves with the world as a whole. The Earth is such a big place that it might as well be no place at all.

If places motivate but the planet does not, a curious paradox emerges. The wrenching global problems that the world's leading thinkers so earnestly warn about—crises such as deforestation, hunger, population growth, climate change, the proliferation of hazardous materials, and the loss of cultural and biological diversity—may submit to solutions only obliquely. The only cures possible may be local and motivated by a sentiment—the love of home—that global thinkers have often regarded as divisive or provincial. Thus, it may be possible to diagnose global problems globally, but impossible to solve them globally. There may not be any ways to save the world that are not, first and foremost, ways for people to save their own places.

If this is true, it means that to seek durable answers to global challenges, the conscientious must—without losing sight of the universal—begin with place, and specifically with *one place*. This book follows such a course, although it does so based on no certainty about these *localist* premises. The book attends to the Pacific Northwest. It does so consistently, even single-mindedly, but it does so without prejudice to other places. It does so as an act of faith in the power of place generally.

## August

After returning to Washington, D.C., from the Philippines, I noticed the seed in my shoe—the burn of that woman's pity—and tried to pick it out. "It's nothing," I told myself. "She was just making conversation." And my conscience said I needed to push on: the health of the Earth, I was constantly reminded, was poor and deteriorating.

For a time, it was easy to ignore the seed. I was swept up in the publication of a book I'd been building toward for years, a book that said Americans could do better for themselves and the planet by—of all things—consuming fewer objects and consuming them differently. The consumer society, I had come to believe, was bringing us up short and squandering our children's inheritance.

The book garnered enough attention to put me on the lecture circuit, the opinion pages, and, briefly, the national airwaves. Being heard was good. It had been my ambition. But it created ever more demand for me to travel. And with each long flight, and each new audience, my sense of unease grew. Where once I had thought of myself as a global citizen, I was beginning to see myself as a carpetbagger. I was beginning to feel uncomfortable telling people from other places and other cultures what was wrong with their lives and their governments. I would return to Washington, D.C., with an empty feeling, anxious to see Amy and Gary, but unmoved by the place itself.

The seed was rubbing my foot into a blister. I shortened my trips. I went to the Netherlands for thirty-six hours once, then to Germany for eighteen. I began thinking up excuses to decline invitations. At the same time, I found myself waking from dreams of rotting logs, banana slugs, and other forgotten fixtures of my childhood. The seed was sprouting.

AGAIN, PICTURE NORTH AMERICA from space. Look again to the Northwest, and allow the political lines to emerge in your imagination as they have on every map you have studied since childhood. The lines that decorate your imagination are familiar, but they are nonsense. They were drawn casually, almost capriciously, during the 1800s. They were drawn by men not native to the region, nor even, in many cases, located in the region. They were drawn with utter disregard for the divisions imminent in nature and recognized by indigenous cultures.

At the beginning of the 1800s, the United States was decidedly uninterested in this coast. Congress declared, "Nature has fixed limits to our nation; she has kindly interposed as our Western barrier, mountains almost inaccessible, whose base she has skirted with irreclaimable deserts of sand. This barrier our population can never pass—if it does, it becomes the people of a new world, whose connexions, whose feelings, and whose interests, are not with us."

The young democracy quickly changed its mind about the Pacific Northwest. At the time, everything from the Continental Divide to the ocean and from Russian Alaska to Spanish California was the Oregon Territory to Americans and the Columbia Department to Canadians. (What it was to its inhabitants can no longer be known. It was presumably just home.) Spain and Russia also had claims to the place.

The political lines all appeared on the map in the space of eight decades. In an 1819 treaty, Spain signed its claims north of California over to the United States, drawing the northern border of California—and what would later become Nevada and Utah—in the process. In 1824 and 1825 treaties, Russia relinquished its claims south of Alaska, drawing Alaska's southernmost boundary along the way. In 1846, the remaining colonial contenders, the United States and Great Britain, quietly settled their dispute over dominion—they were each preoccupied with more pressing affairs at the time—and divvied up the region at the forty-ninth parallel. In 1850, California's eastern border was drawn with linear perversity as it entered the union as a state.

After that, the Americans parceled out their half of the Oregon Territory as settlers arrived. They carved out the state of Oregon in 1859, bounding it with ruler-straight lines wherever a river channel did not oblige. Nevada, severed from Utah by distant mapmakers, became a state in 1864.

The Americans carved out Washington in 1889, its eastern border drawn to please Puget Sound Republicans by excluding the valley of the Coeur d'Alene River. At the time, that valley was full of Democratic miners who threatened to swing elections against the Puget Sounders. The same year Montana's mining elites reached east and west from the Continental Divide and took as much as they could into statehood with them. Poor misshapen Idaho got the leftovers; it lacked even a passable route from its north to its south. Idaho entered the union in 1890, the same year that Wyoming fell into its boxy little place on the map. Six years later, Utah's borders were set as it became a state.

The British Columbians, for their part, toyed with joining the United States, too; most of their lumber and gold, after all, went to Puget Sound or San Francisco. But the new confederation of Canada won them over in 1871 with the promise of a transcontinental railroad and all the real estate windfalls it would generate.

That is how the map was drawn. The province of the rain forest rivers was fractured into ten jurisdictions. The Pacific Northwest is all of Washington, most of British Columbia, Idaho, and Oregon, the southern and southeastern parts of Alaska, the western part of Montana, the northwestern part of California, and fragments of Nevada, Utah, Wyoming, and the Yukon. Political lines cut dozens of rivers into pieces and made the future management of natural wealth a fractious affair.

For the foreseeable future, the region is stuck with this rectilinear absurdity; no American state or Canadian province has yet changed its boundaries. Yet many longtime Northwesterners, while accustomed to operating within the confines of these geometric polities, have an intuitive sense of their larger home. They may not know exactly where to draw the boundaries of their bioregion, but they recognize them when they see them. In moments of candor, some speak of their home as God's Country, using the phrase, despite the irreligion of these times, without self-consciousness or cynicism.

## *August*

I grew up in Seattle at the end of the baby boom, in inner-city schools, and in the sodden woods that cradle Puget Sound. But later we moved east. My parents eventually returned to Seattle, rejoining one grandmother and drawing another along with them. My sister drifted back, too. But my own sense of place had slipped away.

During the time last year when my urge to settle was increasing, my wife was feeling similar inclinations. Where should we go? Amy was not sure, but she said she couldn't imagine staying in the shifting sands of Washington, D.C. Amy is from the East but had fallen under the spell of the Pacific Northwest on past visits. She was willing to give my old haunts a try.

So our plans were set, waiting only for our second child to be born. Earlier this month—a year after the priestess hobbled me with her pity—I rented a yellow moving van and loaded it full of our possessions. Then Gary and I got in it, accompanied by Amy's father, Peter, and drove away. We left Amy and baby Kathryn behind to fly out in a couple of weeks.

IMAGINE THE NORTHWEST FROM SPACE one last time. Paint the coastal forest a dark and misty green. Trace in the rivers in frigid blue. And pepper the waterways with glitters of silver for the salmon that give the region its spirit. Focus on each in turn: forests, rivers, salmon.

Before newcomers arrived in the region on boats and, later, covered wagons, forests of redwood, hemlock, cedar, fir, pine, and spruce stretched along the Pacific in a nearly continuous band from northern California to southern Alaska. Today, though fragmented by development and logging, these forests continue to stand in much of their range.

Conifer rain forests like these are rare. They occur here because of the concurrence of wet winters and dry summers. Deciduous trees need water during the warm months when they are in leaf, but evergreens grow year-round, so a summer drought is no threat. Northwest rain forests do not have the variety of living things found in their tropical counterparts, but they grow bigger. In weight per acre, nothing can compare.

If you have never traveled these groves, understand that they are not tidy, bare-ground woods. They are jumbled, pungent, soggy, dripping, prickly, almost impassable jungles. The standing trees approach the maximum height allowed by physics—much higher and they could not draw water up to the top. The lowest branches are often a hundred feet up, and the trunks are the sizes of Volkswagens.

The logs lie so thick on the forest floor that it looks as if King Kong has been playing pick-up-sticks. Off-trail travel is more like rock climbing than walking. You crawl or tightrope-walk the length of one fallen giant until the trunk gets too narrow, too rotten, or too high above the ground; then you lower yourself, dangling from old branches, in search of another trunk heading your way. The oldest logs have rotted to the core and melted into the soil, leaving long mossy ridges that look like the ruins of some undiscovered civilization. Biologists call these decaying levees "nurse logs" because they nourish seedlings, sometimes a dozen of them in a row.

Rivers give the Northwest its internal form—its dendritic structure. They play a central role in the continuance of life, and they have always been mainstays of the region's cultures and economies.

Flowing water has carved and built up most of the fertile, flat places where people have always congregated. And today, electricity from river water powers the region.

Before the industrial revolution, rivers were the thoroughfares of the Northwest, and later railroads and highways mostly followed their banks. Most Northwest peoples, like most civilizations throughout history, have flowered by rivers. Many of the languages spoken by Indian tribes from deep forest valleys had two compass points: upstream and downstream. The oceangoing coastal tribes made their permanent homes at river mouths. And the nomadic peoples of the interior plateau moved among riverside campsites. In much of the Northwest, cultures were referred to simply by the names of their rivers.

For Northwesterners, there is power in these names. Many are Indian appellations, or feeble imitations thereof. They are beautiful, nonetheless. Some are simple, like Hoh, Alsek, Stikine, Taku, Kootenai, Skagit, and Skeena. There are repeaters, such as Hamma Hamma, Klinaklina, and Walla Walla, which roll off your tongue. And there are big, intimidating ones, too: Chehalis, Homathko, Chilcotin, Nechako, Okanagan, Skykomish, Skokomish, Snohomish, and Squamish. The crowning name of all must be Tatshenshini.

Other names, coined by French Canadians in fur-trapping times, are bastardized but lovely French: Lillooet, Willamette, Grand Ronde, Malheur, Boise, Deschutes, and Pend Oreille. There are English names too, of course, including some that are sturdy and firm: Salmon, Snake, Eel, Rogue, Copper, Bitterroot, Clearwater, Flathead. And many more names have been lost: today's Russian River was the Slavianka, or "charming one," to early fur traders and Shabaikai or Misallaako, or "long snake," to Native Americans.

These are the capillaries of the place. And, as it turns out, they are not merely a matter of surfaces. Rivers, hydrologists now believe, are the visible trunk of an aquatic tree extending in every direction from the channel, including down. Slow-moving water and the nutrients it carries support soil organisms hundreds of feet beneath the bed. In places like the Snake River plain of southern Idaho, the flow underground dwarfs the streams on the surface.

Where the rivers flow, so go the salmon: totems of the Northwest, the muscled kingpins of the aquatic food web, marathon runners of the deep. They hatch in rain forest rivers, transform themselves into saltwater migrants, travel thousands of miles at sea, then battle as much as nine hundred miles upstream again, vaulting cascades to climb thousands of feet above sea level. They deteriorate as they go because they stop eating at tidewater.

Only the millennial urge to perpetuate themselves, the insistent demands of their DNA, gets them to their spawning streams. And not to just any streams. All but a few strays return to the exact creek of their births, locating that waterway from the thousands of others purely by sense of smell. Many lay and fertilize their eggs within a hundred yards of their birthplaces.

Through the salmon, the ocean penetrates the land. The ten-, twenty-, sometimes hundred-pound fish carry the ocean ashore. The pink flesh embodies the metabolized energy of the herring and other swimmers that the wayfarers devour at sea. These, in turn, are the embodiment of what they eat. And so on down the food chain to the phytoplankton, whose photosynthesis powers the entire wheel of oceanic life.

Once the salmon have fertilized their eggs, they die in stinking heaps, their muscle tissue nourishing bears, eagles, and aquatic invertebrates, some of which are later eaten by the newly hatched salmon fry. When the spawners ran undiminished three hundred years ago, their rotting corpses each year deposited billions of pounds of the ocean's fecundity in Northwest headwaters.

The drama of this cyclical epic is why most longtime Northwesterners—whether their ancestors walked across the Bering land bridge or walked down the jetway of a 747—have strong feelings about the slippery creatures. In the words of Seattle-born *New York Times* reporter Timothy Egan: "The Northwest is simply this: wherever the salmon can get to."

## August

In practical terms, leaving base camp was easy for us. Washington, D.C., the capital of an itinerant nation, is the ultimate itinerant city. Moving on is expected. Most of the friends we had made there had long since left; saying good-bye to those who remained was the task for a single weekend.

In every other way, leaving Washington, D.C., was hard and reckless. Prudence argued against the move. We were jumping for the far coast just a month after Kathryn's birth, and just one week after Amy recovered from life-threatening complications of delivery. Amy and I had a family of four. I had no secure source of livelihood in the West; my vocation of town crier for the planet was not especially remunerative. And we knew almost no one in Seattle outside of my family.

Conscience argued against the move as well. Years studying the prospects for this crowded little planet had packed my head with information that demanded action, yet I was abandoning the one post in which I knew how to make a difference. Wildlife ecologist Aldo Leopold once wrote that ecologists, seeing harm where others see only scenery, live "alone in a world of wounds." That is how it was going to feel, driving across the continent.

So I sat gazing out of the rented moving truck's cab in the neighborhood we were leaving, while marauding facts galloped out of the darkness of my memory. Scary, awful knowledge: more than ten million children die each year from preventable diseases such as diarrhea even while the world has more than two hundred billionaires; following present trends, one-fifth of living species will vanish from the Earth before I reach old age; even modest changes to the global climate caused by releasing carbon dioxide and other gases could become a vicious circle in which dying forests and thawing polar lands exhale new pulses of heat-trapping gases.

What, I wondered as I pulled into traffic on the Capital Beltway, could I hope to do about such tragedies and dangers on my own in a backwater port like Seattle?

Still, the seed in my shoe was more powerful than prudence or conscience. I could not tolerate the idea of staying any longer in a place where I had no intention of remaining. The hunch kept growing that *place* was not only the anchor missing from my life but an anchor missing from others' lives as well—an anchor that might turn the voracious efficiency of our industrial society to the ends of enduring longer rather than producing and consuming more. Greater rootedness, I speculated, might be the force that would deter us from eating our habitat alive.

IN THE SPRING OF 1792, Captain George Vancouver sailed into what would later be named the Strait of Juan de Fuca, surveyed the homelands of the Coast Salish people—now western Washington—and recorded in his log: "I could not possibly believe that any uncultivated country had ever been discovered exhibiting so rich a picture. . . . The serenity of the climate, the innumerable pleasing landscapes, and the abundant fertility that unassisted nature puts forth, require only to be enriched by the industry of man . . . to render it the most lovely country that can be imagined."

Vancouver was not the first outsider enchanted by the region. In early August 1788 Robert Haswell, second mate on the *Lady Washington*, a Boston trading ship, described the Northwest coast as "a delightfull Country, thickly inhabited and Cloathed with woods and verdure with maney Charming streems of water gushing from the vallies."

Ever since, the praises have continued. Fitz Hugh Ludlow wrote to the eastern readers of the *Atlantic Monthly* in 1864 that he had witnessed "from the summit of a hill twenty miles south of Salem, one of the most magnificent views in all earthly scenery." It was, in this case, a parade of Cascade volcanoes. "My friend and I clasped each other's hands before it, and thanked God we lived to this day." Northwesterners take such vistas for granted.

Perhaps that is one of the reasons so many people have come, one of the reasons that the Pacific Northwest is now overwhelmingly a place of newcomers. No one originated here, of course. Even the coastal cultures with longest residence were migrants from elsewhere. But they stayed for thousands of years and became native. Since the mid-1830s, when the region's human population was at its lowest point, newcomers have always outnumbered even second-generation residents: Each end-of-decade census has found more residents born elsewhere than residents born in the region. The second-generation folks around Seattle, getting cocky, have started putting bumper stickers on their cars that read "Washington Native." Indigenous natives, meanwhile, accounted for less than one-fiftieth of the regional population in 1992.

On the other side of the world from the Pacific Northwest, the largest assembly of national leaders in history convened at the Earth Summit in Rio de Janeiro in the spring of 1992. The world's political leaders committed themselves to a new definition of success. They called for *sustainable development*, the proposition that progress should come without harm to the Earth.

People everywhere are struggling to practice that principle, but the Pacific Northwest could be the proving ground. It is more ecologically intact than any other populated part of the industrial world. Make no mistake, the region's natural heritage has been badly compromised, and many of its ecosystems are in critical condition.

Yet the Pacific Northwest has more old-growth forest than any part of Europe, Japan, or North America; it has more temperate rain forest than anywhere in the world; its Fraser River remains the world's greatest producer of salmon. And amid the mountains of the Pacific Northwest lurk the most wondrous of rarities in the industrialized world: ecosystems that still have all their native species, from top predators on down. Among other things, sustainability means ensuring the survival not just of the human species but of other species as well—and of the life-giving ecosystems they form. The Pacific Northwest has the best shot at this elusive goal.

Moreover, the Pacific Northwest is inhabited by well-educated people, a large share of whom care deeply about the natural environment. The Northwest has traditions of participatory democracy and innovation in government and business. It has the can-do spirit of all North America, but it also has, at least in its major cities, a global outlook and a commitment to tolerance and solidarity. Its economy already has one foot in the information age, and its dependence on high-impact resource industries is steadily diminishing. Its population of fourteen million and land mass of six hundred thousand square miles are large enough to matter but small enough to grapple with.

The Pacific Northwest is the greenest part of the richest society in history. If Northwesterners cannot build an ecologically sound way of life, it probably cannot be done. If Northwesterners can, they will set an example for the world. They will demonstrate how to transform a prolific but self-destructive economy into something that can last.

No doubt, the challenges are great. The Northwest has squandered much of its natural wealth, creating the challenge of not just sustaining but restoring the place. And the Pacific Northwest faces the universal challenges of industrialized regions: to turn a consumer economy of throwaways, strip malls, and traffic jams into one of durability, livability, and revitalized community; to convert a natural-resources economy predicated on the extraction of ever-larger volumes into one that adds ever more value; to change an industrial economy constructed around linear production systems into one designed for zero emissions and comprehensive recycling; to convert, in the words of Oregon forester Roy Keene, a culture of "lots now" into one of "some forever."

Success is far from assured. Those who grasp the need for bold innovations are still a minority, and the tasks are daunting. Can the regional hubs of Portland, Seattle, and Vancouver create transportation systems that get them off the treadmill of bigger roads and more cars? Can the region lead the world toward methods of production and consumption that radically diminish the sheer mass of matter extracted from natural systems, processed in industrial facilities, transported, used, and disposed of as waste? Can timber towns and other communities that make a living liquidating natural capital create diverse and resilient economies? Can Northwesterners confront the root causes of the environmental predicament—such as prices that do not tell the ecological truth? And can they forge a political coalition broad enough to outflank those who profit from business-as-usual?

## *August*

After four days on the road in our rented moving van, somewhere in eastern Montana, my six-year-old son exclaimed, "Look, Dad. Mom put a water bottle in my toy bag." At each stop, he refilled it and sipped until he made another stop necessary. Tired of searching for toilets on the northern plains, we were soon pulling the rig off onto the shoulder and letting him out. Gary, a fan of wolves, explained his actions: "I'm marking my territory." And as we went, we got to talking—in six-year-old terms—about hydrology, gravity, and watersheds.

That is how Gary understood entering the Pacific Northwest. At Butte, Montana, beside the cavernous Berkeley Pit copper mine, we crested the Rockies. Gary marked his new territory, and he and I stood imagining the waters plunging to the western sea through the pine-dark gorges and sun-drenched plateaus of the Pacific Northwest.

When we arrive in Seattle, Gary uses his wagon to help me move our belongings into temporary housing: a run-down two-bedroom bungalow with thirty-four front steps. My mind remains filled with doubts. Have I sought a new field of battle or simply deserted? Will this place care what I think and say? What do I know about the Pacific Northwest anymore?

Elsewhere in my psyche, however, there is a spreading comfort. The dust smells right as I pack our gear into the basement. The trees cast the right kinds of shadows, and they stay silent—none of the insect cacophony of other places I've resided. The nondescript light from the overcast sky has, I think, quieted something in me.

Having turned in the rental truck and stowed our gear below deck in the basement, I am standing on the porch now and looking out over a drab valley of modest houses on modest lots. I am exhausted from the move and all the upheaval that came before it. I am lonely, knowing only family members here, and waiting for Amy and Kathryn to arrive from the East.

Still, as a light rain begins to fall, I realize that this is the place I should have described to the Philippine priestess. Her place was in the watershed of the Ma'asam River, a tributary of the Agusan River on the island of Mindanao. The cells of her body were made of water and nutrients from that place. Mine is here. I have not lived here in more than fifteen years. My body is constituted by matter from elsewhere, and this neighborhood is a riverless place anyway: the rain that falls here goes through a storm drain into a culvert into Lake Washington and then through a man-made ship canal into the Pacific.

Yet the roots poking through my shoe from the peasant's pity seed find the soil acceptable. The homing instinct is subsiding. This house is a mile from where I hatched. And so I thank her. "My place is the watershed of the ship canal. My homeland is the Pacific Northwest."

*chapter two*

# PAST

## April

**WE HAVE BEEN IN THE** Northwest eight months now. We've been through the gray season. Elsewhere, the moons from September to May are divided between fall, winter, and spring, but in Seattle, there is no difference. Through the whole span of this time, clouds wrap the city, and night wraps the short day. It is the time when outsiders complain about the rain, and it does rain a lot. But the rain is more constant than it is intense, and the darkness is what makes the wet gloomy.

Amy and I were pleased to find the grayness untroubling. We reminded each other of a poem by Denise Levertov, an English émigré to Seattle, that ends, "Grey is the price of neighboring with eagles." Gary claims to enjoy the rain, and Kathryn is too young to know the difference.

Besides, we have been too busy to give the weather much thought. We have conceived another child, and the chores of keeping house have kept us occupied. We have overcome the most basic challenges—securing permanent housing, enrolling Gary in school, and finding a doctor. I have set up a small group to advocate for this bioregion and found kindred spirits to help carry on its work.

Still, we are newcomers here—or newly returned—so we are spending a few surplus days getting reacquainted with the place. We have packed the kids into our aging Honda Civic to embark on a spring tour.

That's how I have come to be at the place where the Pacific Northwest really *began*: Sandpoint, Idaho. Everything was different then, of course, fifteen thousand years ago. Back then, there was no Pizza Hut. No U.S. Highway 2. No Dairy Queen. The site of the Best Western was under a half-mile of ice—ice that ran over the pole to England and the outskirts of Warsaw.

Sandpoint was in a cold trough where the ice jabbed for the equator. A dozen miles south of here, the ice rammed into the flank of the Bitterroot Mountains and shunted eastward, plugging the valley of the Clark Fork River like a dam. Meltwater piled up, turning western Montana into a serpentine lake.

Then the dam burst. All at once, as much water as is in Lake Ontario lunged for the Pacific. Three hundred eighty cubic miles of water blasted through Sandpoint in a matter of days: the largest flood in the geologic record. It packed the punch of two hundred Hiroshima bombs and ran like sixty Amazons, four hundred Mississippis, or a thousand Columbias. It was ten times the combined flow of every river, stream, and drainage ditch now on Earth. You could have seen it from space.

From here in Sandpoint, under the dam, you would not have seen a thing. You would not have known what hit you. The site of

Sandpoint was blasted oceanward, and not for the last time. After the deluge, the ice lobe choked the Clark Fork again, meltwater pooled, and the dam failed. Forty times or more it happened, hitting this spot every fifty years or so.

No great loss, some might say: modern Sandpoint is an armpit of a town. But I disagree. Earlier tonight Amy and I watched sunset stain the snow of the Bitterroots as we pulled into town. Gary and Kathryn slept in the back seat. In the near distance, Lake Pend Oreille picked up the glow on its undulating surface. Up close, everything was gritty pickups and wet gravel, gas pumps and highway strip.

And it was appealing: unpretentious, normal, Northwestern. The smoke from the town sawmill was sweet above the fumes at the Texaco. So when the luminous yellow sign fifty feet high and two blocks away beckoned, "Best Western," this road-weary family accepted.

Now I have been awakened from sleep by a dram of that monster wave. The image of that cataclysm crashing down on this room—Amy and I in the bed with Kathryn between us and Gary on a cot—has me wishing we had pushed on. I am thinking of higher ground.

**THE PAST OF THE NORTHWEST** is replete with floods, both literal and figurative. Ice Age floods of water rearranged the landforms of much of the Columbia Basin. And metaphorical floods— enterprising people arriving, mostly from Europe, to extract natural resources—have rearranged the landscape of the entire Northwest just as they overhauled the rest of the New World.

Reaching this place two centuries ago, these human floods have produced fabulous wealth and a culture both vibrant and diverse. The floods' power has derived from the people—both native and newly arrived—and the quirky blend of traits they displayed generation after generation: outlandish idealism, irrepressible ingenuity, and brute stamina. Sadly, the floods have exhausted a large part of the ecological endowment left by evolution.

Here, as elsewhere, the human floods have come in waves, most of them waves of commerce and industry. But the most lethal wave, and the earliest, was microscopic; it was a flood of diseases. The germs arrived before the Europeans themselves. Smallpox first appeared in the region in the 1770s. It spread from longhouse to longhouse, probably originating in Spanish California. As everywhere in the New World, the death toll quickly rose into the tens of thousands. In some places, whole clans and villages took sick and died. Early outside visitors to these sites felt they had happened into a mortuary. Bodies littered the beaches and cluttered the townsites; settlements stood empty, reverting to ferns.

The pox broke out again every thirty years thereafter, laying low roughly a third of the original Northwesterners in affected areas each time. Malaria, measles, influenza, dysentery, whooping cough, typhus, and even syphilis augmented the misery. No one knows how many people lived in the region in 1770, but a reasonable estimate is half a million. In 1870, indigenous Northwesterners numbered one-tenth of that. Sometime around 1835, after the third smallpox epidemic and before settlement from outside began in earnest, the Northwest's human population was probably at its lowest point in five thousand years.

The other waves of the human flood have been less ghastly, more mundane. They have been intentional; they were industries, rising and falling in succession. Each threw its force against the place in its own way, laying a distinctive imprint on nature's fabric. But most played out their energy according to the same principles: a natural resource would come into favor somewhere outside the region. Faraway investors and governments would support entrepreneurs with the audacity and skill to travel to the region and extract the resource. The entrepreneurs, as often as not, would conscript other men—often with darker skin—to do the manual labor. The region's money economy would boom and then, when demand or the resource ran out, bust. The investors would put their money elsewhere, and those who had come to do the physical labor would dig in or move on.

During the repeated waves of flooding, money operated according to its own logic. It sought the highest return. It sought to grow. Where the most growth would occur by trapping beavers—and where no power of government existed to regulate the trade—the near-elimination of the beaver was inevitable. Where the most money could be made by washing away hillsides to get at trace quantities of one shiny metal or another, the hillsides' elimination was unavoidable.

Each industrial wave made more headway than the previous one. Some of them boomed just once, while others rose and fell repeatedly. But all eventually subsided, their role in the regional economy diminishing. Fur, metals, fish, grass, soil, water, timber— each gave up its wealth in turn and fell away. Each was tapped, exploited, its products packed and shipped. Each was commodified, cashed, transmogrified into money—into new money. Whatever form the natural asset took, humans behaved in the same way: they dug it up, cut it down, netted it, plowed it, dammed it, diverted it. They used it, and it became money. "I hated to kill the [beaver]," confided a nineteenth-century trapper, "but says I, 'it is $5.'"

This was not unique to the Northwest; it was the story of most places on this continent. Still, the particulars of the region's past matter. They matter because the challenges of the present flow directly from the past. Just as the prehistoric floods shaped land-forms in much of the Northwest, the human floods left behind them the ecological conditions, economic structures, legal precedents, political alignments, cultural norms, and habits of mind that both constrain and fuel the region's current efforts toward a durable way of life.

The idealism, ingenuity, and stamina that powered the liquidation of so much natural wealth are now turning to the reconciliation of people and nature. The human floods were not, after all, so much corrupt as they were ill-guided. They operated on the assumption that nature was endlessly bountiful and that human welfare improved in direct relation to the domestication or "development" of the lands and waters. Most of the people involved in tapping the Northwest's natural capital did not see—indeed, they could not conceive—that a time would come when a forest would be worth more standing than felled. They did not understand that the sheer productivity of human enterprise would both imperil the bounty of nature and allow people to care less about additional material commodities and more about immaterial ones, such as healthy air to breathe and wild birds to watch.

The rapid and incomplete transition from an economy of extraction to an economy of preservation may explain the intensity of conflicts in the region over environmental issues. But the transition has taken place. In the Northwest—and here is one critical difference between this region and many others—people stopped themselves while ecosystems still had a chance. They came to see their destiny as different. They came to believe that nature, wildness, and raw beauty ought to survive. And so, despite all the resource development, the Northwest retained a larger share of its ecosystems in a viable state than did other places.

## April

Tonight, still wide-eyed with nightmares of floodwaters, I am listening to the throb of traffic on Highway 2 outside the window. The mattress of the Sandpoint Best Western is too soft, troubling my back. I am contemplating my family's past.

A minute particle of the Northwest's current human population, we exemplify its origins. We are one man and one woman, each twenty-nine years old. She is pregnant. With us are one boy, six, and one girl, less than a year. All are Caucasian.

The man's ancestors include New England Puritans, Irish laborers, and Polish merchants of Jewish heritage. The woman's include midwestern Roman Catholics of German and Irish descent. The children carry traits from all of these sources. If we were dogs, we would be called mutts.

Like most inhabitants of this place, we are recent arrivals and frequent movers. Like most newcomers, we are a heavily schooled bunch—which is not to say we are truly educated. Like most Northwesterners, we are better trained in consumption than in nature. We can confidently navigate any shopping center in the bioregion, but can still name few of the local plants and animals.

We are in this place because I grew up here. I grew up here because my father was mesmerized by the terrain in the summer of 1948. On vacation from college in New England, he went west to cut timber in the redwoods of northern California. The jobs dried up, and he wandered north. The farther he went, the more he wanted to see. He made it to Seattle before his time and money ran out. The beauty and fecundity of the place imprinted themselves on his cells. A decade later, he and my mother—daughter of Ohio missionaries-turned-college-professors—went back to live. They drove west in a Volkswagen Beetle, seeking in the Pacific Northwest an unspoiled landscape, a place worthy of their ideals.

If the Northwest is my homeland, therefore, it is because my father needed money for college, and cutting the redwoods was where the money was.

Inside the rooms up and down the motel's dimly lit corridor are more of our kind. I recognized them earlier when I was checking in: a score of businessmen, a handful of families and older couples. Most, I am willing to wager, love the Pacific Northwest with a deep but little-spoken passion. Most, I am equally certain, have provided for themselves by selling things—laminated wood products or mill flue cleaners, cash registers or video arcades. They have done what they had to do.

My family shares their instincts: work hard, respect authority, do not complain, put something away for later. What I find so painfully difficult is that all of us in this motel—as honest and, I would submit, as likeable a bunch as you would find anywhere— are the working parts of a suicidal economy: an economy whose success ensures its failure.

THE FIRST WAVE OF RESOURCE extraction—the fur trade— hit the Northwest coast in 1784. For decades, China had been buying sea otter pelts from Russia—which stripped them from Siberia and the Aleutian Islands. But in 1779, two ships limped into Canton from the Northwest coast, carrying a few hundred otter skins.

The ships were the remains of English mariner James Cook's last round-the-world voyage, absent the deceased Cook. The previous year, the navigator had been heading for Russian Alaska in search of the legendary Northwest Passage. During a stopover on Vancouver

Island, crew members traded for otter furs from the Indians, preparing for the frozen North. These furs were still on board when Lieutenant James King went to visit the mandarins in Canton. He took twenty with him and came back with eight hundred dollars in silver.

News of the price could travel no faster than the winds in those days, but other traders soon enough headed for the Northwest coast. Anchoring in Nootka Sound and other bays between Spanish California and Russian Alaska, they traded nails, blankets, and beads for the prized fur. Flotillas of canoes met the tall ships, full of Indians eager to do business.

The fur rush depressed otter populations, and prices spiraled. By the early 1800s, a good otter fur could sell for as much as two thousand dollars in Asia. Small wonder that the species was on the verge of extinction by 1810, after just twenty-six trading seasons. In that time, the human flood had energetically dispatched roughly a quarter million of the playful mammals' skins to market.

The otters' extermination likely tore a hole in the food web of the coastal waters. Recent studies show that otters eat spiny sea urchins from the ocean floor, keeping the urchins' numbers in check and preventing them from devouring the kelp forests that otters prefer. When the world economy siphoned off the otters, urchins likely proliferated. To this day, sea otters are rare on the Northwest coast, and hundreds of miles of coastline are what scuba divers call sea urchin barrens. No one knows for sure, but many ecologists suspect that in the centuries before the fur rush, an underwater jungle of kelp paralleled the coast—a mirror image of the onshore jungle of cedars, redwoods, and spruce.

As otters dwindled, the fur trade moved inland, responding to the demand for beaver fur around 1800, when beaver-felt hats came into fashion among the ruling classes of Europe. Once its skin won favor as headgear in London and Paris, the industrious beaver of the mainland Northwest was as doomed as its curious relative on the coast—and the major river valleys of the region were destined to be transformed by the near-eradication of these dam builders. In 1804, Meriwether Lewis and William Clark described the land they traversed as "richer in beaver . . . than any country on earth." Less than four decades later, in 1840, a traveler named Frederick Ruxton reported, "Not a hole or corner but has been ransacked."

Most of the Northwest's beaver fur was sluiced from the region through a spillway called the Hudson's Bay Company, a British partnership chartered by the king with monopoly rights to trade with American natives. In return for this privilege, the company was to serve the interests of the British Empire—making it a sort of for-profit government. The boundaries of its Columbia Department coincide almost exactly with those of the Pacific Northwest bioregion.

The double personality of the company, as both corporation and Crown representative, accelerated the liquidation of the beaver. Between 1812 and 1846, the Columbia Department, or—in American parlance—the Oregon Territory, was under treaty as the shared property of Great Britain and the United States. (The Indians who lived there, of course, had other ideas.)

The result of joint sovereignty was unbridled competition. Anxious to impress the Crown and secure continued monopoly rights, the company used scorched-earth tactics to prevent American expansion. In 1824, the company instructed John McLoughlin, chief of the Department, to dispatch into the Snake River country— the area closest to American territory—enough men to eliminate marketable fur. The men were to dispense with buying pelts from Indians and trap the animals themselves. They were to trap pregnant females and juvenile males in addition to adult males. They were to turn the American approaches to the Northwest into a fur desert.

McLoughlin quickly assembled the Snake River Brigade, which McLoughlin's supervisor George Simpson later described as "the most unruly and troublesome gang . . . in this or any other part of the World." In four years' time, the job was done and the brigade's commander, Peter Skene Ogden, could report, "Almost every part of the country is now more or less in a ruined State."

North of the Columbia, the company continued trading with Indians rather than hunting for itself. But by 1840, the industry had collapsed. As the animals got harder to find, the price soared, which helped convince Europeans that Florentine hats made of silk were more fashionable anyway. Still, the damage had been done. From headwaters to ocean floor, everything from hydrology to nutrient cycling was rearranged in the wake of the human flood, and it took more than a century for beavers and otters to make a weak and partial comeback in the land that their furs first put on the map. The flood of fur trading waned, having achieved remarkable if misguided feats.

## April

On our car trip, we first crossed the track of the great flood on the Flathead Reservation in northwestern Montana.

"I've never seen anything like this before," Amy said. We had left the quilt of Indian cattle pastures and upscale retirement bungalows and entered a barren stretch of bedrock. Parallel gravel ridges—dozens of them—lined up on both sides. Each bar was spaced a football field from the next and stood taller than a bleacher. I pulled the car over near one and we all climbed out.

Kathryn grinned at being freed from the car seat and bounced in the pack on my back.

"What is this place?" Gary asked. A guidebook Amy had checked out of the library explained the landform. This valley was under eight hundred feet of water when the Ice Age dam broke. It was part of the great, spidery lake stretching two hundred miles east from the dam. The water split for the coast at fifty-five, maybe sixty miles an hour. Acceleration induced by a low pass to the west created standing waves here, like the ripples at the head of white water. These ripples, each miles long, dug down to bedrock and swept the lake-bottom gravel into tidy rows.

"Will a flood like that happen again?" Gary worried.

"Not like that," Amy told him.

**THE SECOND WAVE OF HUMAN** industry was mining. It started small but grew into a juggernaut by the end of the 1800s. By World War I, it, too, had collapsed in all but a few places.

The geological poking and scratching began in 1852, when prospectors wandered up from the goldfields of California. There, the easily accessible gold was almost gone, and mining had turned into an industrial venture. From the tortuous ranges of southern Oregon the gold panners made their way north, chasing each other from one small strike to the next.

Up the Columbia into Canada they went, then down the Fraser to near present-day Vancouver. There, they found enough gold in 1858 to convince Great Britain that mainland British Columbia deserved Crown Colony status. Next were strikes on Indian lands in Idaho, then in British Columbia's Cariboo district. The latter occasioned the Northwest's first public works project—the construction of a road around the canyon of the lower Fraser River.

Prospecting peaked in the mid-1860s, then slowed despite the 1872 General Mining Act. This law granted miners the rights to pay dirt found on U.S. government land in exchange for a payment of five dollars per acre. The mother lodes were deep underground and required big money to unearth.

Big money arrived in the 1880s. On the Coeur d'Alene River in northern Idaho in 1881, gold turned out to be the appetizer for a feast of silver that lasted decades. Silver poured out of Milo Gulch near present-day Kellogg, and from other shafts sunk into what became known simply as Silver Valley. Other gold and silver mines opened to the north, birthing such inland towns as Kimberly, Nelson, and Trail, British Columbia. For a few decades, Trail had a higher average income than almost any town in Canada.

Perched atop the Continental Divide, meanwhile, the mines of Butte were following chaotic veins of silver through the labyrinth of folds, fractures, and fissures that make up the Montana Rockies. Giant intrusions of copper mottled the lodes, annoying the miners greatly until the advent of electricity. Electric power for homes and factories needed wires to travel through, and copper was just the stuff. Butte converted itself from a second-rate silver town to the continent's greatest copper pit in the 1880s. By the turn of the century, Butte accounted for one-fourth of all copper mined worldwide and had earned the nickname "richest hill in the world."

The mining boom peaked again in the early twentieth century and began a long decline. In the 1980s, a new technique called heap-leaching allowed a minor resurgence: mountains of loose earth showered with a cyanide solution would yield profitable quantities of minerals. But it was nothing like the old days, and by 1993, mining employed just three-tenths of 1 percent of the region's workers. By then the regional economy depended more on the quality of life its natural amenities helped to make possible than on the bulky commodities it exported. And the mining past had become economic deadweight: the minerals and the money were gone, but the region was left with the holes in the ground—and the river-killing acid that drained out of them, and the acres of toxics-laced rock flour piled outside them, and the sulfur-deadened landscapes downwind from their smelters.

Montana's Clark Fork River below Butte won the dubious title of largest nonmilitary toxic waste cleanup site in the United States: 140 miles of poisoned riverbed. In the early 1990s, fish still died each time the rains were heavy enough to wash from the banks another dose of the arsenic, cadmium, and mercury left there by the mining wave. And the Clark Fork was not Montana's only tainted watercourse; not a single major river in the state escaped mining's touch.

The runner-up among toxic waste sites was Lake Coeur d'Alene, final resting place for the sediment of the Silver Valley. When the U.S. Geological Survey studied the lake in 1993, it found some of the worst heavy-metal contamination ever documented. There were seventy-five million tons of sediment laced with toxins. Nearby, at the old Bunker Hill mine, the soil was saturated with lead down to seventy feet below the surface. Estimates of the cost of cleaning up mining's legacy across the Northwest ran to more than a billion dollars.

## April

We next crossed the flood's path heading north through the Columbia Basin Project from the town of George, Washington. The New Deal irrigated this place, painting green what was once dry and brown. Sprinklers, like giant praying mantises, stalked over the fields. One poorly directed unit tested our windshield wipers. Farther on, we passed the town of Ephrata. It was a quiet place— charming, almost—built on farm money. Then, unexpectedly, north of Soap Lake, walls of ancient basalt rose up on either side. Swallows did loop-the-loops beneath the cliffs. We talked about the flood.

When the flood left Sandpoint, its waters fanned out across eastern Washington, scraping everything in their path to bedrock, then scouring through that. The terrain left behind is called the scablands. It was already an unusual place before the water rose. Millions of years ago, scores of lava-spewing fissures opened in the Columbia Basin, turning the area into a Kansas-sized Jell-O mold of solidifying rock. In places, the cooling basalt cracked into a honeycomb of columns—columns that proved easy pickings for the flood. The flood plucked out island-sized chunks and hurled them downstream like so much Styrofoam.

The flood found streambeds and ripped out hundred-foot canyons. It dug riverless canyons such as Dry Coulee, Spring Coulee, and Moses Coulee in a few days. On an old course of the Columbia, it excavated the largest of them all: the Grand Coulee. Fifty miles long, up to six miles wide and nine hundred feet deep, its impossible magnitude confounded geologists for half a century. And we were driving into it. The rock that once filled the trench, I told Gary, got hauled to sea by the flood.

"Like a dump truck?" he asked.

"Like a dump truck."

We rounded a bend and found the Lenore Lake Recreation Resort, advertising jet ski rentals and wave runners. It snapped us back to the present.

**FISHING WAS THE THIRD WAVE** of industry. It pounded into the lower Columbia in 1880, reaching Puget Sound, British Columbia, and Alaska at intervals thereafter. In its heyday, the Northwest salmon fishery caught and canned enough to feed every man, woman, and child in America four pounds a year. Lined up end to end, the one-pound tins would have circled the globe. In those days, salmon was so cheap it got a bad name. It was cheaper than canned tuna. It was cheaper than beef or chicken. It was food for poor folks.

The abundance of the fish inspired the fishermen to great feats. They strung nets most of the breadth of the Columbia, straining out the giant spring chinook and, when those grew scarce, the coho, silver, chum, and steelhead. The fish weighed so much it sometimes took teams of horses to land the catch. A net fisherman who could protect a good spot on the river would get rich. The hamlet of Chinook, Washington, where the fishermen congregated, was briefly one of the most affluent small towns in the country.

The fishermen constructed fish wheels at The Dalles and other Columbia rapids where Indians had always plucked fish from the current. These hydropowered Ferris wheels scooped their slippery passengers out of the water and threw them into a waiting trough. When the chinook were running, a well-placed device could extract fifty thousand pounds of fish a day.

The industry erected underwater corrals called fish traps on the main stem of the Columbia and in the San Juan Islands, where the millions of sockeye of the Fraser River run passed close to shore. To the south, the circle of traps that grew around Whidbey Island approached a hundred miles in circumference in the early 1900s. By then, dozens of trolling boats were combing the coastal waters, bristling with multihooked lines, and a hundred purse seiners were working off the southern end of Vancouver Island.

In the canneries, Chinese laborers slit and cleaned the salmon for a dollar a day, their razor-sharp blades dispatching two fish per minute. The whites kept the Chinese out of other fishing jobs with death threats and beatings, just as they had run them out of the mining camps years before. Later, anti-Chinese immigration restrictions pushed Chinese from the canneries as well. And away from the Columbia, automatic fish cleaners unapologetically called Iron Chinks came along that could clean a fish in a second. They were expensive, though, and had to run at full capacity to turn a profit. To the cannery owners that meant open-throttle fishing.

Overharvesting made the fishing wave crest initially; the catch peaked in 1901 on the Fraser, in 1902 in Willapa Bay on the Washington coast, in 1911 on the Oregon coast, in 1913 in Puget Sound, and around 1915 on the Columbia. But as the century progressed, irrigation projects, clear-cut logging, water pollution, and, especially, dam building accelerated the fisheries' decline. Fish hatcheries ameliorated the losses, providing a temporary substitute for wild fish. But hatchery-bred salmon lacked the genetic diversity of their free-running relatives. They grew to only half the size of their wild ancestors, and, like most domesticated species, proved easy targets for parasites and disease. Over the long run, they proved as great a danger to the fisheries as did overfishing.

By the 1980s, wild chinook and coho populations in the Columbia, Chehalis, and ten rivers running to the Oregon coast were, according to available data, one-sixth their 1900 level. In the lower forty-eight states, salmon were extinct in 38 percent of their historical range and at risk of extinction almost everywhere else. In British Columbia and Alaska, many runs remained healthy thanks to fewer dams and less degraded habitat. Still, the salmon fishery was a declining industry everywhere from Vancouver Island south; its principal asset had been liquidated. Modern catches were a fraction of those that Indian tribes had brought in each year for centuries. And the larger loss to the regional economy was off the ledger entirely. Salmon were so central to the cultures—both old and new—of this place that their loss threatened the Northwest's identity as an unspoiled place. And that identity was a growing part of the region's economic engine.

The Northwest salmon—the thread that bound the region, that pumped oceanic nutrients back on shore, that nourished native bellies and native cultures, that supported a work force of thousands, that defined the place—was on the ropes. On some rivers, fisheries biologists outnumbered migrating fish. On others, the legal briefs weighed more than the allowable catch. And on the Columbia, the aorta of this rainy province, the fish could no longer be trusted to survive on their own. So the U.S. Army Corps of Engineers, which has poured more concrete in their path than any other institution, began hauling young chinook downstream in converted grain barges. "Oh, Mighty Swimmers!" prayed the Kwakiutl Indians. "Freight tonnage," replied the corps.

## April

With Kathryn babbling on my back, Gary and I explored a slope of sagebrush beside Roosevelt Lake, the 150-mile-long reservoir behind the Grand Coulee Dam. The dam is not in the coulee; it is at a bend in the Columbia where the Ice Age flood veered into the coulee. The Bureau of Reclamation—chartered by Congress to irrigate the West—built the dam to raise water high enough that it could afford to pump the water the rest of the way into the coulee. From there, the bureau could run canals to a half-million acres of otherwise dusty farmland around places like George and Ephrata.

Lifting water that high meant a big dam, and the bureau built a whopper: a dam a mile wide and five hundred feet tall, containing enough concrete to loop a sidewalk twice around the globe, generating more electricity than any other source in North America, and creating the largest lake in the Northwest.

Gary was unimpressed. He stopped throwing rocks at the water to complain, "I thought we were going to see a river, Dad."

THE FOURTH WAVE WAS AGRICULTURE. Like mining and fishing, it started slowly in the middle of the 1800s, gaining momentum through that century. It crested later, though, first during World War I and then again after the New Deal dams provided irrigation water. Settlers began following trappers across the Oregon Trail in 1843, and within years hundreds of covered wagons were arriving at the loamy meadows of western Oregon's Willamette Valley. The next decade, settlers expanded north into Puget Sound country, and cattle herders went inland to tap the stockpiled fertility of native grasses.

The railroads, arriving in the 1880s, turbocharged farming and ranching—and all other Northwest industries—by stitching Northwest commerce to the rest of the continent. The Northern Pacific Railroad skirted the Columbia to Portland in 1883, then bored a parallel route through the Cascades to Tacoma in 1887. The same year, the Oregon and California Railroad bound the Northwest with the Golden State, and the Canadian Pacific Railroad reached the sea, giving birth to the city of Vancouver. Later, in 1893, the Great Northern Railroad connected St. Paul with Seattle by way of Spokane.

Only the last of these roads was built without public subsidy. All told, the railroads received grants in the Northwest of twenty-two million acres, more land than the Indians retained in reservations.

To make money, of course, the railroads needed to sell these lands, or the timber on them, along with plenty of passenger tickets and freight fares. So the Northern Pacific set up "immigration bureaus" in Boston, Omaha, and Topeka. It dispatched more than eight hundred agents in England to promise a better life in the Empire of the Columbia.

The sales job worked. The Northwest's population tripled in the first decade of the railroads, and much of the growth was on farms. Railroads brought settlers, who put two and a half million acres under the plow. Fifteen thousand new farms sprang up in the Columbia Basin in the 1880s. The town of Spokane erected a rough warehouse to shelter the ambitious homesteaders. Many went to work in the wheatlands of the Palouse country. There, fine loess soils ground by Ice Age glaciers had piled up to thicknesses as great as two hundred feet, secured only by a hairnet of grasses. The soil packed extraordinary fertility, quickly earning the Palouse recognition as one of the world's best wheat-growing regions. The productivity of the soil allowed farmers there to compete with their Kansas counterparts, despite a thousand-mile handicap in reaching eastern markets. Lucky farmers could earn the price of their land from a single crop. But the cost was world-class erosion. Between 1939 and 1979, Palouse fields lost six pounds of soil for every pound of wheat they grew.

With the railroads to provide transportation, apple orchards filled the rain-shadowed valleys east of the Cascades, and potatoes spread across every acre of southern Idaho that could be reached with a canal. Cattle and sheep herds expanded too. By 1900, more than a million head of cattle and four times that many sheep grazed the rangelands of Idaho, Oregon, and Washington, and the surge continued through World War I. By midcentury, livestock grazed virtually every acre of grassland from the ocean to the Continental Divide. And livestock owners, rewarded with government bounties, had poisoned or shot many of the region's wolves, coyotes, mountain lions, and grizzly bears.

By the late 1980s, three-quarters of the range in Idaho, Oregon, and Washington controlled by the U.S. Bureau of Land Management was, by the agency's reckoning, in poor or fair condition. Overgrazing had left an impoverished array of unpalatable scrub. Native bunchgrasses had given way to sagebrush, knapweed, and exotic grasses.

By the 1990s, the Eurasian plant cheatgrass was, by many accounts, the most common plant in the inland Northwest. Native grass ecosystems had been essentially eradicated by grazing, plowing, and the exotic species both introduced; patches of "old-growth" grassland were more rare by far than groves of old-growth forest.

After World War II, plentiful grain harvests inside and outside the Northwest made possible a final expansion of the region's herd. Idaho, Oregon, and Washington had nearly three million head of cattle in 1950, and the number rose to more than five million in the quarter century that followed. This surge, however, was based almost entirely on resource-intensive grain-feeding of livestock, not on grazing. And as grain supplies got tighter after 1975, cattle numbers fell; from 1975 to 1993, the Northwest herd shrank by 15 percent. By the end of that period, ranching employed fewer Northwesterners than did photo finishing or landscaping.

With the advent of federal water projects in the middle of the twentieth century, crop agriculture enjoyed another surge akin to that brought on by the railroads, raising farm output to levels previously unimagined. By the 1980s, the Pacific Northwest was providing 80 percent of the potatoes for french fries consumed in America, along with large shares of the apples, wheat, and hops. The region also turned out premium wool and a long list of specialty crops.

Sadly, as productive and industrious as the cultivators were, few operated in ways that could last indefinitely. Farms' water consumption accounted for close to nine-tenths of all water withdrawn from rivers, lakes, and aquifers in the region. Tillers too often treated soil as if it grew back. And they relied on an arsenal of agricultural chemicals that—whether or not they were effective—were toxic, resource-intensive, or both.

In 1991, for example, the state Department of Ecology analyzed well water in potato-growing Grant County, Washington. Two-thirds of the wells were laced with soil fumigants; more than half were contaminated with herbicides; and all the wells tested contained nitrates, a dangerous derivative of nitrogen fertilizers and animal wastes.

Farming and agricultural services continued to generate a small but important stream of income for the regional economy in the 1990s. In the sparsely populated inland Columbia Basin, where most farming took place, it accounted for 6 percent of all income in 1993, down from 11 percent a quarter century earlier. The agriculture wave was subsiding. Towns were dwindling. Young people were taking up other professions. Nobody was rushing to the Pacific Northwest to seek a future in farming.

## April

We met the course of the Ice Age cataclysm again, descending from the parched hills of the Yakama Indian Reservation onto the irrigated green of the Yakima Valley. (The tribe spells it with an "a," everyone else with an "i.") This was a backwater, where the flood piled up behind the entrance to the Columbia Gorge—the narrow canyon that threads its way through the Cascade Mountains. Slack water two hundred feet deep filled the valley, depositing some of the fertile soil it had gathered upstream. Now it is orchards, warehouses, and loading docks. The Spanish of farmworkers is the dominant tongue.

A white-sided building big as a barn loomed on the horizon. Block letters the height of the wall shouted "FRUITS & ANTIQUES. FRESH PLUMS CHERRIES APRICOTS ASPARAGUS." We stopped. Kathryn, learning to walk, bolted for the rear of the fruit stand. Amy joked that she could no longer run fast enough to keep up with her daughter.

"It looks to me," said the owner at the register, nodding at Amy's pregnant belly, "like you didn't run fast enough last fall." He was a leather-skinned man, sixtyish, with mirthful eyes and a wrinkled tattoo. We chuckled. Then he told us about his six kids and eighteen grandkids. His face creased in a grin and he spread out his arms toward his merchandise: "Well, the Lord *did* say be fruitful and multiply."

THE FIFTH WAVE DAMMED THE RIVERS for power and irrigation, turning to advantage the Northwest's corrugated topography and heavy precipitation. The region has more water running downhill than any other part of the continent, and it runs down fast. Few rivers on earth can match the Columbia's combination of volume and gradient. Guitar picker Woody Guthrie's "Roll On, Columbia" is wrong; the wild Columbia didn't roll, it fell. And the Columbia is just the biggest of the region's torrents. The Snake is more than twice the size of the Colorado. The Fraser holds almost twice the runoff of all the rivers in the state of California, and up North, the little-known Skeena gathers as much runoff as all of Texas's rivers.

The wave that tamed the rivers crested in the middle of the twentieth century but began with government-encouraged irrigation efforts in the 1870s. The U.S. Congress, eager to settle the West, voted in the Desert Lands Act of 1877 and the Carey Act of 1894, each offering extensive acreages for those promising to irrigate. In Idaho, the Carey Act did the trick, inducing private irrigation companies to divert Snake River waters onto close to a million acres.

The states in the Northwest chipped in the water free of charge. Following other western states, they adopted the principles of "first-in-time, first-in-rights" and "beneficial use." The Idaho constitution, for example, guarantees "the right to divert and appropriate the unappropriated waters of any natural stream to beneficial uses." If you got there first and started pumping, in other words, you could keep doing so forever—provided that you filed the right papers in the state capital and used the water "beneficially," that is, for irrigation. In Canada, water rights were only slightly more difficult to come by.

Still, free water or no, irrigation expanded too slowly for Uncle Sam. In the late 1920s, the Bureau of Reclamation started building irrigation dams in the region, mostly high on the Snake River. Farther downstream, the rivers descended into deep canyons, and the canyons made irrigation prohibitively expensive. But by the mid-1930s, the government—battling the Great Depression—had come to believe that building dams would restore the national spirit.

The idealism, ingenuity, and stamina of the human floods is nowhere more evident than in dam building. Only dreamers could do what was done on the Columbia: concrete poured as never before—anywhere. On the main stem of the Columbia, Rock Island Dam went up in 1933, Bonneville in 1938, Grand Coulee in 1941, McNary in 1953, Chief Joseph in 1955, The Dalles and Priest Rapids in 1957, Rocky Reach in 1961, Wanapum in 1963, Wells in 1967, John Day and Keenleyside in 1968, and Mica in 1973. And those were just on the trunk of the river. Counting the tributaries, thirty-six big dams stapled the arteries of the Columbia Basin, all built within forty years. On other rivers, more concrete was poured. By the early 1970s, the audacious and indefatigable engineers had plugged most of the leaks in the dendritic pattern, and the Northwest accounted for half of North America's hydroelectricity.

The hydropower was cheap, attracting aluminum smelters the way a candle draws moths. Smelting the metal runs high voltages through bauxite ore to break its chemical bonds. Some metallurgists call aluminum "coagulated electricity." Before long, the Northwest was smelting half of North America's aluminum, all with imported bauxite. At first, the smelters worked for the air force. Northwest rivers powered the aluminum plants that fed the airplane factories that supplied the bombers that softened Europe for D-Day. Grand Coulee alone supplied about half of the aluminum in U.S. aircraft during World War II. British Columbia, wanting to cash in on the aluminum boom after the war, handed the aluminum corporation Alcan the rights to the entire Nechako River, a major tributary of the Fraser.

Cheap hydropower also built the bomb. Producing plutonium takes even more electricity than smelting aluminum. The eight reactors at Hanford, Washington, powered by Grand Coulee, generated half the plutonium in the American nuclear arsenal. They also generated, of course, a world-class mess: reactor cooling water emptied into the Columbia pushed radioactivity levels in the river, even as far away as Portland, to three times that currently allowed for drinking water.

Cheap power—a fraction of a penny per kilowatt-hour wholesale—translated into the highest rates of consumption in the world. In the postwar boom, builders installed inexpensive electric heaters in droves, along with electric water heaters, electric stoves and ovens, and electric dryers. Nobody put in gas lines. Nobody insulated. Nobody thought about conserving. Why bother? Electricity was cheap and getting cheaper. A 1958 mural on the Seattle City Light building promised, "Electricity: that man may use it freely as the air he breathes."

Irrigation water was cheap, too. In southern Idaho, farmers in the Bureau of Reclamation's various projects paid dimes, sometimes nickels, per acre-foot delivered to their fields. An acre-foot is 325,000 gallons: enough to flood an acre one foot deep or to supply a North American family of five for a year. Because of the irrigated farms that bordered the Snake, Idaho was soon using more water per citizen than any other state in the union. By the early 1990s it led the world, withdrawing five times as much water per person as the globe's thirstiest nation, the Central Asian republic of Turkmenistan. Soaking that forty-mile-wide strip of Idaho desert with two, four, sometimes ten feet of water yielded bumper crops of cattle feed such as alfalfa and barley, and taxpayers picked up the tab. In the Columbia Basin Project, meanwhile, the bureau charged less than one-tenth of a cent per kilowatt-hour for irrigation pumping—a price so low that in the 1980s farmers were building miniature hydroelectric dams in their irrigation ditches, generating hydropower from pumped water!

The dream that inspired such public works was a nightmare for most native flora and fauna, as it was for the Indian economies they had supported. Grand Coulee alone closed fourteen hundred miles of salmon spawning grounds, slamming the door on dozens of distinct stocks and the tribal economies that depended on them. Millions of dirt farmers and factory hands across the country lost out, too. After the damming of the Columbia Basin was complete, they could no longer get a pound of Columbia River salmon for a dime; the dams cut off those runs.

At the end of the dam-building wave, the Columbia was hardly a river at all. Draining a basin larger than France that encompassed nearly half of the Northwest bioregion, the river was large enough to affect salinity and temperatures in coastal waters from California to Canada. And almost the entire length of it had become a chain of bathtubs. Less than one-fifth of its fifteen hundred miles still flowed free. The rest was a series of reservoirs, each backing up to the base of the next dam. The Columbia River was now the Columbia Waterworks. It was plumbing. But the regional economy was not well served. By overdoing the development of hydropower, the Northwest sacrificed natural services and qualities worth more than the extra kilowatts.

## April

Gary was reading to us as we approached the one-horse town of Lyle, Washington. We were on the eastern side of the Columbia Gorge. Terraces of parched basalt stepped up from the reservoir of the Bonneville Dam, chiseled clean by the flood all those years ago. We had been running the gauntlet of four-by-fours decked with wind surfers. They sped up and down the gorge, chasing the breeze.

"One fish, two fish, red fish, blue fish," read Gary. We poked through town toward the riverfront, passing a stone gate into a meadow of wildflowers, dry grass, and split-rail fences. Gary looked up from his book and spotted a sign. "Have the . . . "

" . . . Columbia . . . " Amy prompted.

" . . . River at your . . . "

"It's a compound word. Try splitting it in half."

" . . . door . . . step."

"Right!" She continued, "Klickitat Landing. Rare waterfront and view sites. Direct access to windsurfing. Tennis courts and pool . . . Priced from $72,000." Thinking no more of it, we drove over a rise and—pinching ourselves—descended on two Indian tepees, a sweat lodge, and an old-fashioned fishing scaffold. Amy guessed it was a movie set. I figured it was a New Age religious site. Gary just said, "Indians!" He was right.

Stopping the car, we walked closer, then hesitated. "Hello?" No answer. We noticed a bulletin board by the sweat lodge. Plastic-sheathed newspaper clippings told the story. This was a fishing controversy. A middle-aged wind surfer was developing the property. The land was also a traditional fishing site for the Yakama people, one of the "usual and accustomed places" to which they were guaranteed access in perpetuity by their treaty with the United States. Most of the other sites were submerged under the reservoir of the Bonneville Dam.

The wind surfer had no argument with their right to fish there. He had allowed a hundred-foot buffer strip for their access to the riverfront. But the Yakama were worried about the long term. Imagine how the residents of Klickitat Landing would feel when, each year, a few dozen Indians rolled in, pitched tepees, built fire circles, unloaded a portable yellow outhouse, and started drying twenty-pound fish on the median strips. The Yakama believed they would be shouldered aside, so they were protesting Klickitat Landing. They had been camping out and fishing there for months, catching the hatchery salmon that had replaced the wild runs. They had brought a halt to construction for the moment—a sort of eddy in the flood.

It was fitting. The guidebook said that there, thirteen thousand years ago, the Ice Age flood came out of a hairpin turn and spun into a giant eddy, a swirling backwater a thousand feet deep that deposited the gravel on which Lyle was built.

We drove on. Gary read, "Black fish, blue fish, old fish, new fish."

THE SIXTH WAVE WAS LOGGING. It surged and flagged during the 1800s and crested only in 1988. It took that long because the forests were incomprehensibly large. The timber was so straight and plentiful that, as the old-timers said, "You can't lie fast enough to keep up with the honest facts." The wood jutting skyward from southeast Alaska to northwest California comprised what was likely the heaviest accumulation of living matter ever to adhere to the surface of the planet. Each acre groaned under the mass of it; in the coastal lowlands, an acre might carry a thousand metric tons of plant matter, including two hundred Douglas fir trees. Each the girth of an elephant and taller than the Statue of Liberty, one of these arboreal Goliaths could supply enough lumber to build a farmhouse, a barn, and a garden fence—or, when the mills cut the boards a little thinner, four two-bedroom bungalows.

The first loggers strayed no more than two miles from sheltered salt water—the distance a team of oxen could drag one of these monster trunks. That hardly limited things, considering the thirty-five-thousand-mile protected shoreline of the winding Northwest coast. At first, markets were few. The wood was damnably cumbersome. But the California gold rush of 1849 helped. The San Francisco fires that followed helped further, briefly elevating Northwest lumber prices to levels not repeated for more than a century. Thereafter, California capitalists, flushed with gold money, financed exports. In the 1870s, millions of board feet of Douglas fir crossed the Pacific. Fir built railroad trestles in Australia and buttressed mine shafts in Peru.

Owning the timber they cut was of little importance to many loggers. They drew their two-man saws—"misery whips"—through the fifteen-foot bases of the trees, heedless of property lines, Indian reservations, or government policies. And rarely did anyone stop them. On the mountainous coast of British Columbia, teams of lumbermen started at sea level and shaved upward until the logs would no longer tumble unaided into the brine. Then they'd move on to the next slope, towing their booty in great rafts behind.

The next burst of logging was spurred by the exhaustion of the white pine woodlands of Minnesota and the upper Mississippi basin. This drew the lumbermen into the Northwest forests decisively in 1900. In that year, German-born timber maven Frederick Weyerhaeuser and a group of fifteen investors purchased nine hundred thousand acres of forest from the Northern Pacific Railroad Company. The company was then controlled by James J. Hill of St. Paul and his New York banker J. P. Morgan. Weyerhaeuser bought the property for six dollars an acre—a high price for the time—and bought it with explicit intentions. "We bought this timber," one of his partners told the press, "not to look at but to cut." As it turned out, they intended to cut it when the market was strong; they waited years before cashing out.

News of the deal set off a stampede. Mill owners, figuring Weyerhaeuser knew something they did not, bolted for the Northwest. They acquired timberland, cut forests, and erected sawmills. One hundred fifty mills went up on the shores of Puget Sound in 1902 alone. They cut five billion board feet in 1900 and nine billion in 1910. They did it with the help of a new device called the donkey engine, a stationary locomotive that reeled in logs as easily as an angler in a trout pond. With the powerful new machine, logging left salt water and pushed up the valleys, seeking unblemished Douglas fir and redwood wherever they stood.

Timber extraction continued its erratic climb, surging to a peak of perhaps seventeen billion board feet in 1929 before dropping during the Depression. By 1940, though, the cut was back to pre-Depression heights and rising in fits and starts: twenty-five billion in 1960, thirty-two billion in 1970. In 1988, it crested—probably for all time—at thirty-eight billion board feet. In 1992, it was down to thirty billion and falling.

This looked like the last hurrah. There were not too many places left to go. Washington never matched its 1929 timber production, nor Oregon its 1952 cut. Idaho peaked in the late 1970s; Alaska, British Columbia, and western Montana, in the late 1980s. In 1987, British Columbia alone clear-cut more than a thousand square miles of woodlands.

The frontier was pushed back, the virgin forests diminished; they had provided roughly a trillion and a half board feet of the finest softwood timber ever felled, but—outside of Alaska and British Columbia—only scattered remnants still stood. Most of the surviving old-growth forest in eastern Oregon and Washington was in stands of less than a hundred acres.

Early in the century, the industry had cleared private land, but by midcentury it was working the public domain, first in the most prolific, rain-soaked stands along the southern coast, then farther north, farther inland, and higher up. Southeast Alaska and British Columbia, where almost all timber was in government hands, did not start open-throttle logging until the 1960s.

Across the region, corporate and political chiefs recited incantations about maximum sustained yield, perpetual timber supplies, and improving the resource base. Many of them no doubt believed what they said. But they were mistaken. The cut in British Columbia exceeded the B.C. Ministry of Forests' estimated long-term sustained yield in the early 1960s and kept growing. Stumpage fees—the negotiated price a corporation paid the province for the trees it felled—were typically a third to a half of what they would have been if the province had auctioned the trees instead. It was a province-wide clearance sale.

In the United States, Congress required the U.S. Forest Service to spend at least $50 million a year building logging roads to serve up southeast Alaska's Tongass National Forest on a platter. And the legislative branch behaved no differently in the lower forty-eight. Every year from 1986 to 1991, for example, Congress ordered the Forest Service to exceed sustained yield in Washington and Oregon national forests.

Planted firs rose in the place of the old growth: fast-growing, genetically improved, carefully tended specimens to be cut after seventy or a hundred years. Good trees, growing well, but in tree farms, not forests. And they would not last their full rotation. The calculus of finance would see to that.

The first regrown trees to approach saleable sizes were on private lands because those were the first lands cleared. In 1980, a little-noticed provision of the Staggers Act freed railroads to sell off subsidiaries. Within months, a few Wall Street raiders were buying acreage long ago granted to the Northern Pacific, stripping off its young second-growth timber, and dumping it on the market again. The logic of business said "sell." Standing trees, if cut and marketed, were money enough to pay for their own purchase.

Sir James Goldsmith, a knighted Englishman, took over Crown Zellerbach, a timber conglomerate with a million acres in Washington and Oregon. He auctioned its mills and a third of its acreage to finance the debt, then set about cutting wood. On the Olympic Peninsula, he mowed down whole valleys, turning salmon streams such as the Pysht into mud plumes that clogged offshore kelp beds. Then, when the forest was off to the lumberyard, he sold the bald hillsides to another English concern. Scott Paper Company's lands north of Seattle were taken over by a newly incorporated entity called Crown Pacific. Nearby, the Trillium Corporation was taking over Georgia-Pacific lands.

The economics of divesting, acquiring, and debt drove the accelerated cutting. In much of the Northwest, timber companies abandoned restraints and pillaged their own immature plantations. Champion International and Plum Creek Timber cleaned out the western larch and ponderosa pine of the Montana Rockies in square-mile sections. The chessboard pattern of land ownership established by the railroad grant was now etched on the land itself.

When loggers first sharpened their axes in the Northwest, they were taking out five-hundred-year-old trunks averaging seventeen feet in diameter. Weyerhaeuser's average tree felled in 1980 was forty years old and twenty inches thick. The industry was now cutting juveniles. In western Montana, trucks that once carried five jumbo logs per load were, by the early 1990s, hauling thirty skinny ones. As *Seattle Times* reporter William Dietrich put it, "The wild and unruly forest of giant trees and silver snags and behemoth mossy logs and secret rot—the titanic Northwest woods . . . —was mostly gone. It had been replaced by a younger, trimmer, smaller, plainer industrial forest."

In the process of liquidating the Northwest woods, the timber industry and forest departments built three times as many miles of logging roads as the region had in public streets and highways. In 1994, approximately half a million miles of logging roads criss-crossed the region's forests, enough to wrap around the world twenty times. These roads bled soil into streams, worsened floods, fragmented habitats, allowed hunters motorized access to trophy elk and grizzly bears, and hastened the spread of exotic species and diseases. They constituted one of the least-noted and most important threats to ecosystems in the region. They also constituted a threat to its identity as the land of salmon: south of the Canadian border, the Pacific Northwest had more miles of roads than streams. In other words, outside of Alaska, motor vehicles had access to more of the U.S. Northwest than did salmon.

Public outcry and court orders slowed logging in the early 1990s, but most of the accessible old forests were gone by then. Their biological wealth had been converted into shareholder dividends, tax revenues, and paychecks. And then, like the fur trade, the mining boom, the fishing industry, the farm surge, and the dam extravaganza, the timber industry slid toward the periphery of the regional job market. By 1993, it employed less than 4 percent of Northwest workers—one-eighth as many as worked in service industries.

The plantation timber industry—an essentially agricultural enterprise, and one that is well suited to the region's soil and climate—could support a modest share of the region's workers indefinitely. But it would never yield the volumes or quality of wood cut in logging's heyday.

In small old-growth timber towns, workers lost jobs and homes. Schools closed. Communities withered and dissipated. Politicians rallied unemployed woods workers by blaming urban conservationists. The logging wave subsided; it had run its course.

# *April*

We stopped in Stevenson, Washington, deep in the Columbia Gorge, where the flood had cut away whole mountainsides to straighten its route to the sea. Above Stevenson, people had cleared off the woodlands with similar intensity. But the logging was over. The owner of the Baker's Oven in Stevenson, a loquacious woman in her midthirties, said, "I've lived here all my life, and look at us. Most of us are on the unemployment line.

"We used to have the timber industry, but that's gone." Her mouth smiled but her eyes said, "City slickers." Uphill, in the national forest named for Gifford Pinchot—America's first trained forester—the timber industry had clear-cut all but a few valleys of the original forests. The Gifford Pinchot National Forest is what Northwesterners call a "working forest"—it looks like a dog with the mange. For decades, clearing the old growth employed Stevenson's people. They never got rich at it; in fact, their county stayed the poorest in the state. Still, logging was honest work. Then, in 1991, a federal judge—a city slicker—shut them down.

Judge Bill Dwyer sat in a Seattle courtroom and listened to scientists testify that the northern spotted owl, a bird few people had ever seen, faced extinction if business in the woods continued as usual. Dwyer checked the statutes on species protection and found them unequivocal. He ordered the U.S. Forest Service to stop selling timber until it produced a credible plan to save the owl. For Dwyer, it was a straightforward matter of jurisprudence. But because of it, he was excoriated, vilified, and burned in effigy in the Stevensons of the Northwest. Dwyer was a scapegoat, of course. The job losses in Stevenson started a decade before his ruling and resulted from the mechanization of mill work and the liquidation of the forest. If Dwyer had not stopped the logging all at once, it would have soon come to a halt on its own.

The owner of the Baker's Oven did not know that we were from Seattle. And she certainly did not know that I used to go trick-or-treating at Bill Dwyer's house. (He was a neighbor.) But the urban-rural divide separated us. She was a touch defiant. "A couple of us started this bakery," she said; it had done well thanks to the traffic from the Skamania Lodge. She pointed beyond the gas station to a swanky new resort overlooking the town. She lowered her voice and leaned toward us to say that the two hundred rooms started at ninety dollars a night. We were in her favor now. Our thrift-store clothes put us squarely in her tax bracket.

The resort helped Stevenson make the transition from lathes to lattes in record time. In 1992, Stevenson's lumber mill shut down, putting 200 people out of work; a year later, the Skamania Lodge opened, employing 230. Attracted by the view and the wind-surfing—inexhaustible resources, if not as lucrative as old growth—outsiders spent their money at the bakery, the convenience store, and the new espresso cart outside the True Value Hardware. Stevenson was no longer a place of extraction. It was a place of consumption.

Later, Amy and I perched on a roadside high above the river, watching a lone jet skier make lazy eights. The flood had been a thousand feet deep here in the western Columbia Gorge. You could see its course plain as day. The high-water mark was the top of the cliffs. Above it the hills lay back under their patchy evergreen blanket. Below it there was mostly what rock climbers call Big Air: vertical walls down to the floodplain. The Columbia River had sliced through the range in a V-shaped valley until the Ice Age flood bulldozed out this foursquare trench.

It was late afternoon and the kids were asleep in the car. The radio was tuned to a station that promised "the hits of the seventies all weekend long." Amy and I giggled, singing along with the Steve Miller Band, "Some call me the gangster of love." We spit watermelon seeds at each other. Across the river a trainload of bright orange Sealand cargo containers moved up from Portland, riding the Northwest's oldest railroad. Probably TVs, VCRs, CD players, and other acronyms from Japan. A prepubescent Michael Jackson was chirping the end of "One bad apple don't spoil the whole bunch, girl," when a red Corvette pulled in. A sunburned, graying couple got out and looked up the gorge briefly. She posed beside the car. He pointed a camera. They zoomed away, having consumed the spot with their Nikon. The radio was crooning, "My highway in the sun . . . "

FOR TWO CENTURIES AND MORE, the economy has been cashing the landscape, converting natural capital into consumer products. Nature displayed so much wealth at first that it seemed criminal to leave it alone. Northwest trees were obscenely large. Millions of fish rotted in mountain brooks. And the rivers wasted oceans of water. Abundance on this scale was discomforting, so the arriving population attacked the place with a vengeance. "It was strangely like war," wrote historian Murray Morgan in 1955. "They attacked the forest as if it were an enemy to be pushed back from the beachheads, driven into the hills, broken into patches, and wiped out."

In two centuries, the flood of people—mostly from the East, and mostly of European descent—transformed the Northwest. From a last frontier, they turned it into a center of world trade, a rising star of the Pacific Rim. Measured in money, their growth was straight out of the tale of King Midas: everything they touched turned to gold. The total cash-valued output of the regional economy—its gross national product—grew from barter goods worth a few thousand dollars in 1792 to more than $300 billion in 1992.

The combined personal income of all Northwesterners, adjusted for inflation, doubled from 1929 to 1949, doubled again by 1969, and doubled again by 1989. In other words, the Pacific Northwest got rich. The regional economy, with its fourteen million participants, makes more wealth each year than the nation of India, with seventy times the people. A quarter of a percent of the world's population, Northwesterners earn more income each year than did everyone alive in the year the international economy first touched the Northwest—1778, when Captain Cook's crew traded for otters. This place is among the richest parts of the richest society in history.

Each of the floods subsided, yet the economy of the Pacific Northwest continued to expand. It did so because the region partly unhitched itself from resource extraction. It hitched onto a different locomotive—human ingenuity, the ultimate source of all economic improvement.

No one knows the value of the Northwest's entire stock of wealth—its income-producing physical, natural, and human capital. But thoughtful economists believe that the sources of wealth are mostly intangible. Human capital—ingenuity, skills, education, shared knowledge, social networks, and human organizations— matters more to national welfare, for example, than does the inventory of factories and equipment. Besides, physical capital can almost always be rebuilt, while human and natural capital often cannot.

Yet across the Pacific Northwest in the mid-1990s, a disconcerting number of people still believed the economy worked as it did when the region was a resource colony. They believed that tangible capital was where the money was. They did not understand that people are the source of most wealth, and that most economic activity consists of people doing things for each other. They therefore gave to the physical manipulation of the products of nature—of matter—far more credit than it deserved.

Industries that extract and process natural resources, called "primary" or "basic" in official economic accounts, were accorded a degree of respect and government support not shared by industries that work with people directly or with the distribution and redistribution of goods or services. The imagery often employed to describe the economy was of the region's farmers, loggers, and factory hands supporting not only themselves but everyone else, through the "spinoff" effects of their production on "secondary and service industries."

This understanding of the economy—that resource and manufacturing industries created wealth while all other industries simply shuffled it around—was both widespread and false. As of 1993, resource extraction and processing had generated declining shares of employment and income in the Pacific Northwest for as long as records had been kept. Most of the regional economy had long since disengaged from the processing of raw materials and production of manufactured goods. In 1993, seven times as many people worked in services as in timber and mining combined. More people worked for government than for all "primary" industries combined. Three times as many people worked in service industries as in manufacturing industries.

Related to the myth that physical production continued to power the regional economy was the baseless notion that goods-producing activities were important because they met needs, while service enterprises merely met wants. This widely held belief was contradicted by the fact that in the 1980s, enterprises that met Americans' biological needs for basic nourishment and shelter accounted for approximately one-tenth of the economy, according to University of Montana economist Thomas Power. To maintain that resource industries were more vital than service industries was to suggest that health care and education were less important than the production of exterior siding or french fries.

Furthermore, extraction and manufacturing did not, as many believed, provide better jobs than services. Many people thought of service jobs as some variation on burger-flipping, but brain surgeons, teachers, and lawyers were all service-sector workers as well. There were miserable jobs in all sectors of the economy, but overall, pay scales in both government and service industries were better than those in extraction or manufacturing. Workers remained with the same organization longer in service industries than in extraction or manufacturing. Workers suffered less occupational injury and death in service industries than in manufacturing or extraction. Logging was especially dangerous; it ranked among the most risky lines of work in North America.

Towns and counties that relied heavily on resource extraction had lower—and less reliable—incomes than towns and counties that relied on services. Resource towns also received less investment, because no one expected them to last. Northwest mining towns, for example, that had channeled millions of dollars to the outside world remained squalid settlements themselves or disappeared completely.

Conventional wisdom's tenet that without "primary" jobs other jobs would disappear was equally unfounded. Across the region, the opposite had been happening for decades. In western Oregon, the early 1990s saw huge court-ordered reductions in logging, along with the lowest unemployment rates in recent decades. Western Montana's economy displayed the same behavior, thriving during the collapse of its supposed economic base. By the late twentieth century, the Pacific Northwest's economic welfare no longer depended much on resource extraction. What it did rest on was the region's quality of life. The Pacific Northwest's economy was moved primarily by human capital—know-how, creativity, social networks, skills. And human capital was mobile; it congregated in places where people wanted to live.

The old, physical production–centered view of the world ignored just how much people cared where they lived. Living in a safe, friendly, beautiful, and convenient locale was among most people's major concerns. This is why areas adjacent to protected landscapes—wilderness, national parks, areas that had been declared off-limits to extraction—showed much more economic vitality than rural areas where the landscape was open to extraction. "Locking up" natural resources did not, on average, impoverish people; it enriched them.

Thus, Northwesterners' ultimate end—quality of life—was also the engine of their economy. The region prospered to the extent that it remained a good place to live, and thus, there was no long-term tradeoff between jobs and the environment. The region could have both or it could have neither. At the local level, environmental protection sometimes brought dislocation and hardship—although rarely as much as its opponents predicted—but at the regional level, protecting nature had almost always proved a smart economic strategy. Economic studies showed that environmental regulations have small positive effects on employment, because both employers and employees are people, all of whom want to live in a safe and healthy environment.

Yet the Northwest did not comprehend this fact, and it did not accurately monitor its true wealth, neglecting to count environmental quality and the health of its communities. The result was that the region continued to make choices in which natural losses exceeded monetary gains. Some additions to gross national product were subtractions from gross natural productivity. As shares of the income and jobs in the regional economy, all of the resource industries—trapping, mining, fishing, farming, power generation, and logging—declined steeply. Indeed, all of them except power generation and farming yielded declining absolute-dollar outputs and shrinking payrolls. Yet the region continued to favor them.

The human flood was impoverishing itself because people failed to grasp the indispensability and ultimate fragility of the environment. They did not understand that all the investment capital was nothing without the hospitable climate, clean air and water, fertile soil, and arrays of foods, fibers, materials, and chemicals that evolution produced. They neglected the fact that all their physical capital was worthless without the biosphere's help in decomposing, assimilating, and rendering useful again the wastes of industry. And they did not comprehend that all human capital was ultimately living bodies—bodies that exchanged 90 percent of their water, carbon, and other chemical constituents with nature each year.

Natural capital, fortunately, was abundant. There was time to learn. Ecosystems proved resilient; they showed they would bounce back if not pushed too far. Have Northwesterners pushed them too far? Probably not. Few species have been lost throughout their range. Few habitats are entirely gone. Few places are irretrievably contaminated.

The present generation of Northwesterners could restore the Northwest if they put their minds to it, if they trained the cash economy to respect its biological origins. That means erecting a sturdy framework of laws, institutions, and social values able to conform the economy to the limits of nature. If Northwesterners put their minds to it, they can build such a framework—indeed, thousands of them are already struggling to do so. They are bringing to bear their outlandish idealism, irrepressible ingenuity, and brute stamina.

The irony, after all, is that this entire flood of human enterprise has been populated with decent, hardworking people. All along the way, individual people have been making rational choices. It has been the system that has been stark, raving mad.

## April

Last week, we got lost in the maze of new ranch houses going up in the city of Vancouver, Washington—the fastest-growing part of the state. Then, finding the way, we walked down a glade toward the reconstructed Fort Vancouver, once the seat of the Hudson's Bay Company and the early focal point of Euro-American industry in the Northwest. The log-walled fort was now sandwiched between a landing strip and the droning rampart of Interstate 5. Beyond were the Columbia River and Portland, Oregon.

The city's tall buildings were up to their necks in shimmering photochemical smog. Fifteen thousand years ago, they would have been up to their necks in floodwaters—up to the thirtieth floor of the First Interstate tower. Leaving the gorge just upstream, the flood spread out and slowed to thirty-five miles per hour. Part bulged south into the broad Willamette Valley; the rest hammered on to the Pacific. By the time it reached this point, it was as much a sandblaster as a torrent. It carried fifty square miles of loess soil, basalt chunks, and other debris. Here and there, garage-sized boulders washed up on mountainsides. This area got remodeled as suddenly as everything inland, and within a fortnight water levels were back to normal. If there were Indians still in the area, those who had gone hunting in the mountains must have returned to a landscape as foreign as the face of the moon. Did they ever know what happened?

A blue-black barn swallow, iridescent and fork-tailed, circled us at knee height once, twice, three times. It banked hard and was gone—hawking off across the grass. A second swallow mimicked the first. Were they mates luring us away from a nest? No, a third and fourth were repeating the dance. Then the entire colony scrambled and flew around us, doing gyroscopic spins that expanded and contracted. They were playing. We were transfixed.

*chapter three*

# CARS

## September

MAYBE IT WAS THE INDIAN SUMMER sun on the bedroom walls this morning that awakened me with a desire to look into Bear Creek again. Something called up a memory of an Indian summer day when my sister, my brother, and I ran out of the yard of Olive Salstrom's homestead cabin.

Boasting of our fearlessness, we crashed through the sodden woods beyond—woods where darkness oozed from the cedars. Boisterously calling, we ran across a field where the grass brushed our elbows. We galloped until Bear Creek, silent behind a curtain of reeds, threatened to swallow us; only fistfuls of grass kept us from tumbling in. And our feet were hardly beneath us again before Jonathan let out a yelp. "There's a bridge!" It was just downstream, half covered with branches and sinking into the water.

"Dare you to go across it," said Susan, the eldest.

"Double-dare you," retorted Jonathan.

The three of us goaded each other onto the rotting boards, first on our knees and then on our bellies. Finally, we craned our necks and peered into the frigid water.

Our taunts subsided. Staring back were dozens of hook-jawed sockeyes—salmon, their heads jet black and their bodies the color of blood. Treading water and eyeing us, they were ghoulish and ugly. Their flesh hung in ribbons from their bones. Corpses littered the creek bed beneath them, and the air was pungent with death.

Sensing that we had chanced upon something too grown-up for us and, at a loss for words, we simply edged backward off the bridge without looking at each other and retraced our steps to Mrs. Salstrom's listing porch.

She opened her door. "Back so soon?" she asked, her eyes twinkling as always. "Did you see a ghost?" She seemed older than anyone I knew, standing there in her doorway, scarcely taller than me and probably lighter. Soft wrinkles covered her face. Behind her in her tiny house, I could see her wood stove and her spinning wheel. I was sure she was ancient. Her car had been parked in the barn so long that mice had moved in. My parents said that she used to be a teacher and a librarian, but that seemed improbable to me: a gnome or an elf seemed much more likely. How else could you explain that magical glint in her eyes?

"There are salmon in the creek," said Susan, to explain our return.

"Oh, yes," Mrs. Salstrom nodded, smiling slightly. "They come this time every year."

"What's wrong with them?" Jonathan asked.

Mrs. Salstrom did not answer. Instead, she cleared a bench in her cramped kitchen. "You children sit here by the stove. I was just about to check my bread."

She rummaged around for a moment. I thought she was ignoring the question. Maybe it was one of those questions that made adults change the subject. Maybe we were not supposed to have seen what we saw. Maybe it was a secret.

"Aha!" Mrs. Salstrom said, finding her oven mitt. She opened the wood stove. Then, in that small, dancing voice of hers, she said, "They come to lay their eggs in the gravel."

From the heart of her blackened stove, she pulled a golden loaf of bread. "First they fight. Then they pair off."

She cut the bread into thin, steaming slices. "After they lay their eggs, they guard the nests for as long as they can."

She served each of us a slice of the bread. I remember the smell of that bread mixing with the wood smoke. She said, "Right now, they're waiting to die. The eggs will hatch in the spring, and the babies will swim away to the sea."

This morning, as I recalled that distant day, I wanted to go look for fish. "Amy, let's take the bus out to Redmond and see what's become of Olive Salstrom's old place—the place my folks used to take me when I was a kid." Amy, on a lark, agreed.

Gary listened to my tale of a meandering creek and phantom sockeye and ran to his room. "I'm gonna catch some!" In a moment he was back, brandishing a butterfly net.

We dressed Kathryn, now a year old, and our new baby, Peter. I phoned my parents, Jean and Marvin, to get directions. They conferred for a while with their hands muting the receivers, then said they would like to come along. I guess it was the Indian summer sun. We agreed to pack lunches and meet on the bus that runs from their neighborhood to ours. Downtown, we could transfer to the line that would take us to Mrs. Salstrom's, whatever was left of it.

**THE HONOURABLE GORDON PRICE**, member of the Vancouver, British Columbia, City Council and a standard-bearer for the more conservative of the two municipal parties, is cruising the streets of his neighborhood—the West End—on a wet winter Saturday. He is doing what keeps local politicians in office: He is staying in touch with the concerns of his constituency. He is mingling.

At the moment, he is stopped in the middle of the road, greeting some passersby. For a politician, this is not unusual. What is peculiar is that Gordon is not in an automobile; he does not own one. Gordon's peculiarity reflects that of the neighborhood—a tree-lined square mile of apartments, condominiums, offices, and shops between downtown Vancouver and Stanley Park.

Gordon says, "We're standing in the middle of the street in the middle of the highest-density residential area in western Canada, and we're not even thinking about traffic." The narrow road—lined with parked cars, leafy trees and shrubs, wide sidewalks, and closely set buildings both tall and short—is empty of moving autos but full of people on foot.

"When I am walking or jogging in the West End, I usually count ten pedestrians for every moving car," notes Gordon. And this ratio explains why he contends that Vancouver's West End, once reviled as a concrete jungle, is "one of the only real answers to the quandary of creating a sustainable and environmentally sound way of life."

The West End has put cars in their place. How it has done so is an important lesson for the entire Northwest, because most of the rest of the region has conformed itself to the automobile—with disastrous results.

Automobiles' private benefits are enormous and well understood. Gordon admits, "They are powerful tools for mobility, providing personal, door-to-door transportation on demand." Yet they are also the source of a disturbing share of the Northwest's environmental—and social and economic—problems. They are the proximate cause of more environmental harm than any other artifact of everyday life in the region.

Cars are to the human and natural environments as cigarettes are to health: serial killers. Traffic accidents kill more Northwesterners each year than gunshot wounds or drug abuse; almost 2,000 people died—and 168,000 were injured—in car wrecks in 1993 alone. Traffic accidents are the leading cause of death among Americans aged two to twenty-four, and children and the elderly account for a large share of the pedestrians killed by motor vehicles.

Cars kill or injure thousands more Northwesterners each year without ever touching them. Air pollution from cars and trucks— and from the industries that build, fuel, repair, and support them—causes respiratory diseases and lung cancer. Motor vehicles release the single largest share of air pollution in the region, more than factories, furnaces, or any other source. In Washington, road vehicles release 55 percent of all air pollution, while in greater Vancouver, Gordon says, they release two-thirds.

"Cars are far cleaner than they used to be," Gordon notes, but they remain heavy polluters. Each year, each typical automobile in greater Vancouver pumps into the air enough sulfur to fill twenty Olympic-sized swimming pools with acid rain. It emits enough carbon monoxide and nitrogen oxides to contaminate the air inside the massive B.C. Place domed stadium to three times the danger level. Its exhaust contains enough aldehydes, arsenic, lead, and other airborne toxic chemicals to fill a coffee cup. And, each year, it emits its own weight in carbon in the form of carbon dioxide—the principal climate-changing greenhouse gas.

To grasp the full magnitude of the harm automobiles do in the Northwest, add the damage they cause to bodies of water through crankcase drips, oil spills, and the great wash of toxic crud running off roads, driveways, and parking lots. Add the billions of dollars of income drained from the regional economy to pay for the region's two largest imports: vehicles and oil. Add the crops stunted by air pollution on farms near Northwest cities—losses valued annually at more than $10 million. Add the fragmentation of every type of wildlife habitat caused by lacing the bioregion with 220,000 miles of public streets and highways.

"Transportation," says Gordon, now standing under a row of street trees on a West End sidewalk, "is a means, not an end. The end is *access*." People want to have access to things—services, locations, facilities. They want to stop at the health club, pick up some groceries, drop by a friend's place, and still get home from work at a reasonable hour. Most of the Northwest has sought to provide this access through greater mobility. The West End has provided it through greater proximity.

Access through mobility has required incredible numbers of cars. In 1994, there were nearly eleven million motor vehicles in British Columbia, Idaho, Oregon, and Washington combined, and the number was growing. It was growing faster than the economy, and almost twice as fast as the population. In fact, the vehicle population was gaining on the human population.

In 1963, there were two people per vehicle—everyone could hit the road and no one had to sit in the back seat. In 1994, there was 0.8 vehicle per person, counting nondrivers; vehicles actually outnumbered licensed drivers by a million. If every driver in the

Northwest took to the roads at the same time, there would still have been a million parked cars.

After 1983, the amount of driving increased even faster than the number of autos. Vehicles in Idaho, Oregon, and Washington covered eleven miles per person per day in 1957. They drove twenty-five miles per person per day in 1993.

Some of this growth occurred because people were driving farther each time they got in their cars, but most of it happened because people were getting in their cars more often. They were driving on 90 percent of all the trips they took. That share had been rising for decades, at the expense of trains, bicycles, buses, and foot travel. And the reason for this shift was sprawl.

The share of people in Idaho, Oregon, and Washington who live in suburbs has risen from just 7 percent in 1950 to 30 percent in 1990. Suburbs overtook towns in population in the 1960s. They passed cities in the 1970s, and exceeded rural areas in the 1980s. And these figures understate the true share of the population living and working in sprawl because they rely on a narrow definition of suburbs used by the U.S. Census Bureau. A true accounting shows that more than half of all Northwesterners live in sprawl.

Sprawl has three defining characteristics. It is a lightly populated, or "low-density," urban form: there are fewer than twelve people per acre. It is a rigidly compartmentalized urban layout: shops, dwellings, offices, and industries are kept separate, as are different types of each, so apartment buildings and detached single-family houses do not mingle. And it is an urban form with a branching street pattern: small streets begin at cul-de-sacs and feed only into progressively larger streets until they meet high-speed thoroughfares.

This kind of urban form was made possible by the automobile; now it has made the automobile indispensable. People who live in sprawl lack alternatives; typical households in Northwestern suburbs own one car per driver and get in their cars ten times a day. Per person, suburban dwellers drive three times as far as those who live in pedestrian-friendly urban neighborhoods such as the West End. They are, in transportation lingo, "auto-dependent."

Getting people out of their cars is no easy feat. After all, this is, in the words of former Washington State legislator and longtime transportation reformer Dick Nelson, "a motorhead democracy." Gordon Price's response is not to pry people out but to entice them out. If he had a car, his bumper sticker would probably read, "Sprawl is the problem. Cities are the solution."

## September

Our lunch packed, we loaded Kathryn and Peter into the stroller and wheeled them out the front door of our house. We no longer lived in the rented bungalow; in April we had moved to a town-house ten blocks downstream in the same culverted watershed. On the way to the bus stop, Gary walked beside the stroller. "When will you let me cross the street by myself, Dad?"

"When you're ready," I said, thinking, *When you're old enough to vote*.

"But I'm ready now," Gary said. "I know how to make sure it's safe."

"I can hear that you'd like to have more independence," Amy said, demonstrating—as usual—her superior command of sensitive parenting. I was thinking, *No way! Not with the way people drive around here!* They drive fast—at least, a few of them do. Most people are careful, I suppose, but occasionally cars blast down our street at highway speeds.

We reached the first corner. "Watch how I look for cars," said Gary. He scanned the four horizons melodramatically, his hand thrown up to shield his eyes.

In seventh grade, I used to walk to school up the street he is about to cross. At the time, this was a depressed neighborhood of small houses and run-down duplexes. The people who lived here in the bottom of the valley included many of my classmates. Some were poor; others were middle class like me. But almost all, unlike me, were African-American. I lived up on the hill, in the white part of the neighborhood.

Now I know that a partition of legal and informal housing discrimination kept us living separately. In the intervening years, the partition lifted. The valley bottom and the hilltop have become better integrated, and this part of the neighborhood is enjoying a renaissance of investment. But the bitter legacy of inequality still roams the streets: disaffected youths in dark-glassed Broncos chase each other through the bottomland, their car stereos thundering like cannons.

Gary turned to me. "The coast is clear, Dad. Can I go?" I nodded. It was safe. Gary stepped gingerly off the curb. He is, I know, old enough to cross the street by himself—except for those Broncos.

On the other curb, Gary turned to Amy and me. "Wasn't that good? Don't you think I'm ready?"

"It *was* good," Amy said. "And we'll keep it in mind when we talk about your request. We'll take your request seriously." Gary looked from Amy to me, then hung his head. I guess he could tell my feelings.

Then he started his sales pitch, turning his gaze back and forth from Amy to me. "If you let me cross the street, I could run errands for you. I could go to the store and get milk for Kathryn's bottle when we run out, Dad. I could get you coffee at the espresso place, Mom. I could even ride my bike to school, so you wouldn't have to drive me." He was hitting all our soft spots. Amy and I have long been saddened by the fact that what was safe for us to do at Gary's age—walk to school alone, for example—is not safe any longer. Traffic was calmer a quarter century ago, and the abduction of children was not commonplace.

Safety was even greater further back in time. Old-timers say that this valley was once a place where people left their doors unlocked, walked to grocery stores, slept on their porches on summer nights, and listened to the songs of the teenagers who skated in the streets. Today, everybody has burglar alarms, the grocery stores have folded, and people sleep locked behind their doors, listening warily for the thumping Broncos.

As Gary elaborated the benefits of giving him street-crossing privileges, we walked another block. We passed more of the old cottages and duplexes and more of the new townhouses that face onto our street. We approached a new park the city has built in a formerly vacant lot. The park is well made, with benches for sitting and smooth paths for strollers. It is one of the best recent additions to our neighborhood.

"If I could cross the street by myself, I could come down here and play ball," said Gary. "Then I wouldn't mope around the house so much after school, Mom; and Dad, you wouldn't have to go up on the roof all the time to get my ball for me." Again, he knew just what to say.

"We'll keep it in mind," I said, "but Gary, even if we let you cross the street, we probably would want you to stay closer to home than this." A glance from Amy told me she was thinking about the same thing: the shabby man we sometimes see riding his bicycle to the park in the early afternoon. He stays there about a quarter of an hour, just standing at the park gate. We do not know what he is doing. Maybe he just likes standing there. But we worry that he is running drugs. The thought of Gary coming here to play on his own does not sit well with me.

For us, as for most Northwesterners—and North Americans generally—the immediate and daily meaning of place is metropolitan. The place to which we are becoming attached, or reattached, through the slow accumulation of knowledge and memories is a neighborhood, not a farm, woodlot, or wilderness area. Our neighborhood is called Madison Valley—an average Northwestern neighborhood, neither rich nor poor, beautiful nor ugly, fortunate nor unfortunate. Like all urban places, it is composed of physical elements that include buildings, landscaping, streets, sidewalks, and parks. The quality of these things, and our ease of access to them, largely determines the quality of our place. For this reason, the fact that Amy and I regard the streets and the park as mildly dangerous to Gary is not merely an inconvenience. It is an affront, a reduction of our range, a diminution of our place.

VANCOUVER'S WEST END IS AN ECLECTIC, urbane, polished, somewhat upscale enclave of high-rise and low-rise buildings. To the eye, there is nothing stereotypically "environmental" about it—no neighborhood compost bins, vegetarian cooperatives, or solar water heaters. The West End is simply a place where things are close enough together that rubber soles work better than steel-belted radials.

His voice the practiced baritone of an academic lecturer, Gordon Price answers most questions about curbing the automobile by talking about the minutiae of architecture and urban design. This is not just a politician's practiced evasion of unpopular subjects. It is a reflection of his understanding of transportation as a means, and access as the end. Access through proximity succeeds, or fails, in the details of design—the sizes and spatial arrangements of buildings, lots, streets, sidewalks, alleys, crosswalks, parking facilities, parks, libraries, and other amenities. Good design, Gordon contends, can create a public realm that is safe, inviting, and conducive to community; bad design creates a menacing and sterile public realm.

Gordon levels his umbrella toward an intersection. "You need a grid system of streets open for pedestrians and bikes, but you must put in diverters now and again to slow cars. Then you green the diverters." There is a raised concrete planter cutting the intersection diagonally. It is landscaped with trees and shrubs. A traditional street grid broken with these diverters provides smoother movement of traffic—foot, bicycle, and even car—than the sprawl model of cul-de-sacs, feeder roads, connector roads, and highway.

His umbrella measuring the length of the block, Gordon continues, "Small blocks and narrow lots make walking more interesting." They create a diverse but intimate ambience for foot travelers, he says. "Narrow streets also slow traffic," he offers, because drivers tend to adjust their velocity based on available road space, not posted speed limits.

Pointing to the curb lane, Gordon notes that parked cars make pedestrians feel guarded against traffic, which is critical to promoting walking. To further encourage pedestrians, Gordon points out, it is important to have a row of "street trees and grass, then the sidewalk, then landscaping, then buildings," in order to "surround the pedestrian with greenery."

He gestures at the buildings, apartment structures of every size sitting close to the street. Small setbacks give human scale, he says, whereas buildings far from the street create yawning, empty spaces that walkers find unwelcoming.

Gordon points at the unshaded ground-floor windows on most of the buildings: "Eyes toward the street give safety." Cohesive neighborhoods full of concerned neighbors and pedestrians, backed by a speedy police force, have proved again and again to be the best defense against lawlessness.

He points out a high-rise tower emerging from a wide, three-story base. "That is an interesting lesson. Low-rise facades on the street make high rises humane for pedestrians, avoiding the concrete-canyon effect." From the street, the triple-decker frontage is all you pay attention to; it is modestly scaled and conceals the impersonal bigness of the tower behind.

When all the pieces are assembled and "you've calmed the traffic down enough," Gordon says, "this amazing thing happens. Pedestrians claim the streets, and cars go even slower." International comparisons have shown that the higher a city's average traffic speed, the less walking, bicycling, and transit ridership it will have, and the more gasoline each of its residents will consume.

Gordon Price is on Denman Street, a commercial avenue where traffic is heavier and the sidewalks, despite the steady rain, are bursting with people. Some West Enders are sitting under canopies at cafes, while others are walking or waiting for buses. It feels like Europe.

Upstairs from some of the shops and bistros are offices; above others are apartments. This mixing of uses—and the close interlacing of the West End's commercial streets with its strictly residential ones—is another ingredient of access through proximity.

In sprawl, zoning codes zealously segregate homes, shops, and workplaces, forbidding apartments above stores, for example, even though this was the main form of affordable housing for generations in North American towns. Mixing stores, homes, and offices creates a more diverse and stable human realm, one where the spheres of life are not geographically fragmented. Mixing uses also moderates the huge fluctuations of population generated by sprawl: residential districts lose their inhabitants by day, commercial districts lose their tenants by night, and automobile populations are kept high to convey everybody on their daily migrations.

Pausing under one of the many canopies that cover the sidewalk, Gordon notes, "West End merchants compete for foot traffic by providing pedestrian amenities such as benches and awnings. Elsewhere, merchants compete for car traffic by providing free parking."

"Bike parking is one of our major problems just now," says Gordon, pointing to the two-wheelers locked to every post and fence. The city's Engineering Department tallied bicycle trips citywide at nearly fifty thousand per day a few years ago, and there has been an increase since. "Bicycles have been coming out of the woodwork, and the city is just beginning to install enough secure bicycle racks."

Sitting in a restaurant on Denman, Gordon Price looks out through the rain at the public waterfront that rings the city and comes to the crux of the matter. "Of course, none of these details of zoning or design work without a sufficiently concentrated population." Well-designed, mixed-use neighborhoods with few inhabitants per acre do little to lessen auto dependence.

Gordon argues, "If we're going to handle growth on a limited land base, one way or another, you're talking about the D-word, density. We're in a massive state of denial in the Pacific Northwest about that." Politicians all over the region hear from their constituents that they want lower density and less traffic, but that is a contradiction. Lower density means more traffic—if not on each cul-de-sac, then everywhere else. "Citizens also clamor for better transit, which is another contradiction, since transit is hopelessly expensive and inconvenient without sufficient density," Gordon says.

Density—population per acre—is the most important determinant of how dependent citizens are on their automobiles, according to studies of major cities worldwide conducted by Australian researchers Peter Newman and Jeffrey Kenworthy. As population density increases, transportation options multiply and auto dependence lessens, especially as density rises above two thresholds. The first threshold is at twelve people per acre. Urban districts that fall below this threshold—including virtually all suburban Northwest neighborhoods, and many urban neighborhoods built after World War II—have populations that are utterly dependent on autos.

In neighborhoods with densities above this threshold, including the older neighborhoods of Northwest cities, bus service becomes an option because there are enough riders to make passably frequent service cost-effective. This frees some households from needing multiple cars, so vehicle ownership rates slip and occupancy rates rise—more people ride in each car. Above this threshold, total distance driven per person falls, often by half, which results in per capita gasoline consumption also falling precipitously—despite the fact that each car's fuel mileage suffers in stop-and-start urban traffic. As density rises, Newman and Kenworthy found, car traffic slows, but public transit speeds up: as more people take transit, cities invest in faster, dedicated bus lanes and rail transit systems. And as density increases, the amount of urban space per resident that must be allocated to roads and parking spaces decreases.

Things just get better as density increases further to the second threshold at forty people per acre. The West End is above this higher threshold, as is Seattle's First Hill neighborhood. Above this higher threshold, destinations are close enough together that bicycling and foot travel flourish; people drive one-third as much as do people living in sprawl; and as many as one-third of households do not own a car at all.

All of this is true, furthermore, regardless of income: poor people in the suburbs drive more than rich people in the city. Above this threshold, air pollution falls off especially fast because the added walking, biking, and transit trips replace the short, cold-engine car trips that pollute the most per mile.

## September

After helping me push the stroller to the bus stop across our neighborhood's main avenue—Madison Street—Gary tugged on my sleeve and whispered that he needed a bathroom. So he and I opened the nearest door, the door to a beautiful stone building trimmed with terraces and festooned with planters. Called Bailey-Boushay House, it is the largest structure in our neighborhood and, to my mind, the most artful. The weather vane at its peak is shaped like a salmon rather than a rooster, and the windows are filled with pottery and crafts. In the men's room Gary asked, "Dad, is this a hospital?" He had seen white coats in the lobby.

I was uncomfortable. "Sort of," I said. "It's a hospice."

"What's that?" Again, I was uncomfortable. Death is taboo.

"It's a place where people come when they are sick"—I looked around to see that we were alone—"and waiting to die."

"Old people like Ma Ma?" he asked, referring to my grandmother, who lives in a nursing home.

"Not so much old people, I think. I think it is for people who have AIDS." A man walked into the bathroom.

"Oh," Gary said. He thought for a moment.

"You know, if you'd let me cross the street, I could take letters to the mailbox for you."

"True enough, Gary," I said, relieved that he had changed the subject. "True enough. Hey, let's get back to Mom before the bus comes."

At the bus stop, a small crowd had joined Amy, Kathryn, and Peter. A young woman stepped far enough into the street to get a clear view along Madison to the crest of the hill. I could picture the view, having stepped into the street here countless times myself: the wide, straight line of asphalt etched between buildings, and, on the hill, the thick greenery and black iron that conceal Broadmoor, an enclave of million-dollar homes and private golf links that was for whites only until my childhood.

"Is it coming?" Amy asked, when the young woman was back on the curb.

"Nope. I swear this bus is always late," she said. "It's the worst bus I ride. It never runs on schedule. I'm going to be late for work." The others at the stop seemed less concerned. They had books and newspapers open or were conversing with friends.

We agreed with her about this bus, the number eleven. A middle-aged man in running shoes standing nearby said, "Well, at least it comes at all. One time I was over in Idaho—Boise, Idaho. It was a Sunday. I was trying to get downtown from the airport. So I asks this guy where the bus stop is, and he points to a corner out in the middle of nowhere. No sign, no bench, nothing. I went over there and stood for about an hour getting cold. Then it started snowing, so I went back to the airport and caught the next flight out of there. Turns out, Boise doesn't even run buses on Sundays."

The man talked on and on about buses he had ridden and waited for, about bus fares, bus drivers, and bus shelters. The young woman stepped a little closer to Amy. I stopped listening and started thinking about bus experiences of my own.

I have ridden a fair number of buses; I try to ride them wherever I go. It is a good way to get to know a place. I suppose this trait of mine comes from Grandma Beth. When I was growing up, Grandma didn't have a car. She rode the bus, senior I.D. in one hand and a wad of schedules in the other. By the time I was ten, she had taught me the system well enough to give me the run of the city. I have been a bus rider ever since. I have ridden buses on four continents.

The man in running shoes had begun talking about pumpkin farms, which he seemed to regard as somehow akin to public transit. The young woman was chatting with Amy and admiring Kathryn and Peter. Gary had pulled out his electronic baseball game and sat down in the bus shelter. I was thinking about Manila, the city with the best bus system I have ever used. The buses were awful—short, smoky, stretched-out jeeps, playing loud pop music—but they ran all the time. I don't think I ever waited more than five minutes for a bus. The secret of Manila's success was that everybody rode the bus.

I bet almost no one rides in Boise. Here in Seattle, a good share of the population rides, at least by North American standards. But the ridership has within it a generous share of oddballs. Perhaps this is why riding the bus carries a bit of a social stigma. Maybe it's not the old people, students, or poor people on the bus; maybe it is the quirky ones.

The man in running shoes looked at his watch, then walked away from the bus stop. Maybe he had something else to do. Maybe he was going to catch the first flight out.

"IF WE ACCEPT THAT DENSITY must increase, how do we do it?" Gordon Price asks. "The City of Vancouver now is emerging as a leader in how to do it." To describe how, he tells his story and that of the West End. The stories intertwine.

He was born in 1950 across the Strait of Georgia, in Victoria, to a family whose ancestors had been in British Columbia long enough to have "lost any other sense of place." He grew up in the sleepy provincial capital "in a small house on a corner lot by a bus stop." His parents were late to embrace the automobile, buying their first one in the late 1950s, and they never embraced it fully. His dad continued walking the three miles to work.

Gordon stayed in Victoria until 1978, when, at the age of twenty-eight, he moved to the apartment he continues to inhabit in the West End. A small-town boy, he was appalled to learn he had moved into a red-light district. Pimps and prostitutes plied their trade on the corner outside his window. Denman Street was a twenty-four-hour sex bazaar. He joined with neighbors who were trying to reclaim the neighborhood, but they met with a strange kind of indifference from official Vancouver. Deviant and antisocial behavior were unavoidable, officialdom believed, in a zone of so many high rises. High density itself bred criminal behavior. "Was the concrete jungle the problem?" he began to ask. "Was the tenth of the city built up in high rises doomed?"

The West End had not always been this way, of course. More than a century ago it held the two- and three-story mansions of the well-to-do. By early in the 1900s, however, these structures had been divided into flats, boarding hotels, and tenements. It was a working-class neighborhood from which laborers could get to their jobs on foot, bicycle, or streetcar. Then, in June 1956, the Vancouver City Council rezoned all of it for multifamily residential buildings, and by 1962 a building boom was taking hold. Towers went up left and right, filling with renters as quickly as they could be completed.

Despite the concrete towers popping up like horsetails, the West End's population density rose surprisingly little during the building boom. From 1941 to 1971, the number of housing units in the neighborhood quintupled, while population increased by just half. "The old West End was crowded in frame houses," notes Gordon. "The new West End is uncrowded in tall buildings. This is important, because much of the force behind sprawl is the desire for larger living spaces, not the growth of population.

"Interestingly, the population of the West End is about forty thousand in a square mile. The city of Florence in 1400—at the beginning of the Renaissance—was also a square mile within its walls and had a population of forty thousand. I'm looking around here for a Michelangelo."

In the early 1970s, the citizens of Vancouver brought construction screeching to a halt. In the Kitsilano neighborhood, across an inlet from the West End, a developer tried to build an apartment tower in early 1972, setting off a rebellion among that neighborhood's residents. The uproar swelled into a political wave that realigned municipal politics and shut down new building in most of Vancouver's close-in neighborhoods. The urban vision of these opponents of high-rise development was, in Gordon's words, "1956, with good restaurants."

Of course, enforced low density in the city did nothing to stop development. Population was growing, the number of households was growing faster, and demand for additional floor space was growing fastest of all. The building boom was shunted beyond city limits, and the metropolis expanded like a supernova up the Fraser River valley.

Years spent fighting the sex bazaar taught Gordon that density was not the enemy. Lawlessness and moral decay had nothing to do with the density in the West End and everything to do with public policy. Prostitution flourished there because officialdom, from the mayor to the cops on the beat, tolerated it there.

Overcoming this thinking required the politicization of the West End, which happened gradually over a decade. "A community takes that long to gain a sense of itself as a political force," Gordon says. In 1986, having finally won the prostitution fight, he ran for city council, convinced that the West End was not the problem but the solution to much that ailed Vancouver.

On the council, he has helped approve far-reaching development plans for two other areas on the fringe of downtown, plans that will double the residential population of the city's central core. "The West End is full. We have to create new West Ends. The single-family neighborhoods will never let in new development, so we had to encourage building on underused industrial land around downtown."

"Living in apartments or condominiums, especially high rises, is not for everyone," Gordon offers. "But it is an option in much greater demand than is commonly recognized." Citizens who object to apartment developments tend to talk about how children need yards. Yet families with children make up just one-third of households in the Northwest, while nearly half of residences in greater Vancouver are detached, single-family houses, as are 58 percent of residences in King County, Washington—the county in which Seattle is located and the most populous county in the Northwest. Adding row houses that have yards to the detached houses would push these figures substantially higher.

"We ought to be recycling the single-family neighborhoods," Gordon says, "by enticing most house owners who do not have children into better alternatives—whether high-rise, low-rise, or whatever. There is a phenomenal market for urban living," he asserts. "Most new apartment and condo buildings within walking distance of downtowns—whether in Vancouver, Seattle, or Portland—fill almost immediately." The limit on growth of this type of housing is usually political, not economic. Neighborhoods of single-family houses are vehemently opposed to multifamily buildings, especially rental units. In neighborhood meetings throughout the region, the phrase "high rise" is spit like a curse. Most single-family neighborhoods even object to homeowners renting out excess space in their houses as accessory apartments—"granny flats" or "mother-in-law" apartments.

This sentiment has complex roots, Gordon believes. Partly, it is fear of the other. House owners assume apartment dwellers are different—young or old, very poor or very rich, gay or minority. They assume this difference will destroy the cohesiveness of the neighborhood and undermine the house owners' quality of life, property value, or both.

Even deeper than these sources of resistance, however, is what Gordon calls "the myth of the garden"—a cultural attachment to an agrarian idyll. Northwesterners, like most North Americans, believe their roots are rural. They glorify rural life—even while new suburban developments overtake miles of usable farmland each year. In opinion surveys, they say their ideal town would be extremely small, even while they live in huge metropolises. They love to hate cities, thinking of them as symbols of moral decadence and separation from nature. And apartments, condominiums, and other residences that do not evoke images of free-standing farmhouses get wrapped in this stigma. High rises are especially suspect, because they evoke the defining symbol of urbanism: the skyscraper.

Others share Gordon's diagnosis. James Howard Kunstler, in his critique of American cities, *The Geography of Nowhere*, notes that the American Dream itself has been redefined over time to be anti-urban. Once, the American Dream meant freedom from religious persecution, equality before the law, and an entrepreneurial economy where only your merit mattered. By the 1950s, it had come to mean "a detached home on a sacred plot of earth in a rural setting, unbesmirched by the industry that made the home possible; a place where one could play at cultivating the soil without having to rely on husbandry for a livelihood; a place that was, most of all, not the city."

Fortunately, there is another strand in North American culture, one that is manifest in the West End. There are elements that value urbanism, that exult in the energy of public spaces: the combination of intentionality and coincidence, of commerce and pleasure, of people from all walks of life interacting in a realm defined by artfully conceived and well-placed structures.

There is no question in Gordon's mind that, if Northwesterners truly understood the quality of life that is possible through access-by-proximity, they would beg for higher density. "The problem is that when we hear the word 'density,' the myth of the garden takes hold. We think of crime-infested public housing projects—vertical slums."

If anything, sprawl undermines public safety. It forces people to drive more, and driving is among the most dangerous things Northwesterners do. And it removes people from tightly knit communities where residents watch out for one another.

What Northwesterners ought to think about, Gordon suggests, is the West End. Or Paris, which has three times the density of Seattle. Or Amsterdam, Copenhagen, London, Munich, Rome,

Stockholm, or Vienna—all places with vastly higher density than Portland or Vancouver. In cities like these, fewer than half of all trips are taken by automobile, not the 90 percent of Northwest cities.

As dusk falls, Gordon sprints two blocks up Denman, chasing a bus that is headed for one of the new West Ends he has helped create as a member of the city council, Yaletown—a derelict warehouse district half-converted to a mixed neighborhood of youth clubs, restaurants, art galleries, and condominiums.

The streets in the new zone have a raw feeling that is absent in the West End. "The trees and landscaping will take about ten years to fill out," he acknowledges. "And these buildings are a little too massive and uniform. But every building that's been finished has filled immediately. And when the new neighborhood is done, there'll be another West End's worth of people here."

Then, standing out of the rain under another canopy, Gordon reveals his grand political strategy. "What happens when all these developments are completed? Think about it. The business district will be *surrounded* by pedestrian neighborhoods."

Weaving his fingers together, Gordon proclaims, "It will go just like this!" He locks his fingers, then pulls his hands tight against each other. "In a decade they will become politicized. They won't want high-speed through-traffic in their neighborhoods." They will say *enough* to the 175,000 cars that drive into their city each day. No longer dependent on internal combustion, they will become a pedestrian voting bloc.

Throughout the Pacific Northwest, people like Gordon Price are moving to dethrone the car. Block by block, zoning hearing by zoning hearing, they are fighting to refashion their cities, aiming for a future where cars are accessories to life, not its organizing principle.

From Portland to Seattle to Vancouver, the Northwest's major cities are engaged in far-reaching planning efforts, all of which are strikingly similar, at least in the vision they paint of the future.

According to this new vision, most population growth will concentrate in central cities and in satellite hubs rather than in undifferentiated sprawl. Downtowns will once again be surrounded by dense middle-class neighborhoods, with low-income and high-income housing mixed throughout rather than concentrated in pockets of poverty and affluence.

This model amplifies the sense of civic community—the notion people have that despite their diversity, they are all in it together. It does so by promoting interaction among classes, ages, and races. Sprawl, on the other hand, arranges people geographically according to their economic standing, insulating the affluent from fellow citizens who are poor and isolating the poor from the social networks that bind together the affluent. Physical segregation wreaks havoc on fellow feeling.

In the new model, new development will be mixed-use rather than monocultures of residences, shopping palaces, or office parks. Streets will be designed to accommodate pedestrians, bicyclists, buses, and trolleys as well as private cars. Rail transit will knit the city together, with each station surrounded by tightly clustered workplaces, shops, and apartment buildings, grading outward to townhouses and finally to detached houses on small-sized lots. Each station will have its own identity and sense of community.

This, at least, is the officially sanctioned ideal. Whether it will materialize is another question.

## September

The number eleven bus slid to the curb and threw open its doors. We climbed aboard, and Kathryn squealed to see her grandparents seated up front. I happily handed her to them and went back for the stroller. Then Amy and I sat down on the seats my parents had saved by spreading out their sweaters. Gary paid the fare and asked for transfers, just as we had rehearsed. Turning away from the fare box, he was surprised to see his grandparents. He had somehow missed the fact that they were coming with us, "Grammy?! Where did you come from?"

"We got on the bus by our apartment because we wanted to see you," she said, hugging him.

"Well, we're going fishing," said Gary, showing them his butterfly net. "We're going to a creek my dad knows about. It's in Redmond."

"That's why we came," said my dad. "We wanted to see if there are any fish. We used to take your dad there when he was your age. Our old friend Olive Salstrom used to live there."

"Is that true, Dad?" Gary asked.

"Yep!"

"Where does she live now?" he asked.

"She died several years ago," said my mom.

"Was she old?" Gary asked.

"Oh, yes. Quite old," my dad said. "She grew up where we are going, too, when it was wild country."

"In fact, Gary," my mom said, "you know our neighborhood of Madison Park?"

"Uh-huh."

"When Mrs. Salstrom was a teenager, Madison Park was a little beach community with a ferry dock. It was in the middle of nowhere. Mrs. Salstrom's first job was to teach school in Bellevue.

To get there, her father drove her in his buggy from Redmond to a ferry dock in Kirkland. Then she'd ride the ferry across the lake to Madison Park, turn around, and take a ferry back across the lake, but farther south, to Bellevue." Gary looked at her disbelievingly. He said, "Ferries? On the lake? No way."

"It's hard to imagine how things were back then," said my mom.

"Nowadays, the difference between Redmond and Bellevue is four freeway exits," Amy laughed.

The historical connections between my parents' neighborhood, our neighborhood, and Redmond run deep. The ferry terminal at Madison Park was a link in the route across cut-over hills from the brothels and mills of Seattle to inland places such as Redmond. The other links were a cable railroad station at Madison Park and a cable railroad along the current route of Madison Street.

The community of Madison Park grew up around the rail station, before cars were common. Because its main structures were built for easy access to that station, Madison Park is compact and walkable today. That—plus its waterfront property—gives it charm, desirability, and high property values.

The community of Madison Valley grew up later, as an outpost of mostly poor, mostly black workers. It never gained the pedestrian character that Madison Park had. The presence of Madison Street worsened things. The street was built around the cable railroad to expand freight hauling to the interior. It was built to pass through, not to weave things together, and as such, it was made wide and fast. It remains oversized to this day, creating a barrier to community cohesiveness in Madison Valley. My sister Susan and her family live five blocks from us. But Madison Street makes walking there treacherous. We would never let Gary walk to Susan's on his own.

**IS SPRAWL GOOD FOR ANYTHING?** It is good for the legions of industries ranging from oil companies and car makers to lube shops and drive-through restaurants. It is good for speculators in real estate, and real estate is the big money in transportation. And, because buying influence is a normal cost of business among real estate speculators, it is good for campaign contributions. Perhaps that is why sprawl continues despite the best intentions of urban planners.

## September

The bus lumbered uphill out of the bottom of Madison Valley. At the next stop, a tall, statuesque man with silver-tipped hair and the charismatic looks of a model got on the bus. On his feet, he was wearing slippers. He sat by the driver, clutching a cardboard box labeled "Shrimp-Flavored Chips" on which he had scribbled endlessly with a dull pencil. His eyes roamed across the seats and he began enunciating in staccato phrases, to no one in particular, "That's when they tried to hook me on their dope. 1983. In Hawaii. But I said, 'Get that dope away from me. I ain't no junkie.'"

Gary looked to Amy for reassurance. She put her arm around him and whispered in his ear. Kathryn watched the man for a moment, then resumed climbing on the seats. Peter cooed in his grandfather's arms.

The man turned his head in another direction, still unseeing, and flared his nostrils. "They tried in Vietnam too. I had to go to Vietnam. They couldn't make me take their dope. There's dope pushers all over." He delivered his lines well, with clear, measured passion.

The bus, filling at each stop, climbed uphill to the abandoned hall of the ship scalers union. The shrimp man was still giving his monologue. "I had to get out of that rooming house. It was full of drug dealers."

The bus reached the building that used to house a methadone clinic, where my brother Jonathan and I washed windows one summer. "I've been to Brazil. They tried to rob me, but I ripped 'em all off," the shrimp man said, then laughed loudly.

A block farther and still rising, the bus passed the old grocery store, long since closed and converted to a Planned Parenthood clinic. "They're killing children. 1994. Five teenagers, one nine-year-old—shot and killed. Dope."

The bus passed the parking lot that—in the 1980s—was an open-air drug market doing a hundred thousand dollars' worth of business a day. It is gone now, though a few fiery-eyed addicts still wander the block. "You look at him and you lift him three times and he's 450 pounds—same height as you are—and you say, 'I'll see you tomorrow. I'll see you tomorrow!'"

The bus topped the hill and slid down the other side, crossing what urban geographers call a zone of discard—a neighborhood of storage units, thrift stores, and repair shops. The shrimp man's soliloquy ended. He had fallen asleep with his chin tucked into his chest.

Still descending, the bus crossed a bridge over I-5, the interstate freeway constructed in the 1960s that cuts Seattle up the middle and siphons its energies to the north and south. Among the steel and concrete skyscrapers of downtown we got off the bus, leaving the anxious woman late for work and the sleeping shrimp man.

The eleven, I often think, cuts a transect through the sedimentary layers of class, race, sanity, and sobriety in my city. It is never a dull ride.

**HOW DID A PLACE LIKE** the Northwest end up with an unworkable urban design? Some argue that it was the result of millions of people's informed decisions interacting in a free and fair marketplace. To bemoan it, they argue, is elitist. To try to change it is "social engineering." A look at history suggests otherwise; government policies have been as important as market forces in shaping the urban Northwest.

If cities in the Northwest were founded in the 1800s at the junctions of water and railroads, and if they were given form by the routes of electric streetcars, they were remade by the motorcar. Cars increased in number from essentially nil in the region at the turn of the century to nearly one million in 1929. In the wide-open Northwest, they sold like hotcakes. The expanding infrastructure of roads came at the expense of streetcars. Then, when the Great Depression hit, the U.S. government began pumping billions of dollars into road construction, battling a slack economy with miles of asphalt. Similarly, President Franklin Roosevelt created the Federal Housing Authority (FHA) to shovel money into the construction industry. The idea was that since house building declines when the economy slows, government incentives to build houses—by guaranteeing home mortgages—would make the economy speed. And where better to build these new houses than beside the freshly surfaced roads?

The easiest homes to get approved for FHA loans were the reliably uniform new ones going up outside town. Rowhouses, duplexes, and anything else where people shared walls had a harder time qualifying. Meanwhile, entire neighborhoods of old city houses, increasingly occupied by people with African or Asian ancestors, were disqualified outright. It was called redlining. And it was only the latest flavor of discrimination used to segregate people by their skin color. Neighborhoods like Seattle's Central District were, in effect, relegated to decline.

During World War II, industries and military bases oriented toward the Pacific had brought hundreds of thousands of people to the region, and many of them stayed on afterwards, using FHA and new Veterans Administration loans to buy cheap houses in the suburbs. In the decade after the war, roughly half of U.S. home sales were financed through these government-insured mortgages.

Across the span of the century, a provision in the federal income tax code grew to be an even more powerful stimulant to sprawl. Almost from the beginning of the income tax, Washington, D.C., made tax deductible the interest on personal loans—the largest of which are home mortgages. Every dime an owner paid to a bank in interest on a home loan could be subtracted from his or her income before calculating the taxes due. Early in the century, the U.S. income tax was a minor revenue source affecting mostly the rich. As the tax grew to become the principal source of federal money, the incentive to buy bigger, more expensive houses— which often meant suburban mansions—increased. Cementing the subsidy, when all other personal interest payments were made taxable in 1986, mortgage interest remained deductible. This loop-hole is one of the largest handouts in the U.S. tax code, and a huge indirect subsidy to sprawl.

Then came a powerful new decentralized force for sprawl. Beginning in the 1950s, civil engineers began packaging generic

zoning and urban planning codes and distributing them to jurisdictions across the continent, which passed them into law, often
after the most perfunctory of reviews.

Sadly, the consequence was that the same suburban model began
replicating everywhere: residential lots big enough to hold fire stations and impossible to connect into a walkable community; off-
street parking requirements that ensured most new retail buildings
would be islands in seas of pavement; highway designs that con-
signed acres of open space to cloverleaf interchanges and yawning
medians, along with mathematical models that "proved" the necessity of more expressway lanes than could possibly be built; and
neighborhood streets the breadth of county thoroughfares that
swirled and twirled through curlicues, flourishes, and all the forms
of the rococo masters.

At the same time, a second powerful force in favor of sprawl
appeared on the scene—this one highly centralized. In 1956, Congress approved construction of a national system of interstate
highways. President Dwight D. Eisenhower first proposed the
system, inspired by the autobahns he had seen in Germany. The
interstates would be a network of divided, limited-access speed-
ways of four or more lanes that would tie the country together,
lubricate commerce, open the countryside, and let all Americans
experience the convenience, exhilaration, and freedom of gunning
their V-8s. If a stingy Congress balked at the price tag on Eisenhower's requisition, there was always the threat of the bomb; the
new roads would hurry evacuation of the cities in a nuclear attack.

Freeways were good Republican politics: a giant public works
project, arguably larger than anything created by the New Deal,
dedicated not to Roosevelt's union man but to Ike's Chevy-owning
company man. And they were good pork barrel: the federal funds,
covering 90 percent of the tab, would be spread to almost every
congressional district in the country.

Considering the gargantuan scale of the endeavor, debate over the interstate highway act was paltry. In Washington State, there was a brief effort to leave space for a rail transit line in the middle of the planned Central Freeway, now called I-5, but auto interests on the State Highway Commission squelched such talk easily enough. Indeed, few had anything bad to say about the freeways even while they were being built. During the 1960s, hippies loved their microbuses as much as ROTC recruits loved their Mustangs. Most of the reason for the lack of debate was that nobody had any idea what interstate freeways would do to cities.

It was almost too late before some Northwesterners realized that putting a freeway through your city to improve transportation is like putting a hole through your heart to improve circulation. Urban freeways drew people, money, and vitality out of town; as the interstates were built, the cities deteriorated. The interstates were a monstrous, taxpayer-funded sprawl accelerator that helped make the midcentury move to the suburbs the largest migration in U.S. history. Freeways weakened urban retailing by feeding the growth of the shopping mall. By the late 1980s, the Northwest's shopping centers outnumbered its high schools.

The 1970s were a period of uncertainty for the car. It was being criticized for the first time, because of its environmental faults, even while the price of its fuel was gyrating wildly. In the United States, its military significance came briefly into prominence. After the Iranian revolution and the Soviet invasion of Afghanistan, President Jimmy Carter made explicit what had previously been unspoken: any attempt by a foreign power to consolidate control over Middle Eastern oil fields would be treated as an act of trespass against a U.S. national security interest. The Pentagon began to spend tens of billions of dollars each year maintaining readiness to fight wars in faraway deserts.

Despite all the unease about automobile dependence, a demographic revolution in the Northwest was pushing auto numbers up more quickly than ever before or since. Middle-class women joined their working-class sisters in the labor force and, given the already dispersed form of Northwest cities, that entailed second cars for millions of families. From 1973 to 1980, the car population rose from less than six million to almost eight million. During this time, government regulations were making cars cleaner and more fuel efficient. When fuel prices finally dropped in the mid-eighties, the real cost per mile of fueling an automobile was lower than ever before.

With the 1980s came the Reagan administration and a time of sprawl by yet another means. President Reagan deregulated the savings and loan industry, freeing hundreds of thrift institutions to start investing the savings accounts of schoolteachers and sales clerks in exurban office parks and strip malls. This constituted another mammoth subsidy to sprawl, since the federal government was underwriting these loans through the deposit insurance it provided. At the peak of this folly in the mid-1980s, new shopping centers were opening nationwide at the rate of one every four hours. Many of these projects were white elephants. When they failed, they pulled down scores of thrift institutions, landing the debts on the U.S. Treasury.

Meanwhile, the thrift regulators stepped in and auctioned off the exurban commercial and retail space at liquidator prices, undercutting urban buildings that had not benefited from the bailout. Sprawl had again been served and, adjusting to the new requirements of life, the people of the Northwest bought more cars, raising the total to more than ten million by 1990.

Then came the 1990s and a fast-forward replay of the previous two decades. In rapid succession there was an oil war in the Middle East, a flowering of environmental consciousness and support for limits on sprawl, and a political pendulum swing to the right.

Sprawl was not inevitable in the Northwest, as the differences between British Columbia and the American parts of the region demonstrate. From the beginning, British Columbia was less enamored of the automobile. Canada never built an interstate; there are a quarter as many lane-miles of urban freeway per capita in Canada as in the United States. British Columbian drivers pay higher taxes on vehicles and fuels than other Northwesterners, get no income tax deduction for mortgage interest, and pay more for auto insurance too. They use a road network two notches less developed than that south of the border. They cannot go quite as fast. Consequently, cities—while still far from compact enough for sustainability—are less sprawled. There are fewer cars per capita, less driving per capita, and more use of transit. In the 1980s, greater Vancouver converted less rural land to urban uses for every additional resident than any other Canadian metropolis. And it sprawled at one-third the rate of Seattle, despite comparable population growth.

The fate of Interstate 5 illustrates the differences within the region. In Seattle, this freeway cuts a canyon through the heart of the city from north to south, swelling to as many as sixteen lanes and two decks, bisecting downtown, hardly turning, rearranging the city according to the dictates of what traffic engineers call "high-speed geometrics." In Portland, the freeway veers wide of downtown, skirting its periphery and not exceeding eight lanes. In Vancouver, I-5's continuation—Highway 99—turns from a limited-access expressway to an average-sized arterial street when it crosses the city limits.

Was sprawl inevitable? Look at the difference in decision-making for rail transit and highway construction. The United

States, and to a lesser extent Canada, chose to invest in—and sub-sidize—cars and roads rather than cities and transit. No voters any-where ever approved the interstate highway system or the state and provincial highways constructed at taxpayer expense. And no amount of local initiative could turn that tide. The voters of greater Seattle, for example, were asked in 1958, 1962, 1968, 1970, 1988, and 1995 whether to build—or rebuild—a regional rail transit system. A majority usually voted yes, but never the 60 per-cent required for approval of bond measures. Portland, with dif-ferent voting rules, finally succeeded in re-creating a rail transit system in the 1980s, but on a scale that could hardly compete with the road infrastructure.

As Henry Richmond, former head of 1000 Friends of Oregon, and Saunders Hillyer of the National Growth Management Leader-ship Project in Washington, D.C., write, "Sprawl was not decreed by God, nor is it an immutable expression of the American char-acter, love affair with the automobile, or dream of a house in the suburbs. To a great extent it has been shaped by public policies." Governments—not the invisible hand or the American Dream—gave the Northwest sprawl. And governments can give the North-west something better.

## September

Downtown, we found the stop for the 251 to Redmond. When it came, the driver had an attitude. She greeted us by glaring at the baby stroller. "You can't come on here with that if you don't break it down!" It was a flag-snapping Saturday, she was alone on the bus, and my watch put her three minutes ahead of schedule, but she was acting as if she was ten minutes late during Monday rush hour. My mom snatched Kathryn, Amy gathered up Peter, Gary grabbed the diaper bag, and my dad and I wrestled the stroller to the ground. She watched, her fingers tapping the wheel. She careened onto the highway, practically burning rubber, and sped across the floating bridge that crosses Lake Washington.

We looked out the windows, across glittering waves, at the hulking glacial pile of Mount Rainier and the other floating bridge. That was the bridge that did Seattle in. Completed in 1940, it was the conduit that bled off the city's upper-class tax base to Bellevue and beyond. The population inside the city limits peaked shortly thereafter, never to recover. The city of Seattle now houses less than half of the population of the metropolitan area to which it gave rise.

The bus carried us through the old suburb of Kirkland and over the hills sprouting new colonials and contemporaries—Grass Lawn Park Estates, Heights Rentals, James Place, Manhattan Square—to Lake Sammamish, Redmond, and finally Avondale Road.

IF VANCOUVER'S WEST END SHOWS how attractive the heart of a city can be—vibrant and livable, environmentally sound and safe—the question remains of what can be done in a suburb. In Portland, the answer is emerging: fill it in, mix it up, reconnect it. Turn it into a city. Not into a high-rise neighborhood like the West End; that would be too much too fast. Rather, turn it into something like an old-fashioned street or neighborhood. In the Northwest, this idea of unobtrusively filling in the urban universe with walkable, low-rise neighborhoods goes by several names, among them "urban villages," "mixed-use, medium-density development," "transit-oriented development," and "pedestrian pocket."

Downtown Portland is probably the best case of good urban planning in the western United States, combining all the elements of successful cityscapes from near and far: small blocks with shop windows and small businesses at street level; narrow streets; crosswalks laid in brick to demarcate the realm of pedestrians; parks, fountains, and statues sprinkled throughout; and a vibrant mixture of social classes and of uses—offices, stores, and residences.

Talk to almost any of the architects of Portland's revitalization and you will hear that it started with the proposed Mount Hood Freeway, part of the interstate system that would have bulldozed 1 percent of the city's housing. A grass-roots coalition called Sensible Transportation Options for People (STOP) rallied opposition to the freeway in the late 1960s and early 1970s. By all accounts, it was a contest for the soul of the city, pitting a generation of Young Turks against the old-guard proponents of progress by civil engineering. The Turks prevailed.

With the leadership of Republican governor Tom McCall, Oregon passed the nation's firmest farmland protection and growth management law in 1972, and Portland set about doing the opposite of what every other city was doing in the area of land use—a pattern that has since continued. In the 1970s, when other cities were condemning whole neighborhoods to put in freeways, Portland was demolishing an expressway along the Willamette in favor of a two-mile riverfront park. When other cities were approving scores of downtown parking garages, Portland put a moratorium on downtown parking growth and converted a parking lot into a town square. That quadrangle, Pioneer Courthouse Square, has become the undisputed hub of the metropolis.

During the Reagan administration, while other cities were slashing bus service, Portland reinstalled tracks in its streets, breaking ground on a light-rail system called MAX. Wildly popular, MAX has since gained the approval of Oregon voters by lopsided margins each time it has sought additional funds. Within the downtown, Portland made buses free, put up shelters at all stops, and took a main arterial back from cars to make a central transit mall. All the changes made a difference. Between 1970 and 1990, the number of jobs downtown increased by half, the share of downtown workers riding transit rose to more than 40 percent, car traffic entering downtown stabilized, and the air got cleaner.

Outside of downtown, the City of Portland was promoting multifamily housing aggressively and declaring war on traffic. Earl Blumenauer, public works commissioner from 1986 on, earned himself a reputation as the Earl of Speed Bumps. He had city workers begin installing speed bumps, speed humps, traffic diverters, traffic circles, and street-narrowing curb "bubbles" almost on demand. Said Blumenauer, only the fire department—which did not like to slow its million-dollar trucks for anything—stood between him and speed-bumping the entire city. (The City of Boise has recently caught the speed-bump fever from Portland, installing sixty-two in the first half of 1995 alone, and watching traffic velocity drop by a quarter at each.)

Yet Portland proper, like the cities of Vancouver and Seattle, is now but a small part of the metropolitan area it anchors. Its suburbs consist of hundreds of square miles of compartmentalized, low-density sprawl. And greater Portland is expecting a million newcomers in the next few decades.

The definitive challenge for Portland is Washington County, the frontier of sprawl west of town and a farm district that grows bumper crops of winter wheat, berries, fruits, nuts, and wine grapes. On this fertile soil, partisans are re-enacting the Mount Hood Freeway fight. Road builders want to pour concrete around the city to form a Western Bypass route. A group of grass-roots opponents, naming themselves STOP after the earlier organization, took issue with the plan and started to make a ruckus. Eventually, other groups were drawn to the cause, including the state's veteran land-use planning advocate, 1000 Friends of Oregon—or "Thousand Friends." Thousand Friends decided to make Washington County a test case, so the group pulled in experts from across the country to cook up a less auto-bound alternative to the bypass-plus-sprawl then on the menu.

The resulting plan goes by the acronym LUTRAQ, short for "Land Use, Transportation, and Air Quality." Under the LUTRAQ banner, the experts proposed a future for a hundred square miles of Washington County that would look like the old streetcar neighborhoods. They meticulously revised the transportation models that aid government planners in Oregon. These widely used computer-simulation models are fairly good at projecting car traffic under conventional suburban land-use planning, because their assumption that people do not have feet might as well be true in such settings. The experts used the revised models to compare the LUTRAQ option with the bypass-plus-conventional-land-use option. In the computer simulation, LUTRAQ reduced total driving, the share of driving that was done alone, traffic accidents, traffic congestion, the share of households with more than one automobile, and per capita consumption of gasoline. It also allowed twice as many children to walk and bike to school.

Meeky Blizzard, one of the instigators of the new STOP, is touring the route of the proposed Western Bypass and talking, over the traffic noise and the squeak of the windshield wipers, about LUTRAQ. Meeky delights in describing herself in the words of her adversaries, as an "old hippie with good facts." Before growth management took over her life, she was a free-lance technical writer and mom who, with her husband, built a house in rural Washington County. By the time she did so, in 1978—the same year that Gordon Price moved to the West End—she had already lived in a half-dozen other states. A decade later, the prospect of the bypass steamrolling her piece of the countryside drew her into politics. Now she has learned so much about urban design that she is thinking about moving downtown.

Her tour begins on the Sunset Highway, a corridor of industrial parks where Intel, Sequent, and other high-tech firms have been setting up shop. The county is pining for more and has set the table, so to speak, by laying miles of new road network across vacant farmland. Almost everyone who works in this "Sunset Corridor," Meeky says, drives here from other counties. The wages in these plants are fairly low, and Washington County brags about its lack of affordable housing—or at least it did back when Meeky and her ilk were keeping their noses out of land-use planning.

The LUTRAQ solution to the Sunset Corridor, Meeky says, is a simple if radical idea: "Put the housing and the jobs in the same place." Once, industrial zones needed to be kept miles from housing because they were full of smelly factories that menaced public health, but today, many high-tech facilities cause less pollution per acre than a housing development. After six years of pressure from STOP, Meeky proudly notes, "The radical thoughts are coming back to us from the folks who have the microphone." Affordable housing is now part of the plan for Washington County.

Next on the sprawl tour is the Tualatin Valley Highway, a major east-west route connecting Portland to fast-growing Forest Grove. It is a run-of-the-mill commercial strip. "Imagine getting off a bus here," Meeky says. "There's poor lighting, two lanes in either direction, and a suicide lane in the middle. For bus stops, there are no shelters, just signs on telephone poles beside the ditch. And the traffic lights are easily a quarter mile apart. The fire and rescue people call this Big Gulp Gulch, because people are routinely hit going across the street to the 7-Eleven. And despite how hard it is to take the bus here, this particular bus route has one of the highest riderships in the system." The residential areas nearby house many families who cannot afford second cars.

On the surface, Meeky argues, LUTRAQ's plan for this area is simple: "The pedestrian infrastructure is not complete—no sidewalks, no crosswalks, no bus shelters." But there is a bigger issue, too—what Meeky calls "building orientation." Regional-planning rules in greater Portland say that new commercial buildings must be located the "minimum practical distance from the street," but on commercial roads like this one most stores sit behind their parking areas. Big-box retailers such as Wal-Mart and Safeway customarily stand five hundred feet from the curb, which makes walking to them a bit like crossing a firing range. LUTRAQ, Meeky says, would put all commercial buildings at the sidewalk. According to research by Thousand Friends, just putting all the commercial buildings at the street, with parking facilities tucked underneath or behind, reduces driving per person in a neighborhood by 15 percent.

The next stop on the route is zoned residential, a housing tract called the Highlands. "Take a look at this," Meeky commands, shaking her head and pulling off the highway. It is a street of brand-new houses, or, more precisely, of brand-new garages. From her vantage point, she can see the driveways spreading out from the street and the double garage doors lining up toward the horizon. "Can you see any front doors or porches?" None are visible. "For all you know, cars live here. 'Snout houses' is what a friend of mine calls them. The only way to figure out which one is yours is to go down the street pressing your garage door opener." Front porches, according to Meeky, are built on the assumption that people will be arriving on foot. They are superfluous here because no one could possibly arrive on foot. You can hardly even leave this subdivision without an automobile.

Furthermore, sprawling neighborhoods like this multiply water consumption, since watering big lawns and washing multiple cars take up so much water. They also multiply energy consumption for heating; the clustered buildings and apartments common in cities shelter each other from the cold, but detached suburban buildings do not.

The LUTRAQ answer to the Highlands is in evidence at a place called Tualatin Commons, a "pedestrian pocket" in the city of Tualatin. It is a tight cluster of townhouses, flats, and single-family homes—some with actual porches—facing inward onto a common open space. Walking paths crisscross the community, and parking is concentrated at the rear. A community center is planned along with office spaces and footpaths to stores and transit stops. LUTRAQ calls for communities like this one at every MAX station.

Meeky talks about gradually changing what is already built, too. Four decades of subdivisions need to be filled in, she says, first with granny flats and later with smaller lots, townhouses, and multifamily units mixed among the single-family ones. The subdivisions also need to be mixed up, with pockets of stores and workplaces inserted into them. And, finally, they need to be connected; the maze of suburban cul-de-sacs needs to be turned into a functional grid. How to do this is unclear, but maybe narrow, single-lane roads, pedestrian routes, transit-only streets, and other low-traffic rights of way would do the trick.

Of course there is strong opposition to these ideas. Still, Meeky believes people will jump at the opportunity for change when they are confident it will be for the better. "Communities are used to the county coming in and building three-lane connector roads, or building sidewalks that are barely four feet wide, are right next to the curb, lack a buffer of parked cars, and have utility poles interrupting them. Why should any community have faith in the county?"

Instead, she proposes a participatory approach that works slowly and meticulously, block by block, fixing easy problems first and building trust all around. She praises Portland public works commissioner Blumenauer, for example, for his "neighbor walks." He hijacks a few city staff members, invites a photographer, and meets local residents for a Saturday walk around their neighborhood. Together, they look at problem street corners, vacant lots, school zones, and traffic patterns, and make plans for improvements.

Another part of the solution, Meeky insists, is pictures. STOP has a set of slides that illustrate the choices that lie before Portland, pictures of both good and bad urban design. When people are shown the slides and asked which images they prefer, she notes the results are always encouraging. People from the city and the suburbs all want the same things. They want safe, convenient neighborhoods with a sense of community. "What we're talking about isn't from outer space, it's something old and well liked. It's the kind of thing that people travel across the country to see in quaint New England villages, or even fly to Europe to see."

## September

Our bus had stopped. "This is it!" barked the driver, the bus doors exploding open with a sigh of relief. We looked around. We were thirty blocks from our destination. This is it? My father went up front, braving the storm. We overheard, ". . . don't know who told you that . . . Saturday schedule . . . road construction . . . last stop . . . projects at 95th."

We had no choice but to get off the bus. And so we bundled up beside a right-turn lane on Avondale Road at 95th Northeast. On one side of the four-lane road was a low-income housing project called the Colony. "That used to be an air force missile facility," said my mom. On the other was Friendly Village Retirement Park, a mobile home site "for 55+."

The stroller fully loaded, we began walking north, passing signs for housing developments that had recently sprouted: "Cherry Brooke 31 New Homes" and "Summerwood." Peter let out a hungry cry, so Amy unbuttoned her shirt and walked with him pressed to her breast. Gary, pushing Kathryn in the stroller, lost heart. "This is dumb. We're just walking by a big road." We had three miles yet to go. "Where's the creek?" Everyone agreed with him.

After six long blocks, at 100th Avenue Northeast, we left the built-up area and entered lands on the verge of development. Everywhere we looked was another white placard marked "Proposed Land Use Action." At 106th, for example, there was a sign announcing plans to subdivide a property into fifty-four lots. Another sign announced plans for thirty-two lots, another sixty-eight. Every brushy hillside seemed to have one of these plywood billboards stuck into it. Designed to keep nearby residents informed of possible changes in their neighborhood, the black-and-white diagrams surrounded with small print were only faintly legible from the sidewalk. From a car, they must have been blurs.

The road narrowed, but evidence of road widening began somewhere around 108th. Expanding Avondale Road from two lanes to four would speed the trip from the new houses to the nearby office parks and shopping malls of Redmond and other Seattle suburbs. We came to a Texaco convenience store pulsing with minivans and stopped to buy a pint of milk for Kathryn's bottle. I stayed outside with the stroller, breathing fumes and enduring the quizzical looks of drivers rushing in to pay for fuel. They seemed to regard me, an obvious pedestrian, as a freak of nature.

Beyond the Texaco, the sidewalks ended. We traveled on the edge of the road, on a graded but unpaved lane separated from the heavy traffic by orange plastic cones. Kathryn contentedly sucked on her bottle. Peter, however, was getting fussy and quieted only when the stroller was moving at a steady clip. Gary, meanwhile, was lagging and complaining. So we adults divided up. Amy and Jean stayed with Gary, keeping him going with equal parts encouragement and distraction.

Marvin and I went ahead, letting velocity calm Peter, and we got to the site of Mrs. Salstrom's cabin early. At first, we weren't sure if we were there. So much had changed. "There's no house," I said.

"But that looks like her old barn," said Marvin.

I remembered it being bigger, of course, but it did look familiar.

"And those trees could be the remains of her orchard," he said.

"I remember climbing in her orchard and picking apples to take home," I said.

By the time the others had caught up with us, we had our bearings. We had identified the pump house and garden fence. This was the place where Mrs. Salstrom had given me bread from her wood stove.

The house, however, was gone. In its place was a freshly cut ditch, and in the ditch was a lustrous sewer pipe. The pipe flushed waste from the tracts of new houses farther along Avondale Road. The crews widening the road had buried Mrs. Salstrom's front yard under gravel.

I don't know what I had expected. Mrs. Salstrom's mossy roof had sagged even in my childhood, and she had died, I knew, in the late 1980s. I suppose I had expected not to recognize the place at all. What was troubling was that it looked as if we had missed seeing her house by just hours.

As Gary climbed trees in the orchard, Amy and I followed my father to the entrance of a private road that led onto Mrs. Salstrom's land. We read the names on the mailboxes. A car pulled in. My father introduced himself and asked if the fish were running. The driver, a woman, remembered him, and invited us to her house before driving away.

"How do you know her?" Amy asked.

"Alan hasn't told you the story of Mrs. Salstrom's land?"

"No, except that you used to bring him here to play."

"Well, Mrs. Salstrom came to me for legal help." As a lawyer, Marvin took many environmental cases. "She was in a bind. She didn't have anything to retire on. All her years as a teacher and a librarian left her unprovided for, and she didn't have any kids who would care for the land. It was the midsixties, Boeing was gearing up to build supersonic airliners, and the real estate people were beating down her door. She had sixty acres here on Bear Creek with many old trees still standing. See that great big cedar back there?"

We were all walking along the private road now, between vine maples and big trees. Gary and Jean had joined us. "Mrs. Salstrom's father was a man named Thomas Provan. Mrs. Salstrom always said that he dreamed this land would become part of a greenbelt, like the greenbelts around the English cities where he grew up."

My father and Mrs. Salstrom tried to sell the parcel to the parks department or the university for an arboretum, but to no avail. In the end, Mrs. Salstrom asked Marvin to buy it and "develop it right." He sent her to another lawyer and, with a friend, bought the land. They divided it into lots of five acres and larger, retaining the part Mrs. Salstrom lived on. After she died, that parcel could be sold, but until then, it would be her home. They filled the deed with restrictions on subdivision and tree cutting, named it Provan Woods, and put it on the market. The parcels went slowly at first, then faster. Mrs. Salstrom got a modest retirement. And the proceeds helped pay for my college education.

We walked down the private road, passing two mock French chateaus set among the vine maples. "I never imagined what people would build on these lots," Marvin said, shaking his head. Looking at their triple garages, I saw for the first time that we had participated in the sprawl economy. Creating five-acre lots, Marvin thought, would preserve the trees as Mrs. Salstrom wished, and it did. But it also chained the residents of Provan Woods to their automobiles. In a small way, we had aided in the dissipation of our city.

**ON THE OTHER END OF METROPOLITAN** Portland, the city of Gresham is putting the pieces together. Meeky Blizzard's Washington County co-conspirator Terry Moore, and Terry's husband Willy, are riding the light rail out to see Gresham. Terry is a woman whose energy level is all out of proportion to her diminutive size and physical ability. "I broke my neck when I was nineteen in 1969 and I ended up in a wheelchair," she laughs, the words zipping along at about the speed she must have been going on the toboggan that did her in. "They said, 'You're going to live to be seventy-five years old. Have fun.' I went out into the world and I couldn't go anywhere."

To that Terry traces her interest in transportation. For years, she threw herself into making the world safe for wheelchairs, but her concerns spilled over to people without wheels on the day a dumbstruck neighbor showed up at a neighborhood association meeting with condemnation papers from the county. They were going to take over his front yard. "All we'd been told was that the county was going to install a traffic light. What kind of traffic light took a whole yard?"

So she and Willy got the planning documents and spread them out on their living room floor. It turned out the county was going to expand the intersection, apparently in preparation for widening the road to five lanes. The Moores invited their neighbors in, and soon everyone was talking war. If the road gets widened, said Terry, "Kiss your cats good-bye, your dogs, your kids, whatever. We don't need right-turn lanes and left-turn lanes and middle lanes. There's a grade school down the street. We need sidewalks." Her little group of neighbors took on the county, banding together with others who were discontented with the car-happy ways of local government. "Our little intersection," she realized, "was a microcosm of all the bad things that were going on in Washington County."

But she and her allies lost, and the road crews rolled in. "Not only did we lose, but we were so rudely treated by the county board of commissioners that I said, 'Obviously, this is our problem; we're not electing the right people.'" So she and her neighbors ran for office. "I drew the straw for Metro Council." The Metropolitan Service District, a little-known but increasingly powerful body, is the nation's only directly elected regional government, encompassing three counties and the city of Portland. To Terry's amazement, she won.

From her seat on the Metro Council, she helped steer to completion Vision 2040, a comprehensive, participatory regional-planning process that managed to get tens of thousands of people across greater Portland to think hard about the intricacies of mixed-use zoning, residential densities, and other arcane details of urban design. It was also the only time any city on the continent, and possibly the planet, extended its planning horizon fifty years into the future. The end result is far from perfect. Growth is envisioned as concentrating in the core of the city, and in eight regional centers. To achieve real reductions in driving per person, however, the latter number would have to be cut in half, and office-park developers would have to be told to go packing, according to Bob Stacey, Jr., urban growth advisor to the governor of Oregon.

Still, the process left Terry deeply optimistic. In public workshops with business leaders, elected officials, and citizens, she asked Oregonians to make a list of the things their community should have in fifty years. "When people put down everything they want, they get a city that's many times more dense than we could ever imagine based on projected population growth. They want to have a movie theater. They want to have their shops, and restaurants, and Starbucks. And they want to be able to walk. And they want to have a community center. And they want to have apartments. And they want to have jobs in their communities."

Terry and Willy arrive at the Gresham rail station in a downpour and find themselves across a football field of parking lots from the nearest building. Having traversed the asphalt plain, they meet up with Gussie McRobert, mayor of Gresham. She apologizes for the dousing. When MAX was built in the 1980s, she explains, Gresham was so resistant that it sent the rail line wide of the business core. "That was before I had any say-so around here," she says, smiling like a Cheshire cat. "Now the downtown businesses are kicking themselves. We're going to put town hall in that parking lot right next to the station, and we're planning a two-hundred-acre mixed-use development nearby." The market for mixed-use, medium-density real estate close to MAX is red-hot, she says. "The only problem is the banks won't finance higher density. I swear they are hidebound by tradition."

Gussie has soft, country tones in her voice, though she has been in greater Portland most of her adult life. Her jewelry and car say "suburban business woman," and she has savvy in spades. In the early 1990s, she launched something called Gresham Vision, a community-wide effort to define what kind of place Gresham ought to be. The conclusion was compact development surrounded by open space—especially on the lava buttes that ring town. So Gussie put an open-space rescue levy on the ballot and used the $10 million proceeds to buy up property on the buttes by the hundreds of acres. In town, she helped reduce the average size of housing lots. "People don't want big yards anymore," she smiles. And she has pushed for well-designed higher density and mixing of uses everywhere else. "If you don't do these things," she explains, still smiling, "you end up with nothing but asphalt."

Eventually the downtown businesspeople "got the fever" of pedestrian-friendly development, Gussie says. Now the center of town boasts benches, trees, wider sidewalks, and traffic-calming "bubbles." Combining density with open space is working so well that Gresham is booming. The city's population has doubled to eighty thousand over the past fifteen years, and fully half of the residents now work in town, rather than commuting to elsewhere. Downtown businesspeople have even begun coming to town meetings demanding greater density and reduced parking. For the future, Gussie wants more of the same—plus, she whispers as if it were scandalous, "I want to put housing right in the middle of our office parks."

On MAX heading back to Portland, Willy Moore is sitting beside a teenager dressed in flannel, jeans, and combat boots. The youth's hair is tinted metallic red, and he is singing a Bach cantata to himself. Willy is complaining about the toll suburbia takes on a typical young person. "If he's fifteen, then his mom is driving him around in the Suburban." The young man breaks his song with a derisive laugh, "Yeah, right!" (Meaning "wrong.") He looks at Willy in the way that only a teenager can look at an adult; his expression says, "How have you managed to stay alive so long without a brain?" What he utters aloud, however, is simply, "Everybody rides MAX."

## September

The woman who remembered my dad—call her Diane—walked us through their parcel of Thomas Provan's woods and onto a wet cedar platform to show us where the fish come. It had been a good year, she and her husband said. About two thousand sockeye spawned in the creek, hundreds on their land. Diane was a volunteer in a program that aimed to help salmon streams in western Washington. She clearly loved the fish and hoped there would be some to show us. But heavy rains, she expected, would have washed the carcasses downstream, and she doubted any live spawners were still around.

Reaching Bear Creek, we gazed down into the yolk-yellow water, and Gary readied his net. There was nothing. Gary consoled himself by concocting a scheme for scooping the eggs from the creek bed with a bucket, carrying them home on the bus, and raising salmon in the bathtub.

But then my mother cried out, "There's one!" She had seen a tail flick. She pointed it out for my father, and he for me, and so on, until everyone could see the fish. We watched his dorsal fin curve and his ruddy torso turn. Even little Kathryn stared into the water. The salmon was a foot-long male, body like blood, triangular head and fins black, spine silver.

Again a cry went up. There was another, a female—her body less red, her spine less silver. She shadowed her mate's movements deeper and downstream. More cries went up as other fish were spotted, some dead and some alive. Two lone males waited, like shadows in the water, in hopes more females would arrive.

Odds were good that these sockeye were lineal descendants of the fish of my youth. Those mauled and proud fighters that had eyed us as children had contributed genes to some of these sockeye. The fish had gone to sea and back to land. I had grown up and had children of my own. And now we met again, eyeing each other through the wrinkled glass of the water's surface.

Our meeting had the same effect this time around, especially for Gary. He had whined and complained during the hike, wishing he had his two-wheeler. "I thought it was going to be fun. This is dumb. The whole thing is dumb. I don't wanna see some dumb creek." But when he caught sight of the fish, the rest of the world seemed to disappear. He reached up to hold my hand, seeking comfort as I once had, and stood stock still with his eyes lost in the depths. His net dangled from his grip, forgotten.

IN TRANSPORTATION, nothing is as it seems. Transportation policy is less important to transportation than is land-use policy, because density is the key determinant of automobile usage. The quest for natural living in garden suburbs is antinatural; such suburbs create the illusion of more green space and less danger while decreasing true green space and security. Building more homes and workplaces—and not new roads—is the solution to traffic congestion, except that eliminating traffic congestion is not necessarily a good thing. Congestion slows traffic, and slow-moving traffic is actually good for access, national defense, and the environment; it encourages pedestrian travel, decreases per capita gasoline consumption, and diminishes dependence on imports from the Middle East. Greater density can aid the fight against crime, because watchful neighbors and populated streets prevent lawlessness. Affordable suburban housing is actually more expensive than high-priced in-city housing because of the extra cars suburb dwellers need.

The fulcrum on which all these paradoxes turn is the commonplace confusion between means and ends. Energy analyst Amory Lovins illustrates the importance of the means-ends distinction well: "When you go to the store to buy a drill, you do not want a drill, you want a hole. At home, you do not want gallons of oil or kilowatts of power, you want hot showers and cold drinks." Just so, people do not want cars or transportation or even mobility, they want access to things.

But many Northwesterners, not least of all politicians, miss this distinction—being unaware of the possibility of access-through-proximity—and continue to assume that mobility is the purpose of transportation. This assumption is lethal to cities. To the extent that mobility, a means, is taken as an end, sprawl advances, access decreases, and the amount of transportation—in sheer distance traveled—grows. Conversely, to the extent that access is understood as the end, sprawl ebbs, mobility wanes, and people are able to get done what they need to get done.

Compounding the widespread confusion over means and ends are two other myths in the Northwest's public belief system. The first is the widespread view that property rights are absolute and sacrosanct under North American legal systems. Perhaps the frontier bred this uniquely western attitude toward property. To this day, in the Northwestern states and, to a lesser extent, British Columbia, a considerable portion of the public believes that the prerogatives of ownership are virtually unlimited. The owner of a parcel of property, it is thought, is entitled to do absolutely anything he or she wants on it. This belief has no footing in North American legal precedents; from the beginning, North American law—and English common law before it—was full of delicate balancing acts between private rights and public interests.

When the Northwest was a lightly peopled wilderness, the myth of the superiority of property rights was harmless enough. Today, it is dangerous. In large parts of the rural Northwest, town planning—about as controversial as postal service in most of the industrial world—is regarded as an overt infringement on the right to property. Consequently, in large parts of the rural Northwest, there is simply no planning at all.

For example, on western Montana's Flathead Lake, where retirement—and telecommuter—sprawl is picking up, property owners fearful of planning began to descend on public hearings about draft county land-use plans. By early 1995, there was hardly a political leader around the lake who would speak up for channeling the burgeoning population growth of the region in ways that would make sense for the long haul.

A myth with even greater power in the Northwest, as across North America, is the belief that sprawling, auto-dependent development, no matter how socially dysfunctional or ecologically suicidal, is critical to keeping workers employed, factories humming, and incomes rising. It is hailed as "growth" and equated, literally and earnestly, with the general welfare.

Popular histories claim that converting the continent to internal combustion helped power the economic boom years of the twenties. They declare that emptying the cities into the suburbs helped fuel the economic boom years of the fifties and sixties. They state that going from one car per family to two helped propel the economic growth of the seventies. And they assert that giant real estate development schemes helped inflate the economy of the eighties.

Under this mythology of sprawl-as-economic-engine, each new distant house is seen as a boon to the economy, entailing expenditures—or further debt—for appliances, satellite dishes, furniture, ride-on mowers, and extra cars, not to mention new roads, parking lots, and sewer lines. Indeed, in the years after World War II, mass suburbanization and the consumer spending it induced were taken by some to be the formula for perpetual economic growth.

However erroneous, the equating of sprawl and growth is understandable. When children grow, they take up more space, so would not a growing economy do so, too? Not necessarily. In the terms of orthodox economics, a growing economy is one in which the inflation-adjusted cash value of all goods and services sold increases over time. As the word is usually used, it also means an economy in which this aggregate cash value is increasing faster than population.

Growth is *estimated*—measured is far too precise a word—in a number called gross national product (GNP). When gross national product grows 3 percent faster than population and inflation, an economy is, by conventional wisdom, considered to be "healthy." If it is expanding more slowly than that, it is regarded as stagnant. (The choice of words is revealing: slow-growing real GNP per capita is "stagnant," not "stable," "consistent," or "reliable.")

So, in strict terms, to equate sprawling development with growth is a fallacy. It is to equate physical expansion with an increase in the money-denominated value of amenities bought and sold. A cloud of gas dispersing does not grow, although it may appear to; an economy that spreads itself over a larger area is not, by that fact, a growing economy, it is a spreading economy. Whether needs and wants are better met, whether people are better able to develop their talents, whether individuals are better able to flourish—these are all entirely separate matters.

Even those who do not confuse sprawl and growth—by using the word "growth" to refer to both urban expansion and economic development, for example—often believe that sprawl causes growth. Yet the preponderance of evidence suggests that the opposite is true. Sprawl is a drag on conventionally defined growth. It imposes gargantuan costs—economic, social, and environmental—on businesses and workers, diverting resources from more-productive investments. The engine of the economy is ingenuity, not sprawl. The economy improves when people discover ways to do more with the same—the same amount of land, labor, and capital. The Northwest could have spent the hundreds of billions of dollars it devoted to cars, roads, and sprawl on improving cities, educating citizens, or researching contraceptive technologies, and the results—still measured in the orthodox terms of GNP—would have been much better.

Most important of all is the realization that the hopes Northwesterners pin on growth—the desires for a dramatically better life—are now causally related to neither sprawl nor an increasing GNP. Most of what the Pacific Northwest desperately needs to improve the quality of life of its residents is invisible or appears perversely in estimates of gross national product. Neither sprawl nor money growth is likely to fulfill Northwesterners' strong needs for commodities such as greater personal safety, more job security, improved health, more free time, stronger communities, and a healthier environment. To the contrary, sprawl is detrimental to each of these ends, and many things that improve them actually register as declines in GNP. An increase in the vitality of communities, for example, translates into more people sharing things. When cashless trade replaces market exchange, GNP declines. Indeed, community improves life by reducing GNP.

Is what is happening in Vancouver and Portland and other Northwest cities enough? No, it is not. Vancouver's population is growing by a West End's worth each year, and much of that growth is taking place outside the city. Close to two-thirds of workers in the metropolitan area now commute from one suburb to another, rendering the core less relevant. In Portland, sprawling residential development continues despite the urban growth boundary and the comprehensive plans. And greater Seattle, despite a tough statewide growth management act and a well-regarded comprehensive land-use plan, has still sanctioned the development of four hundred square miles of rural land by the year 2020. In places like Boise, western Montana, the Canadian Okanagan Valley, and the sunny side of Vancouver Island, sprawl is rampant and population is growing at record rates.

The Pacific Northwest has changed its vision and begun to change its policies, but it will take a while to see the results on the ground. To unlearn myths such as property-rights-as-inviolable and sprawl-as-growth, and to change attitudes like the deep resistance to in-fill development in single-family neighborhoods, will take an especially long time. But step by step, change is happening.

Northwesterners transformed the urban landscape in the half century since World War II. And the transformation has not slowed. In the next half century, they will undoubtedly rebuild much of what now exists. The question is what they will build. If they choose wisely, they will end up with a human habitat worthy of its creators. They will create cities with vital economies, safe and secure neighborhoods, diminishing impacts on the global environment, and flourishing communities. They will create cities where—with almost no one noticing at first—automobile numbers stabilize and then begin to drop. If they choose wisely, perhaps some day most of their politicians will, like Gordon Price, own no automobile.

## September

Diane gave us some apples from her fruit trees and we ate them in crisp slices as we left Provan Woods, walking back along the shoulder of Avondale Road. On the way, Gary raced and played. He stopped to look at a horse, and he and I explored a dilapidated shed. "Definitely a bad-guy hideout," he told me. Kathryn and Peter slept in the stroller. We stopped to buy coffee at the Texaco. And we finally arrived back at the bus stop by the projects with thirty minutes to wait. There, we sat with three teenage girls as they debated shopping malls.

"I don't wanna go to Bellevue Square if nobody's gonna be there."

"I'm not getting on the bus if we don't know where we're going."

"I wanna go to Seattle."

"My mom would kill me."

"Let's go to Kirkland."

"There ain't nobody there."

"I don't wanna go to Crossroads. God!"

"Let's go to Bel-Square. But if there ain't nobody there, I'm leaving."

"I wish I had a car."

"If I had a car, I'd never wait for no bus."

"If I had a car, I'd be out of here."

"Oh my God! There's my sister! What's she doing here? Her boyfriend's got a car. What's he doing here? Why they riding the bus?"

*chapter four*

# STUFF

## December

**IT IS 2:30 ON A SUNDAY MORNING**. Peter is crying in his crib across the room. The pine-tossing wind outside has cooled our house, and the furnace has been running more than usual. I fumble for my glasses, knocking the alarm clock to the floor. I pull myself groggily out of bed, hoping to get to Peter before he wakes Kathryn, who is sleeping in her crib close by.

I lift him to my chest and wrap a blanket around him. I wipe his nose with a tissue. He screams. I jostle him. "All done, Peter. All done." The moon has gone down, but frost on the roof tops brightens the view from our window by reflecting the light from the street lamps. Peter quiets. I lay him down to change him, wishing diapers were fluorescent. He screams.

Peter has a cold, so Amy and I have not slept more than four consecutive hours in a week. We have not had a good night's sleep in close to two years.

His diaper changed and its contents flushed, I wrap him in the blanket again and set him in the bed beside Amy so he can nurse. I collapse onto the mattress.

The alarm clock is going off, but it is still dark outside. I search desperately for it on the bedside table, then the floor. Peter, still in our bed, is stirring. Kathryn rolls over in her crib. I find the alarm. It is set for 4:30. Kathryn must have played with it yesterday. I close my eyes.

Amy is patting me on my chest. "Alan! She'll wake up Peter." It is 6:00. Kathryn is awake in her crib, kicking the headboard and singing, "Pop! Pop! Pop oh weasel!" I pull her into our bed in desperation, handing her last night's bottle in hopes she will be quiet for another half hour.

"Hi, Dad!" she says. She is well rested.

"Mamma oh seeping," she tells me, accepting the bottle. "Pederr oh seepin! Where Gary go, Dada? Oh no! Lost? Gone?" This is a game we play. I am not amused.

"Gary's sleeping, Kathryn. Shhh. Everybody's sleeping. Here, lie down in the bed and drink your bottle " She lies down and drinks for a moment. I pull the covers up and close my eyes.

"Gary-ary?" she calls out. I open my eyes. "Gary-ary, Gary-ary," she sings.

"Shh."

Too late. He has heard. There is a flurry of footsteps on the stairs. "Gary coming!" she says, grinning and sucking on her bottle.

He bursts into the room, his voice all sunshine. "Hi, Dad! Hi, Kathryn! It's almost Christmas! Merry Christmas!" He leaps over me into the bed and then hides under the covers by my knees.

Kathryn squeals, "Where Gary go?" and crawls after him. They wrestle. I am balancing on the edge of the mattress. Kathryn's foot catches Peter in the ribs and he wakes up crying. I pat him on the back to comfort him. He quiets but stays awake. He rolls onto his back and begins poking his fingers into my eyes. Amy is somehow asleep again.

"All right!" I groan. "I'm getting up."

I am thinking, "Coffee."

JENS MOLBAK IS AN URBAN miner. He runs a high-tech operation, employing computerized remote sensors to extract zinc, copper, and nickel from the landscape. But Jens, whose family has long been in the Northwest, does not follow buried veins. He mines the tops of bedroom dressers and the bottoms of kitchen junk drawers. His company, Coinstar Inc., based in Bellevue, Washington, makes computerized coin-sorting machines and installs them at supermarkets. The sorters count change dumped in a hopper and dispense vouchers good for cash at the checkout stand. In 1994, the company's first full year of operation, Coinstar's three-score machines recovered seven hundred tons of pennies and other coins. That was seven hundred tons of copper and other metals that did not have to be mined, smelted, and minted. (Someday, Jens says, "We'd like to shut down the penny mint.") It was also seven hundred tons of coins that no longer cluttered people's living spaces.

Seven hundred tons of metal, in a regional economy that gobbles metal by the mountainside, is hardly worth mentioning. But Jens Molbak is the perfect metaphor for the new economy emerging in the Pacific Northwest, an economy that knows waste is money—money lost, money waiting to be made.

His company's existence, and that of the increasing number of companies making a profit by recycling various "waste" products, is a lucid demonstration of the fact that there is a lot of money lying around. Wasted money. Money in the form of discarded pocket change, and money in other forms: unused nickel, copper, and steel; discarded wood, cardboard, and glass; plastic, paper, and concrete; yard clippings, plaster, and rags; food scraps, methyl bromide, and every other unwanted substance. Even sewage sludge is money in disguise.

A similar idea applies to things—or qualities—that, while not yet discarded, could be designed out of existence. Think of excessive packaging, planned obsolescence, quick-changing fashions, and disposability; these are "waste" because the same end could be achieved with less stuff. Again, ultimately, all waste is money—money lost, money waiting to be made. The trick, as Jens Molbak's coin counter illustrates, is to figure out how to mine the waste and turn bad money into good.

Put it another way. Think of the economy as a giant organism, as does Herman Daly, professor at the University of Maryland and dean of ecological economists. Money is its circulatory system. Money goes round and round, from businesses to households to businesses to households. There is also a digestive system. It is a one-way trip from ingestion to digestion to excretion. What matters to the world outside the economic organism is not the circulation of money but the digestion of resources. What matters is what the organism eats and excretes. Daly calls this combination of input and output "throughput."

Throughput is a useful word. It fills a hole in our language. It is a way to capture in two syllables the entire process from extraction to manufacture to consumption to disposal for everything from virgin timber to tiddlywinks. It encompasses cement, stone, and gravel; fresh water and farm produce; coal, oil, and natural gas; wood, paper, and cardboard; metals, chemicals, and plastics; textiles, rubber, and road salt; and everything else that is animal, vegetable, or mineral.

The sheer quantity of throughput in the Northwest economy is staggering. On average, it amounts to 115 pounds of mineral, agricultural, and forestry products per person per day. That amounts to a lot of stuff.

The trick of sustainable economics, argues Herman Daly, is to keep the circulatory system going round and round while putting the digestive system on a diet. It has got to be quite a diet, considering that billions of poor people around the world need substantially more than they now have, and considering that world population will grow for decades because most of the world's people are very young—even if all couples immediately decide to have no more than two children.

At the Wuppertal Institute in Germany, economists and ecologists have calculated that, for these reasons, the only thing that will suffice to turn humanity off its collision course with planetary ecology is to increase by a factor of ten the efficiency with which industrial countries use natural resources. For each dollar in the Northwest economy's circulatory system, the region needs to send one-tenth as much stuff down the economy's digestive tract. For each published word read, for example, the region must devise ways to use one-tenth the paper, and for every trip taken, the region must learn to use one-tenth as much fuel. The Northwest must do across the board what replacing bulky copper wires with ultralight fiber optic cables has done in telecommunications: improve the quality of service while reducing resource consumption by an order of magnitude. So *sustainability* means, achieving a "factor-ten economy": an economy that extracts a better quality of life from a daily resource diet of just 11—rather than 115—pounds per person.

Factor ten may sound impossibly ambitious. In any event, there is room for dickering over numbers. Make different assumptions about population, poverty, economic growth, and the resilience of the biosphere, and you will get to as much as factor one hundred or as little as factor four. For the present generation, however, these arguments hardly matter. What matters is the need to multiply the efficiency with which the economy uses throughput. What matters is the challenge that coin counter Jens Molbak latched onto: how to create what salespeople call *value* through what garbage people call *reduction*.

Other Northwesterners are accepting the challenge too. They are using brains and bytes instead of pounds and gallons. They are sharing and repairing rather than disposing and replacing. They are substituting recycled for virgin, reusable for throwaway, and safe for toxic. They are designing into oblivion gigawatts of power. They are planning for durability rather than obsolescence. Whether it is in feeding themselves, clothing themselves, sheltering themselves, or meeting their other needs, Northwesterners are inventing ways to mine waste and wastefulness.

## December

It is 7:00. I have showered. The children are dressed. The oatmeal is cooking, and while Gary plays with Peter on the floor Kathryn is "helping" me brew coffee. We measure the beans into the grinder, then grind and dump the coffee into the filter.

We fill the carafe from the spigot and pour it into the coffee-maker. I point to the switch, and Kathryn turns it on. She flips it back and forth four times, watching the little red light go on and off. We get out a mug and spoon in some sugar and creamer. Kathryn steals some sugar for herself, then notices the coffee dripping into the carafe.

"Cottee! Yay! Cottee!" I suspect Kathryn was a coffee roaster in a past life. She claps. Peter imitates her. Gary tries to teach him how to "high-five."

The coffee finishes brewing. I pour it into the cup and sit down to drink it on the floor beside Peter and Gary. Kathryn climbs into my lap. Leaning back against the dishwasher, I am content. The children are happy. The oatmeal is making little plopping sounds in the pan. I take a sip of coffee.

My sleep-deprived mind reflexively reconstructs the events that led up to the cup of coffee I hold in my hand. The beans, I know, came from a mountain farm in the watershed of Colombia's Cauca River, a place once cloaked with cloud forests—now among the most endangered types of tropical forest. The farm workers probably sprayed the beans three times with insecticides, some of which were synthesized in Europe's Rhine River valley. I know that long stretches of the Rhine are now deprived of aquatic life because of toxic releases from chemical plants. I know the beans were picked by hand—I've seen it done—and removed from the fruit that encased them by a crusher fueled with diesel oil.

"My turn," demands Kathryn. I give her a tiny sip. "Mmm. Cottee." Her impish smile suggests she knows it's "not for children." I take another swallow.

The beans crossed the Caribbean on a freighter made in Japan. And the Japanese shipyard likely used Korean steel. The Korean steel mill used iron ingots mined in Australia, I speculate. And the ship was fueled with petroleum from Venezuela, probably pumped from the ground in the humid basin of the Orinoco River. At New Orleans, above the mouth of the Mississippi, the beans were roasted for thirteen minutes over four-hundred-degree flames of Oklahoma natural gas. The cooling beans were packaged in a four-ply bag made of aluminum foil from the Columbia Basin and nylon, polyester, and polyethylene—all plastic resins synthesized in New Jersey and Missouri from Mexican oil.

"My turn," demands Kathryn. I give her another sip. Peter is now trying to pull himself upright by clinging to his brother's ears. "Peter," Gary giggles, "let go!" I drink again.

From the Mississippi watershed, the beans traveled to the Northwest in an eighteen-wheeler fueled with Middle Eastern petroleum. I bought them in the grocery store and brought them home in a brown bag made of unbleached paper from the Willamette Valley of western Oregon. On the five-mile round-trip to the market, our car burned one-sixth of a gallon of gasoline—refined at Cherry Point in northwestern Washington.

Amy comes down from her shower. Gary asks her, "What are we going to do today? Can we do something fun?"

"Like what?"

"Let's go to Discovery Park and look for eagles!"

"Oh, I don't know. I'm so tired," Amy says.

"We could stop and get you a mocha." Gary's got Amy's number. I drink again.

In the kitchen, we had pulverized the beans in a grinder assembled in China from imported steel, aluminum, copper, and plastic parts. The coffeemaker was assembled in Taiwan, also from imported parts. Our filter is a reusable gold-plated mesh made in Switzerland, probably from Russian ore. The grinder and the coffeemaker were powered by electricity generated at Ross Dam, on the Skagit River near the Canadian border. The water came by pipe from the Cedar River, on the west slope of the Cascade Mountains.

Gary, his wits about him, draws Kathryn to his cause. "Kathryn, do you want to go to a big park?"

"Big pa-ark!" beams Kathryn. "Big pa-ark!" She toddles toward the door asking, "Where my coat go?"

Amy sighs, "Not yet, Kathryn. Later. We'll go to the park later."

"Yessss!" says Gary.

"First," I say, "I want you to go through your toys and decide which ones to send to the consignment store. There's no reason to keep the stuff you don't play with anymore. Do a good job and we'll go look for eagles."

I drink again, draining the cup.

My morning libation took about a hundred beans to brew. At one cup a day, I go through the harvest of a coffee tree every six weeks. I am also responsible for the dozens of direct and indirect uses of fossil fuels, metals, and chemicals that brought the beverage to my lips. I think of these effects rippling out across the globe like the wake of a boat—an ecological wake. It isn't just coffee. Everything has an ecological wake. The T-shirt I bought yesterday on sale. The newspaper on the doorstep that I won't get to read until after the kids are in bed tonight. The burgers and fries we got Gary for dinner last night. The oatmeal on the stove. The stove. The floor I'm sitting on. Everything. Some wakes are big; others are small. Coffee's, I suspect, is medium-sized.

**THE QUESTION IS HOW** to get the coffee—and all the rest—with less wake.

From his perch, John Hess has a million-dollar view. He could turn his close-set eyes in just about any direction and fill them with bracing vistas of Rocky Mountain spires combing the Idaho sky. But he does not much care to: "It's pretty tough to eat," he says, wiping his brow with a wide, grease-stained palm.

John's perch is an upturned bucket in the tool-strewn yard of his farm shed. What he cares to do is farm, and talk about farming. At the moment, he is talking—between tirades against politicians, environmentalists, agribusinessmen, and others he perceives as enemies of his guild—about how he is cutting his farm's consumption of water, energy, fertilizers, and pesticides. He is talking, in his own way, about lowering throughput, mining waste, and moving toward factor ten.

John's original goal was a 25 percent reduction in farm inputs. He is working toward that target by getting control of what goes where. And he is doing that by spending a lot of time in his shed. "When I got started into this thing, there was nothing I could do. With the equipment that we had, if I could get within 40 percent of my target rate of application to the soil with fertilizer, I was doing as good as could be done." The farm machinery manufacturers, to his mind, were missing the boat. And he—who never quite finished agricultural college—figured he would have to do the job himself.

Tinkering was not new to him. "There's very few pieces of equipment on my place that haven't seen the attention of my torch," he boasts. From the looks of him, this statement is not hard to believe. His hands, sleeves, and pant legs are stained with grease and dusted with the sandy soil of the Snake River plain. His round shoulders and broad back look as if they have pressed a fair bit of metal into shape.

Peering into his shed confirms the impression. It is a metal-worker's cave of Ali Baba. The size of a high school gymnasium, the corrugated structure is piled to the rafters with belts, bins, scrap iron, wires, spanners, clamps, hoses, pipes, barrels, and the hulls of derelict machinery.

During the long winters of the early 1990s, John Hess went into the shed and rewired his combines, splicing and welding in electronic controls and monitors that John Deere never dreamed of. To save fuel and stop compressing the soil, he devised a way to seed and treat a field in a single pass of his tractor. He coupled three trailers into a train behind his largest tractor. From his cab, the rig stretches backward for fifty feet and outward twenty feet to each side. In the cockpit, displays, readouts, and toggles monitor and adjust the rate at which each substance is spread.

As his shed work continued, he found he was getting better control of fertilizers and pesticides, enabling him to spread precisely as much of each chemical as planned. In the process, John cut his annual use of farm chemicals enough to save twenty-five thousand dollars, a quarter of his bill, and the initial success gave him bigger and better ideas—ideas that he could not carry out alone in his shed.

John Hess is not an alternative farmer. He does not subscribe to *Organic Gardening* or have any special affinity for biological diversity. But his motives do not matter. He is striving for low-impact farming because high-impact farming is killing him at the bottom line.

Across the region, a growing minority of farmers are doing the same. From snap bean farms in the Willamette Valley, to raspberry fields near Vancouver, to dryland wheat farms in the Palouse, cultivators are cutting back on inputs, concentrating on improving their soil, and making a good living. The incipient transformation is evident all the way down the region's food chain, from farm field to packing plant to grocery to kitchen—and on to toilets and sewage treatment facilities. Northwesterners are learning to feed their personal digestive tracts without sending as much stuff down their economy's agroindustrial digestive tract.

"The next big mistake that we all make," John says, "is getting an even application across the field." He tilts his powerful head toward a potato field. "Most people think a field full of dirt is a field full of dirt. It's not. Between here and the hill over there, the Soil Conservation Service said that there was one class of soil. We've found over a hundred."

"Soil is alive, it's literally *alive*." He speaks with a rich, rural cadence: "lit-rully ali-ive." Wiping a thin tuft of steel wool–colored hair off his forehead, he is momentarily in awe. "The microflora that is in a cubic foot of soil is absolutely staggering. Damned if I know what's all in it!" He rumbles with a belly laugh. "All I know is if I go out there and put the recommended rates on all of my ground, about half of it hasn't got enough and the other half has got too much."

Variation on this scale was a challenge that even John's tinkering skills could not meet, so he hooked up with scientists from institutions such as the University of Idaho and the Idaho National Engineering Laboratory. Together, they aimed to apply advanced technologies to agriculture's economic and environmental problems, using John's farm as a test run. "Farming is still 85 to 95 percent artistry," John says, arching his bushy eyebrows. "We've got to get more scientific."

The team began analyzing John's farm by the square yard. They drilled core samples, ran electric currents through the dirt, tested soil magnetism and moisture, and equipped his harvesters to weigh the crop as it came off each furrow. On his tractors, they installed global positioning systems—navigation devices that pinpoint location through satellite telemetry. (The U.S. military used this technology to find its way around the desert in the Persian Gulf War.) The team then fed their findings into a geographic information system (GIS), a computerized mapping technology that allows data to be sorted and analyzed spatially.

The computerized maps turn the uniform fields into stained-glass mosaics. The maps show the diversity of growing conditions and yields, revealing, for example, that parts of John's wheat fields grow 143 bushels an acre while others yield just 3 bushels an acre. Applying this kind of intelligence, John will be able to dispense inputs more precisely.

John is not doing this for the sake of natural ecology; he is doing it to stay in farming. "All I am is a farmer. First, middle, and last. I've farmed for thirty years. I'm receiving the same dollar price for my commodities today as the day I started to farm." But his costs keep rising: "I've absorbed thirty years of inflation." He is driving across his spread in a gutted Datsun pickup, the smallest wheeled thing on the farm. It cramps his large frame.

If he wanted to, John reflects, he could get out of farming. He owns a long stretch of river frontage that would sell for summer homes at twenty thousand dollars a lot. If he sold it, he could pay off his debt, lease his remaining land, and retire to a more forgiving lifestyle.

His current life is anything but forgiving. "You gotta be about three-quarters crazy to be a farmer. Every time I leave the house, everything I own is in my back pocket. It's my butt against the blaze," he grins, showing two rows of teeth perfect but for one jutting incisor. "And for what? I've lived on nine hundred dollars a month for the last twenty years."

John is not about to sell out, though. He could not live with himself. In 1906 or 1907—no one can remember which—John's grandfather Horace Arnold Hess came to Idaho from the Mormon heartlands of Utah to work for a relative. His summer wages were forty acres of unwatered land worth ten dollars at the time. The next year, Horace brought his wife back from Utah in a boxcar. In the middle of their acreage, they built a soddy—a cabin made of sod—and set to watering their land. When they grew old their son Horace Eugene took over the spread, and John, born in 1938, took over from him when the time came. John has quadrupled the size of the farm, from the five hundred acres he inherited to two thousand acres, and he says he will have to triple its size again.

John will to have to "swallow three of my neighbors" to survive the continuing shakeout in agriculture, he says, and he also must become more efficient. The research on his farm is aimed at producing results that pay for themselves in lower costs, not just for John but for all farmers. He is still paying out a hundred thousand dollars a year for chemicals, the bulk of which miss the crops and end up in the soil, in the groundwater, or downstream. He pays fifty thousand dollars in electric bills to pump irrigation water onto his fields; again, much of it does not reach the plants. And he is still soaking his land with irrigation water by the vertical foot.

In terms of throughput in the regional economy, the water on John's farm is especially important. Irrigation takes 86 percent of the water withdrawn from Northwest aquifers, lakes, and rivers. The bulk of that water is withdrawn in Idaho; nearly half of the Northwest's irrigated acres are in that state, most of them here on the Snake River plain.

Yet for John Hess, the water itself is not a financial concern. There's no incentive to conserve, he points out, taking a grease-stained hand from the wheel to pull a hat onto his head. The hat is leather; it looks as if it might have come with Horace from Utah. Because Horace got here early enough to secure ample water rights, John has plenty of free water. If he conserves it too effectively, he could theoretically lose it, under the "use it or lose it" principle in Idaho water law. John pays just $2.45 per acre per year—less than five thousand dollars a year for the entire farm—for water storage and distribution. He saves water only to conserve soil and energy.

The pickup truck crests a rise from which most of the farm is visible, and John gets out. Looking around, he unveils his hopes for a future in which he will grow crops with a lot less throughput. In winter, he will turn the data stored in the GIS analysis into a prescription tailored for each zone of each field—a prescription for seed, fertilizer, pesticides, and water. He will program that prescription into the controls of his farm machinery and center-pivot irrigators. He will retrofit those irrigators to allow a variable rate of spray from each nozzle. Eventually, "we'll be able to put moisture and nutrient sensors in those zones, and when that pivot comes across the top, it will broadcast what that area needs. I'll probably not even know what's happening. But we'll stop putting stuff where we don't need it, and start putting stuff where we do. I'll cut inputs by a quarter, hopefully more. Yields will rise."

The owners of other irrigated farms on the Snake River plain are also saving water. Over the past decades, most have converted from ditch irrigation to sprinklers in order to slow the soil loss and salt buildup that are sapping fields of their fertility. (Snake River plain topsoil was eroding three times faster than it formed from subsoil in the early 1980s, according to the U.S. Department of Agriculture's Soil Conservation Service.) Along the way, they cut their water use, sometimes by two-thirds. More recently, intent on conserving electricity, they have been switching from outward-spraying pivots to downward-spraying ones, saving more water by reducing losses to evaporation.

Still, the potential for water savings remains largely untapped. Efficient irrigation techniques such as buried pipes instead of open ditches—used widely in Texas and California, where water is dearer—are neglected here. Idaho irrigation water travels in open, unlined ditches. John knows the result: "Half of my water evaporates or seeps out between the top of the ditch and my place."

Mainstream farmers elsewhere in the Northwest have shown the same kind of savvy as John Hess. Take the farmers of apples, the leading crop of the state of Washington. A conventionally grown

Washington apple—eye-popping red and perfectly formed—looks that way partly due to the routine, heavy use of nitrogen and other fertilizers; repeated spraying with an arsenal of insecticides, herbicides, fungicides, and rodenticides; and doses of chemicals that, among other things, enhance skin color and arrest spoilage.

Since 1992, one of Washington's largest apple packers—Stemilt Growers—has been weaning the orchards whose fruit it handles from the most dangerous of these substances while reducing the use of others.

Stemilt's hulking, whitewashed headquarters sits on the banks of the Columbia River in Wenatchee, a bustling fruit-growing town in the rattlesnake hills east of the Cascade crest. Here, and in buildings like it up and down this side of the range, Stemilt stores, packs, and ships nearly $100 million worth of apples, cherries, and pears a year. The fruit grows at 250 independently owned orchards.

"From start to finish, Stemilt is looking for ways to be a responsible company," says Nate Reed, the company's director of research and development. Since 1992, Nate has enrolled most of Stemilt's orchards in a program he calls "Responsible Choice." A university-trained plant physiologist who grew up on an Indiana farm, Nate is simultaneously defensive about conventional farming and enthusiastic about sustainable agriculture. "We don't have all the answers. This isn't organic farming. We need chemicals to farm this basin profitably. But we can still do the right thing." He tilts his chair back behind his metal desk, his frame out of proportion to his small office. Ten yards away, through a thin wall, hundreds of women, aided by French-designed robotic production lines, are washing, sizing, sorting, stickering, and packing apples by the bobbing flotilla.

"Instead of going in in the spring and fall and putting thirty to forty pounds of nitrogen fertilizer down, we're only applying it as needed. Instead of spraying by the calendar—every seven days, twenty-one days, whatever the label says—we're spraying when we need it." Nate has clicked on his desktop computer, and its glow is picked up by his wide glasses and milky complexion. "We're getting smarter. It saves cost. We're not driving excess fertilizer down into the water table. And it's better for the trees."

In 1989, the apple industry was rattled by sudden, deafening public opposition to one of its favorite chemicals, a color and growth enhancer called Alar. Most of the industry was incensed and bitter. Alar, they argued, was a safe and useful chemical. The public was not convinced. Stemilt knew, as Nate says, that "perceptions are reality."

Stemilt founder Tom Mathison resolved to turn the Alar scare to his advantage by putting the company on the leading edge of environmental responsibility. He hired Nate Reed away from the U.S. Department of Agriculture's Wenatchee station and handed him the job of doing a systematic, detailed investigation of each chemical used in the industry. Nate combed hundreds of government documents and scientific articles. He boiled down his findings into a scoring system, with more points assigned to chemicals that posed greater risks to workers, consumers, and the environment. Then he put out a guidebook to responsible orchard management, reporting each chemical's score and recommending earth-friendly strategies for everything from codling moth infestation to soil-nutrient deficiencies.

The point system, Nate acknowledges as he drives across town to visit a grower named Duane Pert, can never be perfect. For one thing, it quantifies imponderables: is a fish worth more than a songbird or the other way around? For another, there are big gaps in risk data. Thus, assigning points is an attempt to compare little-understood risks to workers, for example, with little-understood risks to aquatic invertebrates. Still, farmers needed some way to assess the environmental effects of their choices, and Nate's analysis was at least informed by a careful review of the evidence. The point system let farmers "grab the fuzzy cloud" of ecological responsibility. Besides, points help motivate because "people are competitive by nature." Nate slows the car and turns into the lane of an orchard outside of Wenatchee. Short apple and cherry trees march toward the horizon in perfect columns.

Duane Pert, manager of this spread, is squatting near his white Sonoma truck, pinching some dirt between his fingers. Two-thirds of the Stemilt farmers, including Duane, have embraced the Responsible Choice program, keeping their guidebooks handy in their pickups and tracking their scores over time. They have done so for two reasons, says Duane, a toothpick dangling from his lip. "We've come to a time where we have to be accountable for our actions. And besides, I save money."

Accountable farming is cheaper because it substitutes intelligence for chemistry. Standing in the shade of a Gala apple tree near Duane, Nate shortens his scientific sentences to farm-boy fragments, "Say you got a bug. If you're gonna just hammer it, hey." He shakes his dark locks. "Boost resistance. Never work. Gotta farm smart." He ticks two fingers along the row. "Get bug traps. Monitor 'em. Only spray when you need it. Use biocontrols—confuse the bugs with sex pheromones. Hammer 'em with predatory wasps, ladybugs, lacewings, whatever." He juts his chin. "Same for fertilizer. Test the soil. Apply by the tree, not by the calendar." Duane, a bronzed and barrel-chested native of the Wenatchee Valley, nods quietly.

Using records from each grower, Stemilt has monitored progress. The average point total fell by a quarter between 1991 and 1994—representing, in rough-and-ready terms, a 25 percent reduction in throughput per apple grown. That trend is likely to continue. In the short term, improvement will come as more farmers adapt and perfect Responsible Choice techniques. In the long term, technology will help reduce the throughput involved in growing Washington apples. "They're coming out with infrared goggles to spot tree stress," says Nate, so farmers will be able to apply chemicals as precisely as doctors prescribe medication.

Stemilt's Responsible Choice efforts extend from the farm to the packing plant. There, Nate led Stemilt to halve the use of color-preserving diphenyl amine—"We just stopped using it when we didn't need it, from August to April." He began experimenting with naturally occurring varieties of bacteria and yeast that might provide a substitute for the fungicides spread on fruit after the harvest. He sought a method for recycling the ozone-eating methyl bromide used to fumigate apples before shipping them to Japan and Korea. He found a technique never previously employed for apples, one that makes use of naturally occurring minerals called zeolites to filter the methyl bromide from the smokestack. When heated, the zeolites release the methyl bromide back into the fumigation chamber. And his company helped establish a "pallet pool"—a sort of corporate cooperative for the reuse of wooden forklift pallets. Since it draws fruit from more than twelve thousand acres, and a good acre of apples yields thirty tons of fruit, Stemilt uses a lot of pallets.

For most growers, Responsible Choice has been a money-saver, especially after a first shakedown season. For Stemilt, however, its cost has run to six figures. And to date, "there has been no reward in the marketplace. Our fruit sells for the exact same price as everybody else's." Stemilt has been putting ladybug stickers on its fruit to advertise its environmental initiatives, but few shoppers know the difference. Grocers, Nate says, are not about to inform them. "They just want to turn their cash registers." Putting up signs about the superior environmental characteristics of Stemilt fruit would only raise questions about the produce in the neighboring bins.

The transformation of the Northwest food system extends to growers of other crops as well. Hundreds of dryland wheat growers in the Palouse region have been stemming erosion by tilling the soil without turning it—using new conservation-tillage machinery that pokes holes for seeds rather than plowing. Dozens of Palouse farmers have been slashing their use of fertilizers and chemicals by reviving crop rotations used two generations ago. The standard cropping pattern in the Palouse is to grow wheat each winter, with only a spring crop of peas or lentils to diffuse pests and rebuild the soil. Instead, these farmers are orchestrating complicated rotations of three to five years, in which barley, clover, rapeseed, and grass improve soil fertility and moisture while eliminating weeds and wheat pests. Some dryland farmers are even leaving fields in perennial grasses for five to twenty years, allowing the native flora of the Palouse to regenerate the soil before tilling for bumper crops of wheat.

The Northwest Coalition for Alternatives to Pesticides in Eugene, Oregon, reports that in 1994 farmers were aggressively reducing their pesticide use on seventy-five thousand acres of cropland in Washington and Oregon—a huge increase over the past, but still just one-half of 1 percent of all cropland. Since 1990, Oregon hazelnut cultivators, working close to thirty thousand acres, have controlled two of the three principal hazelnut insect pests by introducing parasitic wasps and nurturing native predator insects. Meanwhile, 280 farmers, most of them working small spreads, have entirely converted to organic methods, employing no synthetic chemicals whatsoever. In British Columbia in 1994, farmers employed integrated pest management—an umbrella term for low-pesticide farming strategies—on more than half of all acres given over to carrots, cranberries, onions, and potatoes. Sustainable farming is complicated and challenging, demanding excellent management and information. It is more an approach than a technology.

Growing and packing food without depleting farm ecology is only half the battle. From the farm field, the food has to travel to market—sometimes stopping off in food processing plants for milling, cleaning, peeling, chopping, freezing, canning, packaging, and so on. All along the way, there are Northwesterners trimming throughput. Shippers are recycling and reusing crates and boxes as never before. Processors are seeking leaner packaging and packaging made from recycled paper and plastic. Farmers markets are expanding in most cities, eliminating the need for much packaging and food processing. And some cost- and environment-conscious consumers are buying foods in season, when they can be produced locally rather than shipped from distant lands.

Major grocery chains are increasingly offering organic products, following the lead of food co-ops and natural food stores. Beverage containers—aluminum cans, glass bottles, and plastic jugs—are being recycled at higher rates than anywhere else in North America. In British Columbia, some glass beer bottles are still refilled; sadly, the share of beer sold in refillable containers fell from 97 percent in 1980 to less than 25 percent in 1994.

Small but growing percentages of the nutrients in food scraps are finding their way back to the soil. In Seattle, a neighbor-to-neighbor master composter program has taught hundreds of people to turn food into soil, diverting twenty-eight hundred tons of food scraps and yard waste from the city's solid waste stream in 1993. In British Columbia, dozens of municipalities are planning composting initiatives; the town of Mission collects food scraps curbside.

Even after it is eaten, food is not done generating throughput. Toilets account for the largest share of water consumption inside Northwest buildings. But in the state of Washington, beginning in 1993, all new toilets sold had to be water-wise, flushing less than half as much water as was the norm previously. In some cases, plumbers have installed no-flow johns: Seattle's historic Smith Tower, once the tallest building west of the Mississippi, now sports only advanced, flushless urinals. Instead of washing each ounce of urine in a gallon of purified water, these fixtures hold a few ounces of a lighter-than-water fluid, which forms an odor seal as the urine empties down the drain.

Finally, the food goes to the sewage treatment plant. Conventional sewage treatment methods are a classic case of industrial-age thinking. They take nutrient-packed biological mass—money waiting to be made—and throw more throughput at it: they filter it mechanically, bathe it in reactive chemicals, aerate it with high-power pumps, and finally discharge it as far as practicable from gardens, farms, and forests—which are nutrient-poor.

But here, too, Northwesterners have demonstrated that factor ten is approachable. The town of Arcata, California, uses a newly created wildlife sanctuary to treat its sewage. Starting in 1983, Arcata took seventy waterfront acres, formerly a county landfill and an abandoned sawmill, and turned them back into a wetland by digging ponds, installing floodgates, and planting bulrushes and cattails.

Intense public education and careful monitoring keep toxic chemicals out of the wastewater marsh. Gravity settles the solids from the city's wastewater; Arcata then dries these solids thoroughly and spreads them in nearby forests to improve the soil. Meanwhile, Arcata's sewage engineers release the liquids from the wastewater into a series of marsh pools. In the pools, solar energy, water plants, and carefully managed bacteria and algae populations cleanse the water, digesting most of the nutrients it carries.

For Arcata, low-throughput sewage treatment yields wastewater bills just a third as high as those in neighboring jurisdictions. And it yields a wildlife marsh bigger than the citizens could have otherwise afforded to restore. Two hundred bird species have returned to spend time in the marsh, including bald eagles and trumpeter swans.

In addition, the wetland attracts a hundred thousand human visitors a year. They come for the birds. Many never know that the rushes they are crouching in, and the birds they are watching, are partly made of the Idaho potatoes and Washington apples Arcatans ate last season. And few contemplate the cattails as the final step in a durable system of human nourishment—one that feeds people well with a fraction of the throughput of conventional methods.

## December

It is 8:00. Kathryn wanders under the counter and stands quietly facing the wall. "What are you doing, Kathryn?"

"My pooping, Dada." Kathryn's relationship with her bodily wastes is unsullied by taboo.

I change her diaper and flush yesterday's dinner down the toilet. She stands waving at the toilet bowl, "Bye-bye, my poop. Bye-bye."

In a minute, I return to the bathroom. My body has filtered what it wanted out of my coffee. It is ready to release the remainder.

"COBBLER" IS AN OLD-FASHIONED WORD, connoting a time when kindly old men in leather aprons stooped over their benches to keep their neighbors shod. Perhaps that is why a historian-turned-boot-mender would paint it on his workshop:

"Dave Page, Cobbler." Dave, square-faced and built like a wrestler, explains in soft, crisp sentences, "It is from Old English. It means someone who puts things together so they work." He glances forward briefly to signal that he is done speaking. Then he returns to scanning the shoes piled on tall shelves above his head.

The Northwest's premier footwear recycler is modest about himself but proud of his workers. Seven of them join him each day in a sunlit Seattle storefront to resole mountaineering boots, restitch street shoes, and refinish sandals.

"That's Giuseppe there," Dave says, studying the deft movements of the eldest, a silver-haired Italian who looks a little like Pinocchio's father. Shaking his head in admiration, Dave whispers, "He's a genius. There's nothing he can't do. He's been doing this for forty-seven years. He started as a boy in an Italian boot factory."

Quality, experience, and smart positioning explain Dave's consistent success during a quarter century in which most shoe repair shops—and repair industries generally—have done lackluster business. In 1993, just 117 people earned their livelihoods repairing and shining shoes in the state of Washington, down from 207 forty years earlier. But since 1990, Dave Page, Cobbler, has been growing by more than 25 percent a year, even while the shoe repair industry overall has been stagnant.

There was a time when cobblers, tailors, tinkers, and other fixers of things made up a good share of the Northwest work force—and mending things took up a piece of most people's weeks. But cheap raw materials, mass production, and, later, off-shore manufacturing shifted the balance. "New shoes from Brazil and the Orient are so cheap!" Dave says, examining a new heel on a dress boot. "Go to these discount shoe stores and you can get two pairs of decent-looking shoes for eighty dollars. It would cost more to resole them than to replace them." So the worn shoes, with all the energy, materials, and workmanship that went into them, become dump filler.

The cost of repair commonly exceeds the cost of replacement not only for shoes but for all kinds of manufactured goods: blue jeans, radios, toys, answering machines, dishes, computer screens, auto parts, telephones, books, and even the hand tools used to repair things. The repair industries generally have been in relative decline. In Oregon, for example, the number of jobs repairing things has not kept pace with overall employment; between 1970 and 1992, total employment grew one-third faster than employment in nonautomotive repair services.

Compounding the trend away from repair has been the relentless, marketing-driven expansion of fashion. Two centuries ago, only the rich worried about being in style, and then only for their dress clothing. Today, all classes are afflicted, and for everything from wristwatches to automobiles. Fashion is an insidious form of planned obsolescence: things become useless long before they wear out.

In the twenty-six years he has been in business, Dave has watched fashion overrun first the athletic shoe trade, then the ski boot trade, and finally the trail boot trade. As fashion advanced, repair—and durability—retreated. And shoe designers stopped paying attention to whether a shoe could be fixed. It no longer mattered.

Even in mountaineering boots, a realm so far untouched by fashion, Dave has noticed a decline in durability. "We've resoled some boots from the fifties and sixties five and six times." New boots are lighter and give better performance, but "they don't last as long."

The cost advantages of mass production will not go away, but in a factor-ten economy, designers of mass-produced goods would put as much emphasis on durability and repairability as on style. And cobblers and other repair industries would flourish.

Dave Page, fifty-six years old, was born in northern Wisconsin and came to the Northwest to run the mile for the University of Washington. By the time he had finished his Ph.D. in history, however, he was more interested in vertical miles: he was an avid mountaineer, captivated by the rock and ice of the Cascades. "At the time, only one guy in the country was resoling mountain boots. He was in Colorado. I got tired of waiting the six months it took him to send the boots back."

Dave taught himself cobbling, mostly by ripping apart old boots, and was immediately overwhelmed by climbers wanting repair work done "before next weekend." So he quit his job lecturing to undergraduates on American history and spent five years in his basement perfecting his craft. Word of mouth spread his name to climbers all over the continent. Convoys of UPS trucks began rolling up to his house.

Only years later, after he had hired others and moved to successively larger shops did he expand from boots to other kinds of footwear. "At first we only did it as a favor to the neighborhood. Now we get shoes from all over the city." There are few other places left to go. Most shoe repair shops, one- and two-worker outfits already buffeted by dwindling business, have been unable to keep up with shoemaking technology. Asian manufacturers, for example, use thermoplastic shoe bottoms—consisting of the sole and what it sticks to—that require expensive equipment and advanced adhesives to replace.

Dave grows somber, thrusting out his jaw slightly and lowering his head of slate-gray hair. Scores of good cobblers have given up, he says, selling out to "guys with two weeks of training who have always wanted to own a business. The skill level is way off."

Repair is to recycling as recycling is to dumping: another step towards factor ten. Waste recycling in the Northwest is surging, but repair shops are just beginning to revive, as are other institutionalized forms of reuse—lending libraries, remanufacturing plants, rental outfits, and thrift stores. The integration of reuse into product manufacturing, moreover, has yet to commence in earnest. Even Northwesterners rarely design things to endure, to foster repair, or to accept upgrades as technology improves.

A handful of remanufacturing plants such as GreenDisk buy used manufactured goods in bulk and refurbish them for resale. From its headquarters on the outskirts of greater Seattle, GreenDisk collects computer disks by the truckload and restores them to new condition. Other Northwest companies do the same for telephones, auto tires and parts, electrical equipment, office furniture, computers, machine tools, and laser-printer toner cartridges. Again, remanufacturing works best when products are designed for continuous restoration.

The secondhand trade has experienced quick growth since the late 1980s. Between 1989 and 1994, thrift stores in Idaho, Oregon, and Washington expanded their payrolls by half, to more than five thousand workers at one thousand establishments. Yet these figures may reflect the acceleration of fashion rather than a shift to reduction. In Washington, for example, thrift-store employment has grown thirtyfold since consumerism became the norm in the 1950s. There is just so much new stuff around now that more of it goes off to Goodwill.

In contrast to the rise of secondhand shops generally, used-bookstores have been dropping like flies. The advent of discount, volume bookstores did in ten secondhand booksellers in Vancouver in 1994 and early 1995 alone.

Unmeasured in business statistics is the shadow economy of yard sales, rummage sales, church sales, and swap meets. Possibly larger as a distributor of manufactured goods is the bustle of sharing, loaning, and borrowing between friends and neighbors. Again, no surveys or statistics track this sector of the economy, although most observers of community life believe that these non-market channels of trade have atrophied. Frontier towns and early-century neighborhoods were thoroughly bound in the mutual reciprocity of borrowing and lending. With affluence has come independence: a Northwest homeowner who finds herself in need of a C-clamp one Saturday is as likely to drive fifteen miles to Home Depot as to ring doorbells around her cul-de-sac until she finds one.

Still, Northwesterners do share, sometimes with remarkable creativity. At the Evergreen State College in Olympia, Washington, for example, the student union building is home to a free box where unwanted clothes are left for others to pick over. Entering students often deposit there the new clothes with which their parents have dutifully outfitted them; then they garb themselves in the tattered jeans and T-shirts left by departing seniors. Meanwhile, graduates heading to job interviews pick out the new apparel supplied by the new students, and the symbiosis is complete.

Lending libraries perform the same function in a more formal way: they allow sharing on a countywide scale for books, periodicals, sound recordings, and videotapes. Typical Northwesterners checked out ten books and other items in 1992, up from six in 1970. Of course, many people are not in the habit of using libraries at all; most of the 114 million items loaned in 1992 went to a core of dedicated patrons.

In one Northwest library or another, you can check out board games, cameras, CD-ROMs, computer software, electric engravers, framed paintings, hand tools, movie projectors, puppets, sheet music, tape recorders, and video games. You can also surf the Internet or practice the piano. In Portland, Oregon, Joe Keating of the United Community Action Network created a bicycle library of the streets. He repaired and repainted one hundred junked two-wheelers and fitted them with these instructions: "Free community bike. Please return to a major street for others to reuse. Use at your own risk." Weeks later, thirty-two blue-painted community bikes hit the streets of Victoria as well, and another score showed up in Salem, Oregon.

The for-profit version of the library is the rental center. The Northwest has long had more than a thousand firms that earn their keep by keeping their merchandise. They rent out tools, tuxedos, wedding gowns, party supplies, medical equipment, trucks, skis, beds, furniture, dining chairs, tablecloths, roller blades, place settings, appliances, sound systems, photo equipment, diapers, musical instruments, heavy machinery, costumes, forklifts, boats, bikes, televisions, computers, and portable toilets. Video rental is the comer in this crowd: it grew by half between 1989 and 1993 in Washington, and it employed almost as many Oregonians in 1992 as did the mining industry.

In the end, however, every variety of reuse is limited by the rapid obsolescence designed into so-called durable goods. Consider household appliances. The Washington Department of Community, Trade, and Economic Development brags that recyclers collected, shredded, sorted, and melted down 126,000 tons of household appliances in 1992. What a waste! Most new dishwashers bought in the Northwest are designed to last just ten years. Refrigerators, washers, and dryers last thirteen or fourteen years, and ranges last seventeen. These appliances are cheaper, lighter, more energy efficient, and do their job better than the models they replace, but they do not last any longer; and, because they are assembled, without bolts, from molded plastic parts, they are more difficult to repair or disassemble for scrap. In a factor-ten economy, appliances would be designed to last longer and to be modular enough that repair, remanufacture, and upgrading would be the rule, not the exception.

Stagnation or shortening of useful lives is evident in many product lines. Adhesive-bound paperbacks from the discount bookstore have replaced sewn hardbacks. New toilet seats made with plastic bolts last for years whereas their metal-bolted predecessors lasted for decades. Carpets woven to last a lifetime have given way to glued ones that last eleven years. And this is to say nothing of the hundreds of products, from diapers to cameras to paintbrushes, that are now manufactured to be used only once.

Factor ten comes easiest at the design stage, before an ounce of steel has been forged or an ounce of resin extruded. It comes when engineers begin by looking ahead a century, instead of the ninety days of the warranty, and work backward from there.

Factor ten—the sometimes-Luddite sentiments of environmental advocates notwithstanding—is not antitechnology. It requires a steep technical curve, one that leaves room for simple, time-tested devices such as ceiling fans, clotheslines, and bicycles, but one that also aggressively incorporates new methods and new knowledge.

For reasons less lofty, staying ahead of the technical curve is cobbler Dave Page's first principle. His hands cradling an Italian hiking boot that looks as if it could have walked all the way from the Alps, he explains, "For two thousand years, footwear was a slab of material stitched to an upper. The sandals of Jesus were made that way. Now we use dozens of types of composite, molded soles and fix them to an upper lots of ways." To thrive in the repair industry, you have to study everything the manufacturers are doing, because the manufacturers are not spending any time studying what you are doing.

To keep his shop ahead of the curve, Dave has switched over from toluene adhesives to hard-to-get European neoprene ones because they are less toxic and, with skillful use, work better.

"This summer, I'm going to take the next step," he says, then pauses to watch Giuseppe buff the finish on a pair of clogs with a rotating brush. Looking away again, he explains his plans to switch to new water-based adhesives from Germany. For Dave's customers, it will mean quicker service, because regular adhesives must dry overnight, whereas water-based ones dry instantly. "You spread it on, flash it under a halogen light—that zaps the water—and you stick the boot back together." On Dave's books, the change will appear as lower electric bills, because regular adhesives must be kept warm under infrared lights, and lower rent, because instant drying will save yards of shelf space.

But the real reason for doing it, Dave says, is simpler. Some of his employees are starting families, and water-based adhesives mean "zero fumes." He jests about protecting the gene pool, but his eyes say he is not joking. In his way, he is thinking about a century. Dave has already revealed his partiality to children. Earlier, when a pigtailed girl stopped outside the shop with her mother, the sole-mending professor looked through the glass and murmured, "Do you know what Dostoyevsky said? 'Children humanize our souls by their mere presence in our midst.'"

## December

It is 11:00. I am helping Gary go through his toy box and closet while Peter practices crawling. Gary is passing judgment on Matchbox cars: "Keep this one . . . trash this one—broken wheels

. . . hmm. This one? Consignment store . . . Would Kathryn like this one, Dad?"

We are still settling into our dream house—the one we moved to from the bungalow we first rented. It's an up-to-date, compact, three-story townhouse in an affordable neighborhood. We put all of our savings into it. But hauling the babies and the laundry up and down the stairs has turned out to be hard on Amy's spine. To minimize hauling, we've decided to move everyone onto one floor—the ground floor—and turn the master bedroom on the top floor into a playroom.

To do so, we've got to downsize.

AN OLD WORLD STEAMER TRUNK sits in the corner of Steve and Kris Loken's living room. It is handmade from aged scraps of salvaged pine. The scraps are held together by wooden pegs. The corners are edged in steel, and the whole thing is lovingly painted. In it, Steve's grandparents brought their belongings from Norway to the town of Heartland, Minnesota. Now the trunk looks out over Missoula, Montana, where Steve has lived since his microbus broke down there in 1969. The trunk sits in the living room for three reasons. The first is obvious; the second and third take some explaining.

The first reason is that the trunk, most of a century old, is a testament to the Loken family's tradition of crafting things to last and then taking care of them. The house in which it sits is a testament to the vitality of that tradition in Steve, who is a builder. The house is a stunning leap toward factor ten: it was made with few virgin resources, it was made for durability, and it was made to consume few resources during its operating life. Steve had low-throughput firmly in mind from start to finish.

Steve had another thing in mind, too. He wanted to "hit the soft, paunchy underbelly" of the Northwest's house-buying public. In the Northwest, builders broke ground on 126,440 units of new housing in 1993. Most of these were not resource-thrifty apartments or rowhouses in town. They were oversized, split-level ranch houses with two-car garages on the rural fringe. They were black holes of throughput: small but with unbelievable gravitational pull, able to suck resources from great distances. They were, in Steve's words, "the underbelly."

Buildings are secret leaders in the throughput leagues. Construction accounts for 40 percent of the raw materials consumed by the U.S. economy, according to David Morris of the Institute for Local Self-Reliance in Minneapolis. Northwest buildings use a third of all the Northwest's energy, mostly for light and heat, and manufacturing building components takes up almost another tenth. Construction accounts for nearly half of U.S. copper consumption, two-fifths of wood consumption, and an even larger share of old-growth lumber consumption because old-growth is big enough and strong enough to yield structural beams.

An average new house contains ten thousand board feet of framing lumber; thirteen thousand square feet of gypsum wallboard, plywood sheathing, and exterior siding; fifty cubic yards of concrete; four hundred linear feet of copper and plastic pipe; fifty gallons of paint; and three hundred pounds of nails, according to the National Association of Home Builders.

All together, a typical U.S. house weighs in at 150 metric tons. Demolishing it generates as much waste as its inhabitants would have set out in the rubbish bin during most of its eighty-year life span. When a new house is built to replace it, another seven tons of waste are carted to the dump. In 1993, almost one-fourth of Portland, Oregon's solid-waste stream was from construction and demolition.

Conscious of such effects, Steve set out to erect something that smelled and tasted like the underbelly but lacked the gravity. He wanted to show that reduction could look like the ads in *Town and Country*. So he built an oversized split-level ranch house with a double garage on the rural fringe. But he made it with one-fifth as much virgin wood, a similarly shrunken percentage of most other virgin materials, and a lot less stuff overall: the building weighs in as a lightweight compared to most houses of its size.

The house—which, for all its innovations, cost just 15 percent extra—also outperforms conventional houses in other ways. Despite its draftproof construction, air quality indoors is superb. Despite its light weight, it will likely last three times longer than an ordinary house. It holds heat and coolness six times better than Montana's typical new house, and it is three times as frugal with water. During construction in 1990, Steve and his crew minimized and recycled waste down to a few Dumpster loads.

The Faustian bargain for Steve Loken, who came to building after studying wildlife biology and living briefly on a commune, was that the only way he could jab at the underbelly was to become part of it himself. To get a loan to build the house, he had to promise to live in it, precisely what he did not want to do, preferring a community-oriented urban setting where his two kids would be able to grow up unchauffeured. The banks, however, would finance the project only if it was going to be "owner occupied."

Beyond requiring that Steve buy the house himself, the bank also stipulated that it be big—to guarantee that appraised value, an appraiser's estimate of its resale price, would cover the loan. Never mind what Steve was trying to demonstrate or what Steve and Kris wanted as a place to raise their two children, both adopted from Korea: the appraisers said big houses hold value better than small ones.

Looking out across the pines and grasses of the northern Rockies, Steve shakes his head. "The best living room in the world is just outside your threshold, so why try to replicate that? Just go outside." The median house in Montana is 1,300 square feet, smaller by a quarter than the national average. Steve's house, thanks to the bank, is a whopping 3,000 square feet.

Now, he and Kris are stuck in it. "It's too big. It's not us. Since we moved in here, real estate prices have gone so high I can't afford to stay here or buy anything else either. I'm trapped. It's really bizarre," he says, speaking with quiet rage.

This rage is the second reason for the trunk's prominent placement: it's there ready to pack. It's a statement of intent.

Steve's house flies in the face of North American housing norms. "Laura Ingalls Wilder talks about her father building the front door: hewing the front door from a big tree. The implication is that more is better. Stout is always better. Hail, locusts, winds, snow—this door was going to protect her and her family. Stout— it's imbued in everything we thought we were doing in America."

Steve's own house, built in 1990, has the stout look. Backed into a mountainside and fitted with a slate roof that spreads deep eaves over the broad expanses of south-facing picture windows, it looks as if the sheer mass of it could shelter its inhabitants from a perilous world. And it is strong, probably stronger than its neighbors. But it was built not to be stout.

"Instead of heavy, dense, and stout, what we tried to do was find things that were light, strong, and efficient." Steve's slender form, under six feet in height, now moves quickly through his residence. Rebounding from resentment, he points out features and rattles off their origins, technical properties, and merits like a sportscaster calling a game. "Many of the materials that we chose had principles of engineered air. The wall panels are Styrofoam, so they're 95 percent air. The structural honeycomb floor system is 95 percent air: very strong, durable, wind resistant, has no lateral or horizontal deflection, and it's air."

The only way to make strong building components that are mostly air is in a factory. "Virgin materials are something of the past," Steve says. They were beautiful, but they're gone. In Montana, the diameter of logs harvested has fallen by half, to seven inches, since he arrived by microbus. Much of his house is built of combinations of wood fibers, waste products, and space-age binders, all manipulated, shaped, and industrially cooked. As Steve puts it, "We are down to turkey loaf now."

The mock-slate roof shingles, for example, were made of wastepaper and recycled cement. Fortuitously, the paper content made the shingles light, which allowed Steve to use fewer and leaner roof beams. Meanwhile, the load-bearing part of the Styrofoam wall panels is oriented strand board, a reconstituted version of plywood made by breaking small trees down to wood chips, lining them up, and gluing them back together.

So far, twelve thousand people have driven up the winding Lincoln Hills road to attend open houses and listen to Steve talk. They get an earful. They park on the narrow driveway. ("We kept the road width to a minimum. The city wanted a twenty-three-foot-wide road to the house. They wanted me to turn around a fire truck up here. Well, I said, what's the rush? After the fire is out, you can have a doughnut, then back the truck out. Now the people in land planning in Missoula are talking about keeping road width very narrow.")

The visitors step inside from the rubber pavers in front of the garage ("old car tires recycled, allows water infiltration"). They walk across the threshold ("the door is headed with a composite wood product called Microlam") and step onto tiles in the entryway ("recycled windshields from old cars").

The visitors marvel at the temperature: cool in summer, warm in winter. ("We're bermed into the hill, so we share the warmth and cool of the Earth. The house is superinsulated: R26 in the walls, R60 in the ceiling, floor at R10, basement walls at R24, windows R8. We could leave for a year and it would always be between 62 and 64 degrees in here. We heat with a natural-gas, sealed-combustion, direct-vent boiler that was always used to heat domestic hot water. Now we've got it tied into heat: radiant tubes that are in the floor. The air temperature actually still stays around sixty-four degrees, but the surface of the floor is warmer. Having evolved from reptiles as we did, what could possibly be nicer than lying on a warm rock on a cool desert day with the sun shining? It feels great. Surfaces need to be warm; the air doesn't.")

The visitors proceed across the hardwood floors. ("Reused maple. Came out of an old Christian Science church. It had only been varnished once in sixty years, so it came out real clean. You can see the holes where the pews were screwed down. Underneath, we used engineered I-beams instead of sawn dimensional lumber because it's a much more efficient use of wood. You use 60 percent less wood fiber, and only about 2.5 percent adhesive. By peeling the veneer you get 95 percent utilization of a tree. Sawing square boards from a round tree you get about 45 percent. The structural subfloor is made of low-grade veneers from salvage trees and wood waste, instead of plywood, which uses lots of veneers from higher-value trees.")

The visitors study the kitchen ("the floor is natural linoleum, made from wood and cork flour, talc, and pine resin, extremely durable. The counter is old-fashioned Formica—largely paper, supercompressed and sealed"). They meander across the living room carpet ("recycled wool with a touch of acrylic to extend life.

The carpet pads are made of recycled rubber from tires"). They gaze out the windows at the panorama of the Rattlesnake Valley ("triple-chamber, krypton gas-filled, double-pane units with heat-trapping films and pull-truded fiberglass sashes") and knock on the walls ("the exterior walls are made of polystyrene board that does not use CFCs. It uses pentane as the foaming agent. Yes, it's oil, but I would rather take a quart of oil and turn it into forty quarts of Styrofoam that can be ground up, recycled, turned into a resin, and reused again than take the oil and burn it. Then what do you have? Combustion by-products, and the resource is gone forever. There are no studs in the wall because it's all Styrofoam, so we reduced our wood consumption quite a bit. The interior wallboard is made of 35 percent recycled newspaper and gypsum. It weighs twice as much as regular drywall, so we have twice the thermal mass to moderate temperature in the house at no extra cost. The paint for the interior is from the City of Seattle's waste collection program. They collect leftover paint, remanufacture it, call it Seattle Beige. There's only one color").

The visitors look hard for any sign of a trashy, shoddy, "recycled" look. And they don't find it. Everything looks so normal, so much like the dream-house tours that are offered every summer. They gaze in wonder at the home-beautiful features: the soaring ceiling ("the house has a fairly open floor plan. We don't have any interior walls to cut up daylight and air movement. The ceiling is held up with one long synthetic wood beam, a beam so strong that it effectively replaced hundreds of two-by-fours"), the Scarlett O'Hara staircase ("built from small-diameter trees; they're sawed into two-by-twos and glued"), the soaking tub in the master bathroom ("salvaged. I got a thousand-dollar cast-iron soaking tub for fifty bucks because the guy wanted to get rid of it. It was the wrong color"), and, above all, the gorgeous, clear-grained interior wood trim ("all salvage wood from old rafters, and bleachers, and boards I've collected over the years. I made a specific point to use it. I'm a carpenter. I love wood. . . . We need to use wood smarter, and use wood in places where people can appreciate what it really is. We don't need to use large, old-growth two-by-twelves in a floor system that no one ever sees"). Most of the Lokens' twelve thousand visitors have left enthusiastic about the possibilities, ready to try some of Steve's tricks at home.

In small part due to the house, and in somewhat larger part due to Steve, the building industry in the Northwest has changed quickly since he finished his house in 1990. Other demonstration homes have gone up in Vancouver and Portland. More than a score of stores have opened to buy and sell salvaged building components. Newsletters and conferences have proliferated. Composite materials have swept into the market, shepherded by steep increases in the price of virgin lumber. Portland has aggressively promoted construction-site recycling, quickly diverting half of the construction waste stream away from city dumps. Steve is pleased, but far from satisfied.

Maybe that is because so few visitors, builders, or others pay any attention to the third reason that the old steamer trunk is waiting in the corner—but, again, that reason takes some explaining.

Steve was not born into the Norwegian family who brought that trunk to Heartland, Minnesota. "My birth father was a Swiss Catholic, and my mother was a German-Austrian Lutheran." His steely blue eyes and sharp, ruddy nose would fit in well in the Alps. "That was not a cool thing—for Lutherans and Catholics to be cohabitating. They were in their early twenties. Met at a barn dance." Steve was put up for adoption.

From his adoptive parents, and his father in particular, Steve got his intense "materialism"—his devotion to materials, their properties, potentialities, and functions, their intrinsic stuffness. Steve also learned the values of frugality and thrift that go with this true form of materialism. To Steve's mind, the problem is not that Northwesterners are too materialistic but that they are not materialistic enough. Northwesterners care *about* things without caring for them. They seek the forms of things rather than their substances; they are, in a way, substance abusers, treating all ailments with infusions of new objects.

"When I was a kid, we went to the dump every weekend. We always left with more stuff than we came with." Steve's son Rye is climbing over him as he talks.

"Later, my dad worked for the highway department. When I-90 was going through, we went out for picnics after work, at night, and on weekends. And we would go out with crowbars, hammers, and go to places he knew were going to be bulldozed or burned in a few weeks." Rye is resting his head on his father's shoulder. It's getting late.

"We would take these buildings apart and salvage everything that we could. I had great fun unbuilding when I was kid. We salvaged everything and stored it. On our farm we built our house, garage, and outbuildings as we could afford them." Steve stands up and rocks Rye slowly on his shoulder.

"We started out living in a basement house for six or seven years, a basement with tar paper and mineral-roll roofing. We lived there and continued to build until we finished the house. It was kind of a grow-home. We all got a chance to build and work on it. That's how I learned construction and carpentry. We built our house, three-quarters of it, with salvaged material. Back then it was really excellent wood. And we built that house to last.

"But look," he says, "here's the question: permanency. We have built permanent and stout even though we have a real impermanent, transient population."

Steve's daughter Kyra comes out of her room to get a good-night kiss. She hugs his leg and lingers to listen. "In terms of its resource consumption, the renovation industry is rapidly approaching what we use in new construction." Building renovations are projected to surpass new construction as a source of income for builders by the year 2010 in the United States as a whole, and somewhat later in the young, fast-growing Northwest. Much remodeling is motivated by concerns about fashion rather than performance: Formica countertops from the seventies that have another thirty years of useful life in them are ripped out and landfilled to make way for mock granite that will, by all odds, become trash too, when the next owners come along.

"Maybe modular, lightweight, and movable is the way to go," suggests Steve. "My grandparents' trunk carried everything they needed. That's my ideal."

And that's the third reason for the trunk's place of honor in the living room. It was enough for them, and it was built to fit their migratory predilections.

In at least one small, secretive way, Steve tried to build portability into his house as well. In so doing, he committed an act almost unimaginably subversive in the building trades. He fastened much of his house together with screws rather than nails. "Oh, the house could last 200 or 250 years. But I want my kids to be able to take it apart and move it. They're not going to be able to live up here. This is crazy."

Even after a building is constructed, there are ways to reduce its appetite for resources, especially energy.

Persian-born architect Faezeh Weaver knows where many of the savings are hidden. She is conservation manager for the Northwest's biggest business: the Boeing Company. Boeing makes more than half of the world's commercial jet airplanes. It makes most of them in factories around Puget Sound; the factories are big. The company touts its factory in Everett, Washington, for example, as the largest enclosed structure on the planet. Local mythology holds that the plant generates its own internal weather: clouds form, rain falls, fronts advance.

At the moment, Fay Weaver is on the catwalk of a more understated facility in Renton, Washington—a million-square-foot hangar where, on a sleepy summer day like today, a mere sixteen 737 and 757 passenger jets are in the assembly bays. Fay's head of auburn hair is tilted backward to study the ceiling, hundreds of feet above. Site energy manager Mark Petreye, his thick mustache pointing straight up, is describing the light bulbs that make a grid overhead.

"Those are single-head high-intensity-discharge metal halide lamps. They take a thousand watts apiece—eleven hundred including the ballasts. We took out double-head units to put these in. It cut the power at each fixture in half but gave us better light. There are about a thousand fixtures under this roof."

Lighting takes up roughly 40 percent of Boeing's electrical energy overall, and, despite the region's low power prices, electricity remains Boeing's largest utility bill. So Fay Weaver, trained in architecture at the University of Oregon, spends much of her time worrying about light bulbs. She and her colleagues have surveyed ninety million square feet of floor space, virtually all that the company has, and found millions of wasteful old lamps in wasteful old fixtures arranged in ill-functioning old ways.

In close to a third of that floor space—including this Renton plant and the colossus of Everett—she and her team have changed the lights. They have installed improved fluorescent tubes, advanced metal halide lamps, sensors that turn off the lights when a space is vacant, computerized lighting-control systems, and lighting fine-tuned for each task.

It has been a mammoth undertaking. Since 1991, she and her team have done energy-saving lighting retrofits in an indoor area larger than all the commercial buildings in downtown Seattle. Along the way, they have boosted the efficiency of electric motors and heating, ventilation, and air conditioning systems. And on the side, they have been trimming natural gas and water consumption. Mark's site, Renton, for example, has cut water use by 40 percent.

But lights remain the main event, because that's where there has been the most waste to mine. Mark says, "In this structure, better lighting is saving $375,000 a year in power bills. That's money we can reinvest." Company-wide, the savings are in the millions of dollars.

This may be why the company resolved in 1993 to reduce its electricity consumption by 5 percent each year indefinitely. In 1994, power consumption fell 6.5 percent, saving enough juice to light sixty thousand typical (inefficient) houses. Part of the 1994 decrease was caused by falling airplane production, not conservation. Still, Mark and Fay think the 5 percent goal is achievable.

"Look over there." Mark points to the other end of the building, where a door that covers much of the wall is yawning open. Sunshine is pouring in. "Those doors are open a lot. Daylight is free, but the lights down there are on. We have no way to adjust the lights to compensate yet." Mark, who wrote his masters thesis years ago on solar energy, suggests that sunshine could eventually replace a good share of Boeing's electric lighting.

And for the lights that will remain, Fay is optimistic about a new lighting technology unveiled by the U.S. Department of Energy in late 1994: a globe of sulfur the size of a Ping-Pong ball, excited with a microwave generator like that in a countertop microwave oven, that emits as much light as hundreds, even thousands, of regular bulbs. Light from the globe can be directed down a semi-reflective plastic tube to make a "light pipe" hundreds of feet in length. A handful of these globes and pipes might replace the entire constellation of metal halide lamps above her head, reducing power consumption by, she says excitedly, "an order of magnitude."

If she knew the term, she might say it: "Factor ten."


## December

It is 11:10. Gary is still sorting the cars I line up and drive his way: "Busted . . . busted . . . dumb . . . consignment . . . Hey! Another miniature race car! I didn't even know I had this!" When the cars are all done, we unearth four baskets of doodads and art supplies from his closet, and carry on with the culling.

The pioneers who followed the Oregon Trail in the 1840s traveled in covered wagons that were twelve feet long and four feet wide. They packed only their most prized possessions, but the road was steep and fodder short. They jettisoned heirlooms and fed seed grain to their stock. At trail's end, they were down to the essentials.

For us, the three moves—from the D.C. apartment to the bungalow, from the bungalow to the townhouse, and from the top floor to the bottom—are accomplishing something similar. Leaving D.C., we held a yard sale, took carloads to the Salvation Army, and finally just set things out by the Dumpster. Even so, we barely dented the pile. Years' worth of artifacts were entombed in that apartment. We filled a modern prairie schooner with them: a Ryder Family Van that was fifteen feet long, ten feet wide, and twelve feet tall. We packed its 750 cubic feet of stowage solid as a woodpile, hitched our car behind, and strapped our bikes to the roof.

On our arrival in Seattle, we owned fewer things than we had five years before, but the forces of accumulation began again immediately. West Coast family deluged us with homecoming gifts, heirlooms, and hand-me-downs. We found ourselves responsible for dining chairs, end tables, stools, bureaus, and silverware. We piled them in the basement of the bungalow, then purged again before moving to the townhouse. I called a thrift store to send a truck. It hauled off bushels of stuff we did not want, enabling us to squeeze into another Family Van for the one-mile trip to the townhouse.

In the townhouse, we were resolute: we had enough stuff, any more would be clutter. But clutter kept coming; the world, it seemed, wanted us to have more. On top of the other marketers who had always come after us, a new horde picked up our scent when our name went on the title deed. Catalogs we had never heard of started arriving. Our mailbox was stuffed with ads for bedding, drapes, carpets, lawn care services, garden supplies, and video stores. Our telephone started ringing about burglar alarms, remodeling, and life insurance ("I don't mean to dwell, sir, but have you considered the *unthinkable?*"). At our door, we found hawkers of television cables. On our doorknob were flyers from Chinese restaurants and pizza joints.

We resisted as best we could, but new needs arose and we let things past the barricades—a new bed for Gary, clothes and supplies for newborn Peter, a rocking chair, a push mower, new storage shelves, a socket wrench, two high chairs, a throw rug. Reasonable things, but they added up.

The rule we are now operating by is that if we haven't actually used something since moving to this house, it has got to go. It is a useful rule, allowing us to rid ourselves of wedding presents, baby shower gifts, heirloom china, goblets and vases, and other things that social convention says we cannot possibly give away. It means we will sell or donate most of our personal library—if we ever want to read those books again, we can go to the public library. We are convinced that less stuff will mean more time, and that fewer toys will mean more fun.

NORTHWESTERNERS CONSUMED almost seven hundred pounds of paper and cardboard apiece in 1994, through the workings of the industrial economy. Assuming the same breakdown as in the United States overall, and in round numbers, 340 pounds of it served to wrap things (as packaging), 50 pounds of it served to absorb things (as tissues and towels), and 290 pounds served to hold ink—to convey information. This last use of paper is the fastest growing: since the early 1980s, its rate of growth has outraced gross domestic product.

The cause of this spurt, at least partly, has been people like Paul Brainerd—apostles of the information age, who automated office operations all over the world and, in the process, unleashed a paper flood.

Paul himself had a bit part in the electronic conversion of the office, but his part, and his background, made him think a lot about its consequences. He puzzled over the resulting paper stream: the reams of drafts reprinted for lack of page numbers and the piles of faxes sent because, well, it was easy. And he fretted over the results written on the landscape—forests cleared, streams polluted, fisheries tainted with dioxins, skies filled with smoke. Paper, he knew, is the most energy-intensive of wood products. Each sheet of office paper is like a twenty-watt bulb burning for an hour. And paper accounts for more than a quarter of the solid waste stream in the Northwest. "Electronics—computers—have probably generated more paper than anything else," he says solemnly, almost repentantly, from a glass-walled conference room at his Seattle office.

"We're using more and more paper as a society. But we have an opportunity to change that," he says. An unusual tycoon, Paul speaks softly and thoughtfully.

Paul Brainerd's vision of the future includes the demise of many printing presses, the end of paper telephone directories, and the downsizing of the Post Office. He wants to take most information off of ground-up trees and put it on phone lines, compact discs, and computer chips.

Two things explain Paul's preoccupation with this subject. He spent the 1980s inventing desktop publishing—the place where cyberspace touches organic matter. And he spent the 1950s growing up under the vaulted evergreen canopy of the southern Cascades—a canopy that lumber and pulp demand has since torn to shreds.

The son of photo-shop owners in the mill town of Medford, Oregon, Paul's first career was in journalism. He edited his college and graduate school newspapers and then worked for the Minneapolis daily. As the 1970s ended he went to work for Atex, a company that programmed mainframe computers for large newspapers. His second career, as an entrepreneur, started in 1984 when Atex handed him a pink slip. Along with four laid-off engineers, Paul formed a company called Aldus. He took the name from a medieval Italian who, sixty years after Gutenberg invented movable type, made printing accessible to a wider market. This original Aldus invented cheaper type, a less expensive book format, and a publishing formula that held up for three hundred years: scholars, writers, printers, and binders all laboring under the same roof. It was, literally, a publishing house.

Desktop publishing, as the new Aldus developed it, harkened back to that ideal: a single shop—even a single person—could conceive, research, write, lay out, and produce a finished document. It democratized publishing, putting the power of the press in the hands of anyone who could afford a good desktop computer.

The commercial publishing industry, Atex included, just ignored Aldus. When Paul came knocking, magazines, newspapers, and book imprints snickered at the proposition of desktop publishing. But he soon found himself overwhelmed by interest from churches, community groups, businesses, and others "who had been struggling for years to get their materials produced—that wanted to look professional, of course, but just didn't have the resources." Faint tones of Medford occasionally sound in the back of Paul's voice: of course sounds like "a-course."

Within a decade, Aldus had grown to a thousand employees and $200 million gross revenue. Its products went everywhere. For example, when the Soviet military staged a coup against Mikhail Gorbachev, Russian leader Boris Yeltsin stood before the tanks and held up a sheet of paper calling for a general strike. The proclamation was laid out on Aldus's PageMaker software.

Later, even the commercial publishers converted to desktop software. It had become "more powerful than their systems at a fraction of the price." And Atex rued the day it had let Paul go.

In 1994, at the age of forty-seven, Paul Brainerd quit the software business to start his third career: "giving back." He endowed a foundation with a large share of his earnings and began advocating for the environment full time—acting on the passion that sprang from "my childhood in the Oregon woods."

And, though he was out of the information industry, he kept thinking about how information might be separated from its contrail of paper.

Paper, Paul says, ought to be reserved for important things such as love poems, sacred texts, and great art. Most of the information in our lives would travel better over fiber-optic cables or the airwaves than on airplanes or diesel trucks. Properly used, information technology could allow us to stop hauling mass around the surface of the planet just to share words and images with one another.

It is a radical proposal, leapfrogging the tendentious conversion to paper recycling that has occupied most Northwest mills and municipalities. That conversion has yielded fruit: In just a few years, twenty-six of Washington and Oregon's twenty-eight pulp and paper mills have retooled for recycling, according to the Northwest Pulp and Paper Association. They have spent more than a billion dollars in the process and, on top of that, have spent millions to begin switching from dioxin-forming chlorine bleaching of pulp to a variety of processes less harmful to fish. They are buying less virgin fiber; consumption of virgin fiber in Washington and Oregon pulp and paper mills actually *fell* in the first half of the 1990s. By 1995, one-third of the paper and paperboard milled in these states was made of wastepaper.

Still—and not to belittle these gains—paper recycling is a factor-two proposition. In rough terms, it saves half the energy, three-fourths of the air pollution, one-third of the water pollution and—because wood fibers break down and cannot be recycled indefinitely—about half of the trees.

The information revolution is the region's shot at factor ten. Manufacturing and powering computers, monitors, network servers, and data cables involve sending minuscule amounts of resources through the economy's digestive tract compared to communicating via paper and ink. And those amounts could become even more minuscule if the hardware were consciously designed for durability and modular upgrading.

"The amount of information distributed in electronic form will soon exceed that in traditional, paper forms," Paul says. But few see the change because they misconceive publishing. First, they think of its means—ink on paper—rather than its end. "The real element is not the information itself but the refinement of it. The information itself? There's too much of it around," Paul argues. "The human being was never equipped to deal with the amount of stuff that we deal with today—the number of messages that we get lambasted with." As many books come out each hour now as were produced in a year in the 1700s.

As the amount of information available through various media continues its explosive growth, the importance of what Paul calls "voice" only increases. The essence of publishing is the selection, not the multiplication, of information.

People also misconstrue publishing by thinking of it as something done mostly by publishers. They think of it, Paul suggests, as consisting mostly of newspapers, magazines, and popular books that are sold in the marketplace. But publishing takes place throughout the economy, by elementary schools, government agencies, industrial facilities, corporate offices, direct-mail advertisers, and scores of others. And these establishments consume forests full of paper.

"Boeing is the largest commercial publisher west of the Mississippi," Paul points out. "But in their budgets, it's spread out all over the place in little line items."

Paper could play a diminishing role in the information stream in these huge but little tracked realms of publishing. This is already starting. "One of the standing jokes is that the documentation for the 747 weighed more than the airplane." To provide mechanics on all continents with regularly updated information on every part in the airplane required manuals by the boxcar. With the 777— launched in 1995—all that information is distributed on compact discs. Internally, Boeing has also shrunk its paper use by communicating via computer.

In banking, investing, and other financial services, paper-based transactions are decreasing. In law offices, databases are replacing law books. Commercial newsletters increasingly travel by telephone line to a fax machine or modem, obviating the need for air freight. More and more corporations do their purchase orders electronically. Medical researchers spend more time scanning databases for journal articles than they do among the stacks at libraries. Electronic mail is gaining on "snail mail"—postal delivery. Governments are beginning to make reports, regulations, and, especially, statistics available on electronic bulletin boards. Encyclopedia companies are selling more compact discs than books; the price of the medium is a pittance, so the volumes can be updated regularly. In countries such as Japan and France, telephone directories are made of cables and chips instead of wood pulp: they are display terminals.

In Paul's view, people keep using paper mostly because "culturally, we're very attached to print." Everyone grew up with it and therefore associates permanence and value with ink on paper. This explains why workers print out a document, mark it up in ink, then type in the changes and print it again. He expects the next generation, raised on computers, to be less paper-bound.

Still, there are large practical obstacles to paperless dissemination of information. Computer screens are still hard on the eyes. Not everyone has access to computers. Many communications programs are difficult to use or incompatible with other programs. Most people are just beginning to learn to use new media such as the Internet, CD-ROMs, and the World Wide Web. Electronic displays still don't work as well as paper for some things—you can read a newspaper on the bus, cuddle up with a book in bed, and spread your tax records out across your kitchen table.

But change is happening quickly. Familiarity is increasing, and the technology is advancing at lightning speeds. For a couple thousand dollars, Paul says, "You can now buy a computer that has the computing capacity that, when I started in computing, would have cost $250,000 or $500,000. It was a big deal that used to be in a big room and now, of course, sits on your desk." Within a decade, he expects engineers to perfect portable, flat display panels that make reading from a screen almost like reading from paper. With refinements, they will be able to provide a library full of fiction, periodicals, and videotapes for the weight of a hardback novel.

To date, the information revolution has increased paper consumption. But in the areas where it is most advanced—financial services, for example—paper consumption has long since peaked and declined. Eventually, Paul hopes the same will happen throughout the economy. He hopes that classified ads and then entire newspapers will shift online; that specialty journals and then consumer magazines will stop printing on paper; that reference works and then other books will be published on disks instead of on compressed wood fiber. Paul thinks it possible that information on paper could become the exception, not the rule, and that publishing could sever its ties to the decline of forests.

## December

It is 1:30. I am lying on the living room floor with a yellow legal pad. Gary comes up from his decluttered room. Heading for the kitchen, he spots me and stops. "Dad? What are you doing?"

"Working on my book."

"Writing a book on *paper*?!" He is disoriented. Incredulous. During his lifetime, I realize, I have always written on a screen. At the moment, my computer is on a shelf in a coma. When turned on, it searches for power, fails inexplicably, and sinks back into darkness. Its manufacturer went bankrupt years ago. I have been unable to find a suitable repair shop.

IN 1988, A GARBAGE BARGE from Islip, Long Island, wandered the oceans looking for a place to unload. The incident galvanized public concern about garbage across North America, and the immediate response was a surge in recycling. The Northwest led the pack.

Seattle has the highest recycling rate of any major city in North America, recycling 42 percent of its garbage. Three-fourths of Washingtonians participate in some form of solid waste recycling, giving the state the highest recycling rate in the country: 38 percent of municipal solid waste was recycled in 1993, up from 23 percent in 1987.

The state of Oregon "recovered" 30 percent of municipal solid waste, meaning that much municipal solid waste was either recycled or burned in a power plant. Two-thirds of British Columbians participate in waste-recycling programs, meanwhile, and the province recycled 18 percent of its household waste (a narrower category than municipal waste) in 1992.

Of course, none of these figures say much about throughput. First, "municipal solid waste" refers only to stuff handled by garbage trucks, either a city's own or those it oversees. It therefore does not count sewage, air pollution, or water pollution. It does not count industrial, medical, or hazardous wastes, or a variety of other commercial wastes. And it includes none of the much more voluminous wastes generated farther up the throughput stream, at, for example, distant factories, farms, mills, mines, power plants, refineries, smelters, and quarries.

Second, recycling rates themselves are a poor measure of progress. In Washington, for example, between 1987 and 1993, the state doubled the sheer tonnage of municipal solid wastes recycled, and still the tonnage landfilled grew. Washingtonians generated 9 percent more waste per person in 1993 than they did just six years earlier. Washington recycles more than Oregon, furthermore, partly because Washington generates lots more garbage, a full pound extra per person per day. Likewise, both Washington and Oregon recycle more than British Columbia partly because they consume more and reuse less: empty beverage containers in British Columbia, for example, are more likely to be refilled than anywhere else in the region.

None of this diminishes the fact, however, that in less than a decade, households, businesses, and localities throughout the Pacific Northwest have adopted recycling as a bedrock value. They have distinguished themselves, and the region, as a global leader in the field. For example, the Clean Washington Center, a Washington State agency, spearheaded the introduction of waste materials into the Chicago commodities market, removing a barrier that had previously restrained recycling's growth. Other programs of the Clean Washington Center have become international models of how to stimulate waste-based manufacturing.

At the level of popular consciousness, recycling has become a matter of regional identity. Seattle is immensely proud that it leads the national recycling league, and many of its citizens recycle with great zeal. The city composts Christmas trees, yard wastes, and all the manure at the zoo. Citywide, it collects two kinds of plastic, glass, tin and aluminum cans, all grades of paper, car batteries and tires, leftover paint, used appliances and furniture, motor oil, and wood.

King County, which encompasses Seattle, has spent millions of dollars in a collaborative effort with local businesses to promote recycled products. The county's "Close the Loop" public interest advertising campaign is the largest of its kind ever. Seattle, meanwhile, has undertaken two especially innovative public education campaigns. It prints an annual guide for every household in the city called *Use It Again, Seattle: A Money-Saving Guide to Repairing, Reusing, and Renting Goods in Seattle*. And in 1995, it decided to attack direct-mail advertising that is unwanted by households and thus gluts the city's paper-recycling system. It began citywide distribution of lists of direct-mail marketing companies and gave out thousands of free postcards reading, "Please Remove My Name from Your Mailing List."

In these last actions, the city is attempting the next step, the big one: the step from recycling to reduction. There are tentative signs that public awareness is evolving apace. The Recycling Council of British Columbia, long the province's leading promoter of recycling, now uses its newsletters and conferences to criticize recycling as a stopgap. On all the region's campuses, and now on the streets of its downtowns, refillable coffee mugs are appearing, fastened to book bags and briefcases. A fair number of Northwesterners are hungry for the "unstuffing" of their economy.

In May 1995, a garbage barge set sail from the coast of British Columbia, heading for Haida Gwaii, the long, windswept chain of islands also known as the Queen Charlottes, famous mostly for its totem poles and native Haida culture. Was the barge carrying trash to dump on an indigenous homeland? No. It was going to collect 360 half-buried hulks of automobiles. Decades worth of twisted metal lay rusting in the rain forests there, cluttering the landscape and endangering children at play. Finally, in 1995, somebody figured out that 360 two-ton boxes of steel, chrome, copper, and aluminum sunk into an island in the Pacific was about as close to buried treasure as this world has to offer these days. Waste is money. It is just waiting.

## December

It is 3:00. We're hiking to the beach at Discovery Park, a former military base that is now Seattle's largest parcel of undeveloped woods. The beach trail is steep and punctuated by hundreds of steps made of railroad ties. Peter is on my back in a baby carrier. Kathryn is walking between Amy and me, holding our hands. Gary is hiking out front. "Mom, quiet, there's a robin in that bush." We emerge from the woods at the margin of the sand, beside a complex of mammoth concrete structures.

"What dat, Dada? What dat?"

"Yeah, Dad, what is that thing?"

"I don't know. Can you read that sign?"

Gary reads, " 'West Point Sewage Treatment Facility.' What's that?"

"I guess that's where the poop goes," I say.

"Disgusting!" says Gary.

"Where oh poop go?" Kathryn is puzzled, not seeing any indication of poop.

"Inside those buildings, that's where the poop goes when we flush the toilet," Amy says.

"Oh, great. My poop in dere," she nods, matter-of-factly. She heads for the beach to pick up rocks. (Strictly speaking, I later learn, she is probably right. I call West Point, and an odor control specialist named James tells me that the typical flow rate would deliver wastewater from our part of Seattle to Discovery Park in less than half a day. Peter's 2:30 A.M. and Kathryn's 8:00 A.M. poops, in other words, had probably beaten us to West Point; they were inside when we arrived. Come to think of it, my coffee was in there too.)

On the beach with Peter on my back, I carry Kathryn in my arms. We walk with our eyes scanning westward across Puget Sound. We mostly ignore the hulking poop plant behind us.

Gary and Amy catch up to us on a point by a lighthouse. They've discovered that clams shoot streams of water up into the air when frightened and have been stamping on clam holes with shrieks of glee. Gary is in convulsions of laughter. "Dad, the beach is peeing!" Kathryn joins in. Soon we're all bouncing up and down, looking for clam holes, and getting wet.

*chapter five*

# PEOPLE
# AND PRICES

## January

IT IS A NEW MOON and, in evolutionary terms, I am now irrelevant. I am no longer part of the gene pool. I have been neutered, spayed, fixed, snipped. I had a vasectomy.

It should not have been that big a deal, really. Almost a year ago, Amy and I went to see our doctor, a young guy named Matt. His office is in a converted grocery store where I used to spend my allowance on gum balls. Matt feigned surprise at first. "What? You guys don't want any more kids?" He was teasing.

Amy, the children, and I were now a family of five. Don't get me wrong. I adore my children. I don't regret a thing. But ever since Peter was born, Amy and I just could not bring ourselves to, ah, conjugate our vows, so to speak. I'd look at her. She'd look at me. I'd purr at her. She'd bat her eyes at me. Then she'd whisper, "When are you going to get that vasectomy, honey?" That always seemed to dissipate the testosterone in my blood. Who is eager to contemplate a plumbing overhaul at a time like that?

**THE EQUATION THAT DESCRIBES** an economy's impact on its environment has two factors, population and consumption—how many people times how much stuff. So the quest for permanence in the Northwest, or anywhere, divides into efforts to slow population growth and efforts to turn consumption—and the production behind it—toward low-impact, factor-ten alternatives. But how do you do these things? If consumption and population are the horses pulling the wagon, where are the reins? The reins for population are family planning and—possibly—reconnection to place. The reins for consumption are prices. Take them in turn.

The population of the Northwest is growing faster than the North American population. It is increasing at about the same rate as global population. British Columbia, Oregon, and Washington consistently rank in the top ten for annual population growth among North American states and provinces. Idaho and western Montana surged in the early 1990s. Demographers project high growth rates in the Northwest for decades to come. As population grows, so does the demand for diapers, schoolbooks, houses, jobs, shopping centers, electricity, and everything else in the economy. As it grows, so does ecological damage. A lasting way of life is impossible at present rates of population growth.

The causes of population growth are usually identified as migration (arrivals minus departures) and natural increase (births minus deaths). Historically, migration has constituted essentially all of the Northwest's growth. The aboriginal inhabitants of the region were counted in hundreds of thousands, not millions, and were almost eliminated by Old World diseases in the century after 1770. Virtually all growth since then has been newcomers and their offspring.

Over the span of this century, however, natural increase has contributed almost as much population growth as new migration. And figuring out how to slow natural increase is an easier job than devising a plan to slow migration, because almost half of natural increase is accidental; unintentional pregnancies—those that are mistimed and those that are unwanted—accounted for 44 percent of births in the United States in 1990. Studies in the Northwest reveal similar figures. The share of births that result from unintended pregnancies appears to have increased since 1990, continuing a trend that began in the early 1980s. Rates of unintentional pregnancy need not be so high; they are lower in western Europe and British Columbia than in the Northwest states.

Helping Northwesterners to avoid accidental pregnancies—striving for a future of planned, intentional childbearing—is an urgent priority in its own right. The benefits of preventing unintentional pregnancies, according to the National Academy of Sciences' Institute of Medicine in Washington, D.C., are numerous. They include reductions in infant and maternal mortality, low-weight births, and fetal exposure to alcohol, tobacco, and illicit drugs; fewer abortions, births out of wedlock, and births to teenagers; less child and maternal poverty, child abuse and neglect, and school failure—both for children and parents; decreased divorce, family dissolution, and single parenting; and diminished welfare dependency and income inequality between the sexes. Preventing unintended pregnancies also reduces tax burdens; a public dollar spent preventing unintended pregnancies in the United States saves an average of $4.40 on health, welfare, and nutrition programs.

Overwhelmingly justified on these grounds, public support for family planning also slows natural increase. Between 1980 and 1994, births to teens alone—almost all of them unintended at conception—accounted for one-tenth of all population growth in the Pacific Northwest, including migration. Add unintentional births to older mothers and that figure rises to one-fifth.

Obviously, preventing unintended pregnancies reduces natural increase, but so does delaying them. Consider an imaginary Northwest with a population of fourteen million, in which people live eighty years and women have two children apiece—the first at the age of thirty. If there is no migration, this Northwest has a stable population. Now imagine a sudden change: the age of first-time mothers falls abruptly to fifteen years. Imagine that women continue to have two children apiece and that, as before, everyone still lives to the age of eighty. The younger age of new mothers results in an expanding population. In fact, teen motherhood will double the population to twenty-eight million before restabilizing, because six generations will coexist where only three once did.

Preventing teenage pregnancies slows growth in two additional ways. First, women who have their first child as a teen are likely to have more children during their lives than women who delay their first pregnancy, because teen mothers miss the opportunities for education and personal development that lead many women to have smaller families. Second, teenage motherhood tends to repeat itself through the generations. This is probably because the hardships brought on by early childbearing can entangle families for decades.

Preventing unintended pregnancies among young women, therefore, is an especially effective way to slow population growth, even while it is an especially high social and economic priority. Unfortunately, births to teens in the Northwest, after declining from 1980 to 1985, surged upward in the decade that followed.

The goal of intentional pregnancy for the Pacific Northwest has profound implications. If all pregnancies were intentional, the long-term rate of population growth from all sources—factoring in the influences just described—would be cut by a quarter.

The proximate cause of unintended pregnancy is simply the failure to use effective contraception. The ultimate causes—the reasons for this failure—are as complex as human physiology, psychology, and culture. Among them are the declining age of biological puberty—possibly caused by improved health and nutrition—the rising age of marriage, the decreased interaction between parents and their teenage children that has resulted from increased single-parent and dual-earner families, and changed—and contradictory—social norms about sex. Still, there are proven methods for expanding the effective use of contraception.

Unintended pregnancy happens to all kinds of women, but it is especially prevalent among women who are young, single, poor, or black, in approximately that order. These are the women who are most likely to conceive children without intending to. Despite the popular rhetoric, they are likely to do so not because they are more sexually active than other women. Instead, they experience more unintended pregnancies because they are less likely than other women to use effective means of contraception properly.

A review of scholarly literature by the Institute of Medicine in Washington, D.C., concluded—importantly—that both government-funded family planning clinics and Medicaid-funded contraceptive services work. Both of these politically embattled and underfunded programs moderately reduce the rate of unintended pregnancy. They do so, furthermore, without increasing sexual activity or promiscuity. Fully funding these programs and reducing ideological restrictions on them would help thousands more women avoid unintended pregnancies. The Institute of Medicine also found that Aid to Families with Dependent Children (AFDC) and other U.S. welfare programs do not encourage pregnancies.

The institute found evidence that educational programs can decrease unintended pregnancies among teenagers. School-based sexuality education works, for example, especially when it combines the conventional factual information on human reproduction and contraception with age-appropriate emotional, social, and practical material. Communication skills for young people in romantic relationships turn out to be as important as an understanding of biology and contraception. And information on the prevalence of sexual intercourse helps young people make responsible decisions; many teens are relieved to learn that "everyone" is most certainly not "doing it." Sex education does not, as some critics suggest, encourage earlier sex among young people. In fact, it has the opposite effect.

To be most effective in preventing pregnancies, school-based programs need not only to inform teens about contraception, but to provide it. For surprising numbers of young people, the seemingly mundane process of obtaining contraceptives from pharmacies, clinics, or medical offices is incredibly intimidating. Few abstain from intercourse because they are afraid to get contraceptives, however, thus risking pregnancy and infection. According to Washington's Department of Social and Health Services, 45 percent of premarital pregnancies occur within six months of a woman's first intercourse—before she has obtained contraceptives. In-school contraceptive distribution, when it is part of comprehensive sexuality education, marginally reduces sexual intercourse among teenagers, while substantially diminishing rates of pregnancy and abortion.

Initiatives that promote male responsibility hold promise, too. The fathers of children born to unmarried teenagers are usually older than the mothers. Many of them are adults. Yet scarcely one-tenth of unmarried teen mothers raise their children with the help of the fathers. Holding fathers accountable, at least financially, could lessen the burden of mothering. In addition, the relatively few educational programs that have emphasized male responsibility in sexuality and parenting have sometimes succeeded in changing male attitudes. This is encouraging because one of the strongest determinants of a woman's use of contraceptives is the attitude of her partner.

Safeguarding women's right to elective abortion of unintended pregnancies is also a priority for slowing population growth. An excruciating moral decision for any woman and her loved ones, abortion remains—from a public health perspective—an indispensable medical procedure. Without access to safe, legal abortions, women would again die from botched illegal abortions, as they did in the United States before the nationwide legalization of abortion in 1973. Before legalization, complications of ill-performed, illegal abortions killed between one thousand and ten thousand American women each year. And, of course, if women had no access to abortion, birth rates would soar, along with the incidence of all the problems associated with unwanted pregnancies. Ironically, the safest and most effective way to reduce the number of abortions is not to ban them but to help women prevent unwanted pregnancies. In western Europe, where rates of unintended pregnancy are much lower, so are abortion rates.

In the end, preventing unintended pregnancies will take more than better programs. It will take a cultural reckoning with sexuality. It will require that people think and talk more about contraception and about the responsibilities of sex.

North American culture is increasingly permissive and explicit about sex, but remains prudish about its conduct and consequences. Sex between unmarried but consenting adults, and even adolescents, is now the norm, but there is no consensus on its responsible conduct. Public discourse is schizophrenic: endlessly fascinated with sex but skittish about contraception.

This ambivalence is especially pronounced in the electronic media, which powerfully shape social norms, especially among young people: By midadolescence, average American young people have spent more time watching television than they have spent with their teachers, friends, or parents. The message they get about sex is "do it, but don't plan it, prepare for it, or talk about it." When teens watch television, according to the Institute of Medicine, they are exposed to twenty-five references to sexual acts for each reference to contraception or abstinence. The latter tend to be derogatory; the former, positive. In fact, many media organizations avoid discussion of contraception. Most television stations in the Pacific Northwest, for example, refuse to air even the most circumspect ads for contraceptives.

A sensitive initiative to lower the average desired family size—the number of intended pregnancies—might help slow population growth, too. Creative educational approaches in churches, schools, health centers, and the media could facilitate the spread of a new social norm: "two by birth." No one knows if it would work, but the stakes are too high not to try.

## January

As Amy and I sat in Matt's antiseptic little office back in the spring, he described the vasectomy procedure to us in living color. He talked about shots of anesthetic in the groin, and about locating the vas deferens, which connects each testicle to the penis.

Amy was listening attentively. I was having a hard time concentrating.

Matt talked about slitting open the scrotum and dissecting the tube and vein that encase each vas deferens.

Amy was nodding slowly.

Matt talked about severing, cauterizing, and tying each vas. I was having flashbacks to childhood: I remembered the old grocery store's jolly butcher, waving his bloody gloves at me. Maybe I turned green, because Amy reached over to pat my leg and Matt stopped talking.

"Well, anyway, here's a pamphlet that describes everything," he said. "We do it here in the office. It doesn't take more than half an hour . . . assuming there's no shrinkage."

"Shrinkage?" I asked, my voice cracking.

It seems that guys who get queasy around needles and scalpels can make the procedure harder. Not on purpose, mind you. It's just that we can sort of, um, recede, if you take my meaning, which is a real headache for whoever's holding the knife. If I was worried about getting nervous on the table, Matt said, "I can give you a Valium."

What I wanted to say was, "Can you take me in my sleep and not wake me up until I'm healed?" But what I did say, apparently, was that I wasn't one of those whiners who needs to be doped to make it through a simple snipping. Hey, Amy had endured all that labor without so much as an aspirin. I could handle this.

Matt sent us home to think things over. "Call in for an appointment as soon as you're ready." It was difficult for me to call. For a long time I did not know why. It was more than just fear. Now I think that my resistance was the mirror image of my motivation: it was my children.

**EFFORTS TO SLOW MIGRATION ARE** a necessary comple-ment to efforts to prevent accidental pregnancies, although migra-tion is, from a global perspective, not as serious a concern as natural increase. Migration increases the Northwest's environmental burden but reduces the burden on other places. Still, an economy of perma-nence in the Northwest is all but impossible if current rates of domestic and international migration to the region continue.

Take domestic migration first. What can be done to slow it? Per-haps the solution to this problem lies in another problem, place-lessness—the widespread loss of roots in community and place evident across the continent. Maybe the shifting, migratory lifestyle of North Americans is a manifestation of hunger for connection. It is demonstrably not a simple consequence of job supply, as is commonly believed. The conventional wisdom about how domestic migration works is that businesses locate their facilities based on purely "bottom-line" considerations such as proximity to markets and costs of labor. These decisions supposedly deter-mine the geographic distribution of jobs, and people relocate to take the jobs. Profit, tracked hourly in the fluttering of stock prices, thus puts people in their places.

The truth of the matter is that migrants move to places where they believe their lives will be better. Jobs count in the equation, but so do family, friends, safety, community, and everything else that contributes to quality of life. Migrants make their decisions based on their perceptions before departure—perceptions that, research suggests, can be based on surprisingly little factual infor-mation. A migrant to the Northwest is as likely to arrive without a job and find one as she is to come explicitly to fill one. Ironically, in the process of relocating, she is likely to spend enough of the money that she earned back home to create a new job in the local economy. In other words, migration sometimes drives job creation.

Similarly, researchers have never been able to statistically explain businesses' location decisions based on purely bottom-line considerations. Businesses locate where they do for the same kinds of reasons as individuals do: they set up shop in places that they perceive to be good places to set up shop.

If perceptions of superior quality of life in the Pacific Northwest fuel migration to the region, the only surefire way of forestalling migration would be to reduce quality of life—or worsen perceptions of it. Indeed, if quality of life fuels migration, then the more successfully the Northwest reconciles community, economy, and ecology, the more attractive it will be to potential migrants. Success at home, in other words, cannot be sustained without matching success elsewhere.

How can the Pacific Northwest discourage excessive mobility without restricting freedom? Two first steps are to stop speeding migration through corporate recruitment and subsidies to real estate development. Local governments can also better inform potential migrants of the realities and responsibilities of life in the region. Together, these actions would help ensure that those who come intend to grow roots.

State-funded corporate recruitment aids migrants as much as natives. Oregon offers tax holidays to computer chip manufacturers and other high-tech firms that agree to build new industrial plants. Oregon hopes that some of the jobs will go to Oregonians, although many do not, and that the new money spent by the firms will help other Oregonians. These programs penalize local businesses not similarly favored with tax breaks while subsidizing migration into the region.

Northwest governments could also correct misrepresentation of the region. On the west side of the region, a standard joke has long been to tell visitors, "Enjoy your stay and remember to tell all the folks back home that it always rains here." (It does, of course.) Oregon governor Tom McCall used to tell out-of-state audiences, "Visit Oregon . . . on your way to Washington."

As it turns out, messages like these might actually make a difference. Many migrants choose where to live based on surprisingly little knowledge. They have heard good things, seen a movie, or read a magazine article. A systematic attempt to counteract hyperbolic publicity could go a long way.

Stephen Lyons of Moscow, Idaho, showed how to do this in an essay in *High Country News*. "*Outside* magazine recently picked six or seven towns . . . as great places to live. But those seduced into pulling up stakes by the glossy photos and idyllic promises in July's cover story should first consider a few facts. Here are three days' worth of headlines from the *Spokesman-Review*, the newspaper of record in Spokane, Wash., one of *Outside*'s dream towns: June 25: 'Meth use sparks crime wave.' June 26: 'House near Manito sprayed with bullets.' June 27: 'Police call targeted teen Crips member.'"

Lyons goes on to detail similar tragedies in the other *Outside* towns, then suggests that readers of *Outside* try sinking roots into the community they already inhabit. If they choose to move, he encourages them to "approach slowly with humility and respect. Treat older residents with the dignity they deserve. Learn some history. Don't tell anybody what to do for at least five years. Leave your jet skis at home. Turn your stereos off. Volunteer for everything."

Imagine the results if, every time a magazine or television broadcast idealized the Pacific Northwest, some Northwesterner offered a fuller picture. Imagine if the state offices currently devoted to corporate recruitment performed this function instead.

At a minimum, newcomers would arrive with an understanding of what kind of a place Northwesterners are trying to create.

Over time, other options may emerge—options that encourage rootedness everywhere. In the past, Northwest governments have always been neutral or encouraging toward mobility; they have never intentionally set out to slow it. In fact, in 1994, Portland's multicounty Metropolitan Council commissioned a study on policy options for slowing in-migration; when the team conducting the research surveyed the scholarly literature they found virtually no relevant articles.

Migration increases dramatically with years of education, although no one knows if this is coincidental or if something about advanced education actually encourages mobility. The fact itself, however, raises the question of whether colleges and universities, currently focused on specialized, disciplinary expertise, need to become more oriented toward their own places. If they taught what it means to live responsibly in their particular places, would it make a difference?

Demographers, economists, and sociologists argue over North America's uniquely high mobility. Some view frequent migration as a source of social vitality: it mixes the stew, breaks down the supposedly stultifying grip of family ties, and enhances individual liberty. Others view it negatively, citing its association with both higher crime and higher divorce rates. They see it eroding the human bonds that hold society together.

The Northwest could help end this debate by lending itself as an example—an example of how a place with a sense of itself can be at once invigorating and liberating for individuals and cohesive as a community. In the process, the Northwest could demonstrate how to be the kind of place where people want to stay.

Migration from foreign countries—immigration—is different from domestic migration. The United States and Canada rightfully pride themselves on their openness to immigrants from other parts of the world. Both countries have reasons to continue the admission of newcomers from abroad. Among these reasons are their own identities as nations of immigrants, their continuing low population density compared to much of the world, and the sad historical fact, especially true in the Northwest, that movements for exclusionary immigration policies have often reflected xenophobia and racism.

North America, as the richest place in the world, has a responsibility to help care for the world. Immigration is one way to do so. Yet neither American nor Canadian immigration policies are based purely on this motive. They are ad hoc mixes of self-interest and idealism, and they have allowed immigration that accounted for 14 percent of Northwest population growth between 1960 and 1990—an increment that grows in the second generation because foreign-born citizens tend to have more children than native-born citizens.

Simply reforming immigration laws to make them positive influences on the world would slow Northwest growth. For the United States, truly humanitarian immigration programs—admission of refugees, victims of persecution, and the spouses and minor children of citizens—accounted for half of immigration in 1994. Limiting immigration to humanitarian purposes in North America would likely reduce the Northwest rate of population growth by about 15 percent over the long run. If, at the same time, the Northwest promoted greater rootedness in North America and helped women prevent accidental pregnancies, the regional population would grow half as much as it would without these changes.

And that could make all the difference in balancing the population-consumption equation.

## January

The prelude to my vasectomy began just after dinner on a July evening two summers ago. I was in the kitchen in our D.C. apartment washing dishes, while Amy's parents, visiting from Connecticut, cleared the table. Amy and Gary were in our bedroom looking for something when he shouted, "Mom's peeing!"

"My water broke!" she called out. "My water broke!" This was good news. She was ten days past her due date, and we had already been up two nights monitoring contractions that went nowhere. Now, by hook or by crook, the baby had to come.

We lit out for the hospital, leaving Amy's father home with Gary. With us came Amy's mother, Rita, who had adopted both of her children and had never seen a child born.

About midnight, the contractions began in earnest. I immediately forgot everything I ever knew about Lamaze breathing patterns. When the midwife reminded me, I began whew-ing and ththth-ing so aggressively that I hyperventilated. Amy, meanwhile, just snapped, "Stop breathing on me."

I got one of Gary's favorite stuffed animals out of our bag; he planned to give it to the baby. I set it before Amy for her to focus her attention on, to serve as what the birth people call a "focal point." She batted it across the room and hollered "too soft" at me. By this time Amy was swearing, as her mother later said, "like a sailor." And I was too dizzy—from whew-ing and ththth-ing, out of the side of my mouth—to do much of anything helpful.

That is when Amy's mother pulled a bottle of hand cream out of her bag, planted it in front of Amy and me, and said, "Let's get some rhythm going here." For perhaps the first time in her life, Amy listened to her mother, focused on the lotion, and breathed. "One-two-three-four. One-two-three-four," said Rita. Somehow,

Amy later said, Rita's commanding presence put the pain into a box, where it still hurt but did not control her.

At the end, though, when Amy's cervix was finally open and baby Kathryn began to lunge headfirst into the world, the pain got back out of the box.

**CONSUMPTION IS THE OTHER HORSE**—besides population growth—that is pulling the Northwest economy off the track of sustainability. Carolyn Alkire knows what the reins of resource consumptions are: prices.

To talk about these reins, Carolyn has come to the top of the Yakima Basin in the Cascade Mountains. An analyst for an outfit back East that monitors capital assets for millions of Americans, she is checking on her stock portfolio—salmon stock. She is a resource economist for The Wilderness Society in Washington, D.C.—a faraway city that is home to the U.S. Forest Service, the Bureau of Land Management, and other government agencies that control more than a quarter of the acres in the Pacific Northwest. (Overall, three-fourths of the Pacific Northwest is public land. Victoria leads the acreage league; the provincial government there controls nearly half the bioregion.)

"You see, wild salmon are natural capital," says Carolyn, sitting on a rock beside Lake Keechelus and speaking with the soft tones of the South in her voice. "They're just like financial capital or physical capital. The fish that aren't harvested or killed go off and reproduce and produce new wild salmon in the same way that if you have stocks, you get dividends. In the case of wild salmon, however, we have dipped into our capital; we have harvested and killed many more fish than we should have to maintain a constant stock." Carolyn's hazel eyes, watering from the brisk wind gusting up the valley, scan the hillsides, touch the clear-cuts, traverse the rim of a dam, and tally the boats of recreational fishers. The Northwest would have more wealth, she points out, if it had protected its natural capital.

From here near the crest of the Cascades, the Yakima River surges downhill through pine forests, irrigated valleys, and deep canyons. Then it joins the Columbia. It once contributed more salmon to that fishy thoroughfare each year than any tributary but the Snake, and each year almost a million spawners returned to carry on the cycle of birth and death. The Yakima now waters apples and cows, but few oceangoing fish. The native sockeye and coho, and the summer run of chinook, are gone. The remaining chinook—the spring run—have dwindled to just 700 this year. Fewer than 250 of these reached Lake Keechelus.

To Carolyn's mind, this zeroing out of the capital account is the result of blinkered economics. "A wild chinook salmon in the Columbia Basin is natural capital worth $2,148. A wild coho is worth $488. But on the market, they go for $49 and $10, respectively." She mentions these numbers quietly, in an almost offhand manner, without taking her gaze from the lake. The only indication that she recognizes the radical nature of what she has said is a slight furrowing of her brow.

"As natural capital, you are looking at each fish as what the potential earning value is," she explains, or how much income a fish's offspring would provide over the next century if people allowed the fish to spawn rather than killing it with cattle grazing, clear-cuts, fishing nets, hydroelectric dams, irrigation diversions, and water pollution. Her assessment is conservative, Carolyn notes, because it ignores nonmonetary values. "I know that salmon are near and dear to the people of this region, especially the tribes."

The value of chinook is so high because many Columbia Basin chinook populations are endangered. They should not be killed or caught at all. Yet nobody behaves as if each of the Columbia Basin's remaining wild chinook salmon were a share of stock worth $2,148. The money economy, and government cost-benefit analyses, have long treated salmon as cheap, abundant, and indestructible. This largely explains their near eradication in the Yakima and in many other rivers.

Similar discrepancies between cost and price are woven through the fabric of the Northwest economy. Prices—the money economy's main tool for conveying information—do not tell the truth. They therefore fail to do their job of regulating consumption so as to maximize good and minimize bad. Prices are blind to most ecological and many social costs.

In commodity after commodity critical to the long-term viability of life in the Northwest, market prices are a fraction of true costs. The gasoline burned by the automobile that brought Carolyn over the Cascades from the airport in Seattle was priced at $1.29 a gallon. The full cost of that gallon of gasoline, including such side effects as air pollution damage to human lungs and farm crops, was perhaps $6. The price of using the highway to get here, paid through fuel taxes, was less than one cent a mile, but the cost of using the highway—if you add in tax subsidies from nondrivers and damage to air, water, and wildlife habitat—was closer to a dime a mile. The map that guided Carolyn to the lake sold for $2.50, but its cost—counting the pollution released in making and transporting its paper and ink—may have been three times that.

The list goes on and on. The clothes Carolyn wears, the water that runs past her feet and into irrigation canals or hydroelectric turbines, the airplane ticket she bought to get here, and just about everything else that uses natural resources intensively is also underpriced.

Meanwhile, things that use labor intensively, including health care and most other services, are overpriced. So too are things for which the peculiar nature of the market results in hoarding, speculation, artificial scarcity, and underinvestment. Carolyn's rent, for example, is probably too high by a tenth—a premium amounting to hundreds of dollars a year.

If the Northwest economy is to endure, Northwesterners will have to make prices tell the truth. While laws, regulations, and individual efforts to live ethically are crucial in moving toward sustainability, only prices are powerful enough to fundamentally redirect consumption and production patterns. Look at the record. Study the trends for energy consumption in the Northwest—the best single indicator of the environmental responsibility of the region's economy. Over the decades, the lines have soared upward in great, uninterrupted sweeps, rising even through most recessions.

On the graphs of energy consumption, there is no evidence of the great events of environmental consciousness-raising. There is no sign of the publication in 1962 of Rachel Carson's *Silent Spring*, regarded by many as the birth announcement of the modern environmental movement. There is no sign of Earth Day 1970, when environmental awareness burst onto the public scene. There is no sign of milestone environmental regulations passing legislative bodies. There is no sign of Earth Day 1990, history's largest teach-in. The lines for production and consumption of energy just keep rising. Environmental education, moral exhortation, and government regulation do not visibly alter the curve.

Where there are significant decreases, they are the consequences of rising energy prices. For petroleum, the line dips twice: once after the Arab oil embargo jacked up prices in 1973, and again after the Iranian revolution did so in 1979. For electricity, the line goes flat after the region's disastrous venture into nuclear power elevated most Northwest electric rates in the early 1980s.

Each of these price increases caused inflation and contributed to recessions. They did so, however, because they were sudden, were unanticipated, and siphoned money from the Pacific Northwest to oil exporters and utility bond holders in faraway places. If prices of energy—and of labor, salmon, water, housing, parking spaces, and everything else—were gradually and predictably aligned, upward or downward, to match true costs, and if the money stayed at home, the economy would benefit enormously. Jobs would proliferate even as the environment improved.

This contention may seem exaggerated. Most people believe that they must choose between a vibrant economy and a healthy environment. But listen to thinkers such as Carolyn Alkire. Their message is simple and revolutionary: To thrive—even just to survive—the Northwest must teach prices to tell the ecological truth.

You cannot wave a wand and change the prices of hundreds of goods and services. But there is a way to do it: by partially replacing existing taxes with taxes on the pollution, depletion, and disruption of nature. Prices, realigned through a shift of taxes, are the reins for consumption.

## January

I still vividly recall that time in the delivery room. Each time Amy pushed, she looked as if a blade were tearing at her flesh. It was not supposed to happen this way. Natural childbirth was supposed to hurt less; it was supposed to be intense but exhilarating. Something was wrong. The midwife, previously flexible, nurturing, and tolerant, began telling Amy what to do in crisp commands. "We need you to get on the bed. There's too much pressure standing up like this." My adrenaline curdled into fear.

Amy began to scream with the next contraction. "I can't do it! I can't do it! I'm coming apart!"

"The baby is coming," said the midwife. "She is big and healthy. Tuck in your chin. Hold your breath. Push for a count of ten."

Amy grabbed me around the neck and pulled me to her. I hugged and counted to ten over and over, while she screamed, held her breath, screamed, and held her breath. Amy was clinging to me so tightly that I wondered if I would suffocate. I didn't want her to stop, though, because she was squeezing hard enough that I could not feel the terror. How long this went on I do not know. It might have been five minutes or an hour. Normal time had long since stopped.

Then, all of a sudden, it was over. Kathryn Thein Durning burst into the world in a shower of her mother's blood. The birth certificate says it was two hours after sunrise on July 3. It was a shock to see her. The pregnancy, and then the labor, had seemed so interminable, and Kathryn had seemed such an abstraction, that it was disorienting to actually have her in my arms. Yet there she was, gazing back at Amy and me, apparently as surprised as we were.

The heart monitor strapped to Amy's belly reported that throughout her last night in the womb, Kathryn was fast asleep—despite the commotion, contracting, and cursing. She woke up for her birth but remained almost serenely calm through her birthday. She did not cry when the nurse pricked her heel for blood. She did not complain when I rubbed alcohol on the stump of her umbilical cord. And she took to the breast as if she had been doing it for years. She just watched. Her eyes reminded me of Amy's.

**GOVERNMENTS NEED MONEY TO PERFORM** public functions that the market is no good at—functions such as writing and enforcing laws, providing for the common defense, building public infrastructure, counteracting historic injustices, planning land use, ensuring equality of opportunity, and protecting public health and the environment. Yet the taxes that governments currently use to gather money cause problems—taxes on income, payroll, property, and retail sales discourage entrepreneurship, hiring, investment, savings, and work.

Because they are riddled with loopholes, exceptions, poor enforcement, and straight giveaways, they also encourage sprawl, depletion of natural resources, and pollution of land, air, and water. On balance, at least in the United States, they also make the poor poorer and the rich richer.

Liberals and conservatives both regard the burdensome effects of taxation as necessary evils and spend their time arguing about overall levels of taxation. Occasionally, they debate the fairness of different taxes on rich and poor, young and old.

But hardly anybody yet understands that many current taxes could be phased out. They could be gradually replaced with taxes on land values and on actions that pollute, deplete, or destroy habitat. And those taxes not only would fund government but would actually help the economy, the environment, and social welfare in the process.

Jim Lazar is panting over his bicycle in the Hanaford Valley of western Washington. As usual, the ferns beside the road are soaked from drizzle. His time-worn jacket flaps open as he muscles his way up a grade, explaining, between puffing breaths, the finer points of electric-utility accounting.

Jim Lazar is a resource economist, but he comes across more like a great horned owl—an impressive predator with a look that is vaguely dark. He has green eyes and curly black hair, a broad, hooked nose, and a rufflike mass of beard. He gesticulates with his burly wings to punctuate his speech, which alternates between tirades and jests. He has the instincts of a hunter. Greeting an old lobbying adversary on the grounds of the state capitol a few hours ago, he smiled icily and inquired, "What are you selling? And who for?"

Atop the rise, Jim brakes his Cannondale bicycle and dismounts to take in a view of one of the state's two operating coal mines, a black and tan crater that yawns below the road like the Grand Canyon's evil twin. The coal buried in the earth here is foul, even as coal goes. Jim says, "There are two main seams—one is Big Dirty, the other's Little Dirty."

An ant line of dump trucks is streaming up from the bottom of the hole and unloading at a steam-topped power plant on the opposite lip. It is a big plant, feeding more power into the grid than a large nuclear station. And the power, according to Jim, is cheap, at least according to the one-eyed bookkeeping of the market.

The investment cost of the plant has now depreciated to hardly anything, Jim says, because this plant went on line in 1972. (Jim confides that that was about the time he chased a college girlfriend to the state of Washington from the Midwest. "By the time I got here, she had taken up chewing tobacco, and my romantic interest waned.")

Wiping road splash from his glasses with a flannel shirttail, Jim bites into the accounts of this coal complex: "The capital cost and the operating cost total a penny and a half a kilowatt-hour, and the fuel cost is about a penny." That puts the price of a kilowatt-hour leaving the plant at two and a half cents. By the time the kilowatt-hour travels through the grid to, say, Jim's desk light in nearby Olympia, Washington, its price has risen another two pennies. So "we pay roughly a nickel a kilowatt-hour," Jim says. "But we ought to pay a dime."

The money price does not include the sickness and death caused by air pollutants such as sulfur and nitrogen oxides that spew from the plant's twin smokestacks. In 1991, the Pacific Northwest Laboratories in Richland, Washington, estimated that half a million people breathed sulfur from this plant. Based on toxicology models, the laboratory estimated that each year hundreds of them got sick from the sulfur and nineteen of them died.

The money price does not include environmental damage from this air pollution, nor does it include the climate-altering impacts of carbon dioxide; this plant is the largest discrete source of greenhouse gas emissions in the bioregion, accounting for one-eighth of Washington's fossil fuel–derived carbon dioxide all by itself in 1993. The money price does not include the spoiled landscape and streams around the mine, plant, and power lines. Nor does it reflect the aesthetic losses downwind: the plant is responsible for a third of the sulfur pollution that muddies views for the two million people who visit Mount Rainier National Park each year.

"If the utilities had to consider environmental effects of generation, you wouldn't be seeing steam," Jim concludes. The mine and power plant, which are owned by the Portland-based utility PacifiCorps along with its subsidiaries and partners, would close. They would close because the full cost of a kilowatt-hour generated here is greater than what Northwesterners are willing to pay. This operation is a losing venture, Jim explains; its costs exceed its benefits.

The profits that PacifiCorps reports to shareholders, Jim suggests, are not profits at all. They are actually transfers of wealth from those on whom the operation inflicts half of the costs of production. They are transfers from the Northwesterners who breathe the pollution, suffer the degraded streams and forests, brace for climatic turmoil, and lose the chance—on their once-in-a-lifetime climb up the Big Mountain—to gaze all the way into Canada.

Noneconomists, Jim comments, have a simpler name for these transfers: theft.

If the price of electric power were a dime a kilowatt-hour, a lot of things would change. Jim knows this because a string of events that multiplied wholesale power prices launched his career as an energy economist. He remembers it well. The string of events is referred to locally as "whoops."

In the late 1970s, Jim was a transportation economist on the staff of a committee in the state legislature. He became concerned about grandiose plans—in the long tradition of Northwestern audacity—by a coalition of utilities to build five nuclear power plants in a hurry. The coalition called itself Washington Public Power Supply System (WPPSS, pronounced "whoops").

While many citizens were questioning the safety of nuclear plants, Jim was fretting about the Alice in Wonderland economics that informed WPPSS plans. The more he learned, the less sense it made. These plants would generate power for several times the cost of conserving the same power. "The plan was to buy twelve-cent generation instead of three-cent conservation," Jim says. So Jim helped organize an initiative campaign to require voter approval of public power bonds. He went around the state arguing, "We get to vote on high school stadiums that cost a quarter of a million dollars. Why don't we get to vote on public power bonds that cost $8 billion?" Voters approved the initiative overwhelmingly and knocked WPPSS, already on the ropes, out of the ring.

The campaign steeped him in the arcane details of electric utility regulation and accounting. It also overwhelmed his paying job. He quit, and has been perfecting his knowledge of energy ever since. The main lesson of WPPSS, Jim contends as he pushes his two-wheeler back onto the asphalt, was not about atoms, it was about economics. "The original budget for WPPSS was $8 billion. They said, 'Give us $8 billion and we'll solve your region's electricity shortage.' We gave them $8 billion and our electricity shortage went away. I guess you could call it a success."

He is joking. WPPSS was the largest municipal bond default in American history. Only one of the five plants was ever finished. The budget ballooned to $24 billion. The debt still absorbs every fourth dollar Northwesterners pay on their electric bills. And largely because of this nuclear debt, millions of salmon die in hydroelectric dams and reservoirs on the Columbia; utilities impoverished by WPPSS debt claim they cannot afford to spend the smaller sums it would take to help salmon get past the dams. Between 1979 and 1982, the Bonneville Power Administration, WPPSS's largest stakeholder, had to elevate wholesale power rates from four-tenths of a cent per kilowatt-hour to two and a half cents per kilowatt-hour.

The electricity shortage went away because "when wholesale prices went up more than fivefold in four years," Jim explains, "a funny thing happened. The meter went around slower. The engineers didn't understand this, but anyone who pays their own home electric bill certainly understands it. Loads were forecast to grow at 4 to 6 percent a year. All of a sudden it just leveled off. There was just no growth at all." Jim is cranking his way along the road that circumnavigates the coal pit, keeping one eye on the mine.

The leveling off of electricity consumption was partly caused by a general economic slowdown. Building construction petered out, and power-hogging aluminum smelters idled production lines.

But most of the leveling was a result of price-induced conservation and substitution. It was a textbook example of the demand curve economists have been describing for generations. At higher prices, people buy less; at lower prices, people buy more.

Amazingly, in the early 1980s, many energy analysts were shocked that price increases suppressed power use. They thought electricity consumption was largely unresponsive to price changes. They were mistaken.

High prices told everybody to look for ways to conserve electricity or find substitutes for it. With everybody looking, Jim notes, "All kinds of alternatives kept showing up. People turned down their thermostats. They went out and bought kerosene heaters. They put in wood stoves. They took shorter showers." And it was not just individual electric customers. Soaring prices prompted lawmakers, researchers, and active citizens to take a fresh look at power companies and utility commissions—institutions that had mostly been left to their own devices for decades.

Under scrutiny, Jim recounts, utilities began "some pretty aggressive short-term conservation measures. Utilities distributed water-heater insulation kits. They retrofitted all the streetlights in the Pacific Northwest. Shower-flow-restrictor buttons were being given away like crazy."

This crash course in conservation was the precursor to more sophisticated reforms. Legislators revolutionized energy policies in Oregon and Washington, creating state energy offices that were among the most proactive in the nation. Northwest utilities and their regulators helped develop and demonstrate "least-cost, integrated resource planning," a technique for comparing supply and conservation options watt for watt and dollar for dollar. For the first time, decision makers could look at heat escaping from apartment-house walls the same way they looked at water running downhill or coal in the ground: It was all energy. The question was which source was cheapest.

In 1980, the U.S. Congress established the Northwest Power Planning Council to coordinate the region's power and salmon policies. The council took the opportunity of soaring prices to begin least-cost planning for the entire U.S. Northwest, an achievement unmatched elsewhere on the continent. The council and other agencies pushed least-cost analysis beyond the realm of power companies themselves. They saw that house and mobile-home builders and appliance manufacturers, for example, were making choices that would affect energy consumption for decades. So the council sought to create standards and incentives that would encourage these industries to design in conservation from the start. The Northwest states enacted progressively more ambitious building codes, pushed for national appliance efficiency standards, and underwrote better insulation in all new mobile homes.

Describing the changes in Washington, Jim says, "In 1977 the state passed its first-ever building code. It didn't require double-pane windows." Then came WPPSS. In 1980 the legislature upgraded the code to require the insulating windows. "In 1986 they upgraded the code, and in 1990 they upgraded it again; in 1993, again. We've made tremendous progress."

Many of these measures were based on a new understanding of inherent flaws in the market for electricity. For one thing, consumers will spend money on improved energy efficiency only if it promises to pay for itself within three years. When buying a house or a refrigerator, for example, consumers put little emphasis on life-cycle energy costs. Electric companies, meanwhile, were spending money on power plants that might take thirty years to pay for themselves. Put side by side like this, it seemed obvious that a power company, rather than building new plants, should "buy" electricity that consumers were wasting—by underwriting conservation in homes and businesses—and sell the saved power to other customers. As long as the cost of conserving a kilowatt was less than the cost of generating one, the power company would come out ahead.

With regulator encouragement, Northwest utilities began offering rebates, coupons, and low-interest loans for energy-saving equipment. Some utilities took more innovative approaches, investing in education as well as equipment. With help from regional bodies, for example, Seattle's municipal utility built a lighting-design laboratory. The lab let architects and contractors prove to themselves that new, efficient lighting devices did a better job with less energy than the old standbys, fluorescent tubes and incandescent lamps.

"A lot of efficiency," Jim offers, scratching his bushy beard as he coasts down a grade, "has not happened in response to market prices directly but indirectly, in response to standards and utility programs." The standards and utility programs catalyzed the conservation; the prices motivated the standards and utility programs.

While prices were high, state and utility policies were aggressive. But in the early 1990s, market prices for electricity from new generating facilities were plummeting, and conservation efforts dissipated. "In 1994 and 1995, we have probably lost as much ground as we had gained in any previous two-year period." The main reason was the expanded supply of natural gas from northeastern British Columbia and Alberta, combined with greatly improved technologies for burning gas to generate power.

"The price of gas has come down," Jim argues. "The price of gas technology has come down. The efficiency has gone up. This is an awesome competitor, and it has fundamentally changed the economics." In 1991, the Northwest Power Planning Council issued a plan that instructed the Bonneville Power Administration to "buy" saved electricity whenever it could do so for thirteen cents a kilowatt-hour or less. In 1995, new natural gas–fired electricity cost only a nickel at the meter—as little as the power from this old coal plant.

"It doesn't make sense to spend thirteen cents to save a nickel," Jim says, "unless you add environmental costs to the equation. Then it does make sense." Jim dismounts again outside the power plant gates and eyes the moraine of dark fuel heaped beside the boiler. His commentary grows more venomous in its proximity. Still, he sticks to the accounts.

"If we tax $CO_2$ emissions at twenty dollars a ton, we add about two cents a kilowatt-hour to the equation." With a twenty-dollars-a-ton tax on carbon dioxide emissions, gas-derived electricity would cost seven cents a kilowatt-hour at the meter. With a higher tax, the price would rise further.

Carolyn Alkire was able to calculate the value of a wild salmon as natural capital because salmon are bought and sold. But no one can pinpoint the monetary value of a human life, a stable climate, healthy streams, or crystalline views in a national park. They are worth a lot, but how much exactly is an unanswerable question. "Still, we know the answer is not zero," Jim points out. "We can hardly do worse than the status quo." He uses indirect approaches to estimate the full cost of a kilowatt-hour. He looks at what it would cost to not cause the harm, to repair the harm, or to offset the harm with improvements elsewhere. What would it cost, for example, to reduce sulfur emissions from other industrial facilities by the amount emitted here? What would it cost to trap as much carbon dioxide in regrown forests as this plant spews out? These approaches lead him to put the full cost of a kilowatt-hour around a dime. And even that, he argues, may be conservative.

To stabilize carbon dioxide concentrations in the atmosphere and minimize the dangers of catastrophic climate change, affluent regions such as the Pacific Northwest will need to reduce emissions of carbon dioxide by at least 90 percent. And if a 90 percent reduction is the goal, then the cost of carbon dioxide emissions must be valued much higher than twenty dollars a ton, because a twenty-dollars-a-ton tax on carbon dioxide emissions would not induce a 90 percent reduction. To reach that target, the Northwest will need a carbon dioxide tax that increases each year until emissions have fallen sufficiently—which might not happen before the tax surpasses two hundred dollars a ton. At two hundred dollars a ton, the cost of a kilowatt-hour from this plant is thirty cents.

Jim would be happy to start with a tax of twenty dollars a ton to get the ball rolling. And he would like to offset it with reductions in other taxes.

Imagine an air pollution tax levied by British Columbia and each of the Northwest states. Each major pollutant—oxides of nitrogen, sulfur, and carbon; volatile organic compounds; airborne heavy metals and other toxic materials—would be taxed at a rate set to reflect its relative impacts. Major factories and other polluters would pay the tax based on constant monitoring of their emissions, giving them a strong incentive to pollute less. Medium-scale polluters such as small businesses would be taxed based on periodic checks. Small-scale polluters, such as households, would be taxed based on their fuel consumption and ratings for the furnaces, wood stoves, and other equipment they use.

The tax rates would start low and increase for ten to thirty years according to a set schedule to allow a smooth transition. The tax would be a tonic to energy conservation the likes of which the world has never seen. It would restore and sustain the momentum that the WPPSS-era price hikes created. Businesses would revise their investment strategies and upgrade their plants and equipment. Consumer-product designers would put energy savings on a par with convenience. Utilities would revitalize their conservation programs and phase out coal and natural gas in favor of renewable energy sources.

All of this would happen for motives no more altruistic than those that currently propel the tax-shelter industry—the legions of accountants and pseudo-businesses that exist largely to keep money away from the tax collector. Air pollution tax avoidance, however, would be a beneficent act. And even with everyone striving to limit pollution-tax bills, an upward-ramping levy would generate enough revenue to allow deep cuts in other taxes. Consumers would pay more for energy, but they would save on their income or sales taxes.

Jim mounts his bike again to peddle away from the power plant gate. He mutters, "Maybe I'll have to run another state initiative."

## January

Kathryn had left a broken-glass pattern of lacerations in her wake. That explained the trauma of her grand entrance. But when that was stitched up and we were finally home, Amy developed a high fever that inched up and down for four horrible weeks. The entire family—Amy, Gary, and I, and Amy's parents Peter and Rita—rode the roller coaster of her fever chart. Only Kathryn was blessedly unaware. When the thermometer read lower, we swung into hopeful euphoria. As her temperature rose, we sweated and avoided each other's eyes.

We consulted doctors and more doctors, and Amy endured tests and more tests. A bloom of bacteria, they all surmised, was infecting her body somewhere, maybe her uterus, maybe one of her breasts, maybe elsewhere. And they prescribed antibiotics of increasing cost and toxicity, along with pills to contract her uterus, supplement her iron stores, and cool the fever. I arrayed the multi-colored tablets in an egg carton and constructed an elaborate daily schedule. On it, I noted the readings of the thermometer and every symptom she mentioned to me. I codified her illness and never lost confidence that she would be better soon. I was alone in my confidence. Her father, Peter—who took on the job of emptying the trash—was worrying, he told me afterwards, about having "to put on a black suit. That basket was full of bloody bandages every day." And Amy said, "If this were a hundred years ago, I would be dead."

Late on one of those nights, Amy went into the bathroom and, moments later, called me, in near panic. I went in and she pointed at the toilet. "My God, what is it?" There was a large bloody mass at the bottom of the bowl.

Strangely calm, I said, "Um, I don't know."

"It just came out of me!"

I called the doctor's emergency number, sitting down on the bathroom floor with Amy and staring at the blob in our toilet. Finally, I had a doctor on the line. I told him what had happened. He asked to talk to Amy. They went over things for a while. She was crying. "How big is it, Alan?" I plunged my hand into the toilet bowl and picked it up.

"Tell him it's the size of a tangerine. No, an avocado. Tell him it looks like marbled beef," I said.

Amy gradually calmed and dried her eyes. She thanked him and hung up. "He says it's just a blood clot. He says we should go to the doctor in the morning. He says it just means my uterus still has not shrunk back to size."

The next day, a Friday at the end of July, we were again in the examining room of Amy's obstetrician, a slight, fiftyish woman with a caring but perfunctory manner. I held Amy's hand as the doctor did yet another pelvic exam. By now, Amy was acutely anemic. The doctor poked and prodded for several minutes, looking for a site of infection or some other cause of trouble. Suddenly, blood gushed onto the floor as it had at Kathryn's birth. The doctor began to bark at the nurse. "We may need to move over to the hospital." My stomach seized. I came unglued. All the confidence I had possessed disappeared. As the blood drained from her womb, stark images filled my mind: the pool of blood expanding, Amy slipping away. I was fighting for consciousness, sucking air. Amy needed me now more than ever, but it was no use. I collapsed onto the white linoleum. When I recovered, we were rushing to the hospital.

At midnight a surgeon dilated Amy's cervix and removed fragments of the placenta that had cradled Kathryn but had, the obstetrician had finally determined, failed to disengage. They were the cause of the fever, the blood clots, and the bleeding. They tricked Amy's uterus into behaving as if the baby were still there.

Outside the operating theater, I paced, rocking Kathryn on my shoulder. I rocked her for my sake, not hers. She was oblivious to the fact that her mother was unconscious in the next room. The doctor came sooner than I expected. The retained placenta was out. Amy was awake and waiting for us in the recovery room. Kathryn nursed hungrily. I cried.

My hesitation about calling the old grocery to schedule a vasectomy did not grow from nostalgia for the birth experience. It had been the worst month of my life.

**THE TOLLGATE RAISES ITS MECHANICAL** arm to let out another car, this one a steely gray sedan trailing curls of bluish oil smoke. The four-wheeler pulls away from the darkened booth, glides up a ramp, and disappears into daylight. Leaning against a wall in the exhaust-filled garage, Todd Litman is watching the toll-gate rise and fall. In the building above him are the Victoria offices of the B.C. Ministry of Transportation and Highways.

This is the underground parking for British Columbia's high priests of motorized velocity, and a good place to ponder the cost and price of one of the Northwest's premier resource consumers, the private automobile. It is also a good place to talk about making the price match the cost.

Todd, an economist and principal of the Victoria Transport Policy Institute, spends a lot of time counting things the market does not. The full cost of driving a mile, he contends, is $1.05, but motorists bill one-third of that—34 cents—to others, especially nondrivers, the poor, and taxpayers.

Thirty-four cents in hidden costs does not sound like much at first; it is not even bus fare. But remember that Northwest vehicles travel a hundred billion miles a year. Todd ticks off the hidden costs of driving as the tollgate rises to discharge a sputtering Mercedes. The biggest costs—he tallies them at a nickel or more each—are air pollution, sprawl, congestion, accident risk imposed on others, and subsidies for parking. The smaller costs are worth pennies or fractions of pennies apiece. They include waste generation, water and noise pollution, land values lost to roads and parking facilities, and a litany of auto-related government expenses not fully recovered from fuel and vehicle taxes—expenses such as road construction and maintenance, military protection of oil fields and supply lines, traffic policing, and emergency services at auto accidents.

Underpricing automobile use leads to massive transfers of wealth—and well-being—from people who drive less to people who drive more. "These are not, as many people assume, things that come out a wash," Todd says. Households with annual income under ten thousand dollars drive a fourth as much on average as households with income over forty thousand dollars. Urban households drive about a third as much as suburban households. And everyone who does not have a car—approximately one-tenth of Northwesterners—still pays the hidden costs of driving. Car-less households are disproportionately made up of the disabled, elderly, female, and poor.

Replacing existing taxes with taxes on air pollution, resource consumption, and greenhouse gas emissions would help ensure that drivers no longer shirk one third of the cost of driving. Other changes would help too, because even the costs of driving that motorists already pay are poor incentives to drive less, Todd notes. The problem is that motorists do not pay as they go.

"Owning a car is very expensive," Todd explains. It averages three hundred dollars a month, but two thirds of that covers the purchase price of the car, insurance, registration, residential parking, and other things that hardly change with miles driven. "Driving a car, once you have one, appears very cheap," Todd points out. Drivers pay as they go for little more than fuel—which, after adjusting for inflation, is cheaper than ever. "The total cost of driving," Todd says, "is over a dollar a mile, but the price that people are responding to is roughly a dime."

Slicing up big, fixed costs of driving such as insurance and parking into small, pay-as-you-go costs gives people an incentive to drive less because it allows them to save money.

Drivers pay an average of seven cents a mile for auto insurance—more than they pay for fuel. The more you drive, the higher the probability you will get in an accident. Yet auto insurers put almost no weight on mileage in calculating insurance rates. The California Insurance Department reported in December 1994 that major insurers in that state underweighted mileage in their risk formulas by factors ranging from two to twenty-two. There are several viable ways to sell insurance by the slice, the simplest being to require insurers to account for mileage accurately in their rates.

A more comprehensive and efficient solution, however, is to convert to no-fault, pay-at-the-pump insurance. Motorists would buy insurance through a flat surcharge of perhaps forty cents on each gallon of gasoline—a charge rolled into the listed gas price just as gas taxes are now. State government would randomly divide all registered vehicles into blocks of several thousand each, and insurers would bid to cover each block of vehicles. The state would automatically forward the insurance payments collected by gas stations to insurers in proportion to how many blocks they insured. Because the system would replace the current litigious system with a no-fault regime that paid legitimate costs and losses, but not the legal fees and sales costs that consume roughly half of every insurance dollar today, motorists would actually pay less for insurance. Best of all, because everybody would buy insurance at the pump, there would no longer be uninsured motorists.

Converting parking to a pay-as-you-go cost is a similar opportunity. Todd says, "Americans end 99 percent of auto trips at free parking spaces. No, not free," he corrects himself. "Somebody pays for them." The parking spaces in the B.C. Ministry's garage are among the tiny fraction for which drivers pay for exactly what they use.

Parking is the dominant land use in urban areas. A typical commercial development dedicates more land to parking than to the buildings that the parking serves. The Northwest has two and a half times as many parking spaces as motor vehicles. Parking a car in the various spaces it uses costs roughly seventy-five dollars a month—roughly twice as much as fueling it.

Drivers do not pay per use for parking because antiquated provisions in zoning and building codes have artificially increased the supply of parking—glutting the market and causing the price to drop toward zero. Fixing these flaws would affect the pricing of parking gradually.

Zoning and building codes enforce a tremendous oversupply of parking. In the sixteen most populous counties and cities in the Northwest, off-street parking requirements are omnipresent. Rural and suburban jurisdictions require even more parking than cities. For houses, the requirement is usually two spaces per house. Office buildings are required to provide up to four spaces per thousand square feet of floor space. And in much of the region, retail developers are required to devote more space to cars than they do to people.

To slice up parking costs into pay-per-use costs, the Northwest could strike all off-street parking requirements from zoning and building codes. Deregulation would allow the market to decide how much parking space to provide and how to pay for it. Many new developments would include much less parking, lowering costs, especially for the poor. Including parking facilities in new multi-family buildings increases construction costs by up to 18 percent.

The change would affect existing developments as well. The owners of buildings surrounded by seas of concrete would have new choices. They could expand, sell off land to others, or turn parking into landscaped plazas. Even homeowners would have new options, such as converting parking space to living or gardening space. It might take ten years for the oversupply of parking space to be absorbed by these changes, but scarcity—and a market—would inevitably develop. Employers and retailers would start charging for parking, so nondriving workers and shoppers would no longer subsidize their peers who drive. Prices, in short, would tell the truth.

Todd estimates that if the Northwest converted insurance and parking from fixed to variable costs, motorists would voluntarily forego one-third of their driving in order to recoup the savings. Taxing auto travel up to its full costs would nourish current and as-yet-unimagined alternatives. Cars would be one choice among many, and they would continue to be used on trips where, in the drivers' judgment, the benefits were worth the price. Todd asks, "That is the idea of a free market economy, isn't it?"

## January

Three months after Kathryn's birth, and two months after Amy's surgery, the prelude to my vasectomy resumed. We conceived Peter. Amy was far from thoroughly recovered. She was still mildly anemic, her bones still ached from giving birth, and breastfeeding Kathryn was taking much of her energy. We had made the cross-country move to Seattle in the interim and were living out of boxes.

We took a chance. We skipped birth control once. It seemed like a good gamble at the time. Kathryn was exclusively breastfed, and breastfeeding commonly delays the resumption of ovulation for a year or more. Amy had not had a period since before Kathryn was conceived, and in her weakened condition, we figured her body would not be expending energy on ovulating.

Well, we hit the jackpot. Amy began complaining of morning nausea. One day as I was heading into a press conference, she called my office to say, "It's pink." She had taken a home pregnancy test. "No way!" was all I could say.

Peter was born in Seattle thirteen months after Kathryn. Amy went into strong labor in her sleep just minutes after her due date ended at midnight. I called my mother, Jean, who rushed over to watch Gary and Kathryn. We headed up the steep hill above our house, twelve blocks to the hospital.

Inside the door, with the contractions quickly strengthening, Amy said to the first nurse she saw, "I want drugs. I just did this. I want drugs now!"

"No problem," she assured her. "Let's just get situated first."

At this hospital, laboring women are given private suites with tilting whirlpool tubs. Our nurse, a woman named B.J., asked a battery of questions, then said, "You ought to try the tub before you go to medication. You can't have drugs in the tub." Amy agreed to try it, so B.J. helped her in, tilted her back, and flooded her with hot, bubbly water. The contractions were getting stronger quickly and I wasn't much help, having again forgotten everything about breathing, focal points, and relaxing visualizations.

Amy screamed with the first contraction underwater, tensing her body to resist the pain. B.J. interrupted my words of encouragement and said matter-of-factly, "I know it hurts, but it works faster if you can concentrate on relaxing. It lets the contractions do their job. The pain is just the feeling of the birth canal opening to let the baby out. Tell yourself that. Tell yourself to make room for the baby." I stared at her in disbelief. From me, it never would have worked. Amy would have snarled at me not to tell her what to do. But Amy accepted the advice. It seemed to put her in control of herself, to return her to the center of her body. She never again mentioned drugs. She went limp in the tub, breathed deeply, and said, "This time, Alan, talk to me about the kids. Tell me something happy about the kids."

So I did. "We went to the arboretum. Almost everybody was there: Grammy Jean and Grandpa Marvin, Aunt Susan and Uncle Steve and cousin Ahren. The kids got on the swings down by the playing fields. Then you got in the swing and everybody sang, 'It's time for the baby to come out.' You said you were going to jump out of the swing to get things going. Then we walked a ways down Azalea Way. Gary had his bike and he was riding down the hills. I took a turn on Gary's bike. It was a blast. Then you did it, too. You were a maniac."

The next contraction, I told her about breakfast. The next one, I told her about dinner. Then I told her about the book Gary and I were reading. After the first five contractions, I could not remember anything new to say, so for most of the night, I just repeated the same sentimental anecdotes. Amy did not sound like a sailor this time, and she never once said, "Don't breathe on me."

By six o'clock, the night was bleaching into dawn, the contractions were slowing, and Amy was getting drowsy. The midwife, Janna, took it as a sign that Peter was on his way, but Amy did not want to leave the tub and begin the pushing. She was afraid of the tearing pain. We were both terrified of what would come after the birth. Somehow, Janna convinced her to get out of the tub, and I called my mother. A mile away from us, she scooped Kathryn out of her crib, awoke Gary, and piled them into the car in their pajamas. Up the hill she drove, up the same hill my father had rushed her to give birth to my sister, my brother, and me—up the hill to the hospital where she had birthed three babies and lost her father.

Delivery was different this time. Amy pushed gently and Peter descended. There was no ripping sensation. My mother arrived with Gary and Kathryn, and they sat nearby. Their presence strengthened Amy. "This is scary," Gary said after the first push he watched.

"Yes, it is," Amy said. "But I'm okay, see? The baby is coming." Kathryn watched in her calm, curious way as her little brother emerged—first his head, then his shoulders, then his entire body.

Looking at the bloody goo on Peter and Amy, Gary said, "It's neat but kind of disgusting." Smaller than Kathryn had been, Peter still weighed in at eight and a half pounds. He was inquisitive and energetic and was fascinated by the overhead lights. Holding him, Gary smelled the dark ocean scent of the womb and said, "Peter, you need to take a shower. You stink."

**HOW WOULD A TAX SHIFT WORK?** It would revise the existing tax structure from top to bottom, because that structure has no reason to it. It has an explanation: it is an accident of history, or a history of accidents. It was cobbled together by a century and a half of political compromises, half-baked theories, and special pleading. But it has no reason, no consistent rationale, no underlying principle or unifying form. The local, state, and national taxes affecting the region exist solely to draw money for governments. They succeed at that; they claimed about 30 percent of the region's gross domestic product in 1994, a total of $89 billion in government revenues that was spent in pursuit of various public goals.

Yet the taxes' side effects work at cross-purposes with those public aims. Taxes in the Northwest penalize work, enterprise, and investment, aggravate inequality, and accelerate environmental decline. They give the wrong incentives to almost everyone. They are, to borrow a phrase from energy analyst Amory Lovins, "spherically senseless"—no matter how you look at them, they are nonsense.

By custom, economists speak of land, labor, and capital as the three "factors of production." Whatever a business wants to sell, it needs some combination of land, labor, and capital. In this abstract but useful framework, labor refers to people. Capital refers to physical objects created by people, such as buildings, tools, and machinery. And land refers, somewhat opaquely, to all the gifts of nature—everything that is not created by people. Land includes not only tracts of earth and natural resource commodities but also basic ecosystem functions, such as the cycles of water, nutrients, and energy. These goods are provided by nonhuman forces, free of charge. The mispricing and consequent misuse of these gifts causes much environmental harm.

Taxes on the gifts of nature raise the price of using them, which tells people to conserve these gifts. Taxes on labor and capital tell businesses and households to scrimp on workers and tools—in other words, to practice unemployment and underinvestment. A reasonable tax policy would tax the gifts of nature first and tax labor and capital only as a last resort.

Yet most existing taxes affecting the Pacific Northwest stand reason on its head; they fall overwhelmingly on labor and capital. The Northwest can stand reason on its feet again by shifting the tax burden. Over the space of one to three decades, Northwest jurisdictions could eliminate many existing taxes—most of them levies on income, sales, and property—and replace them with taxes on the gifts of nature.

A tax shift alone will not solve the Northwest's problems. The region will always need a strong framework of laws and regulations against crimes, whether social, economic, or environmental. Taxes are no substitute for prohibition of inadmissible actions. The Northwest will also need to eliminate counterproductive subsidies, such as below-cost and below-market sales of public timber, parking space, and water. It will need to rewrite perverse regulations like those affecting auto insurance. And it will need to make public investments in the human services that meet vital social needs and reduce unintended pregnancy.

Yet a tax shift, more than any other large-scale policy change, would help align prices with costs, putting the power of the marketplace behind the reconciliation of people and nature. The bulk of existing tax revenue in the Pacific Northwest comes from levies on personal income, retail sales, and property values. Each of these forms of taxation is familiar and accepted, but each has inherent negative effects.

In 1994, national governments received about 60 percent of the total revenue collected in the region, most of it from personal income taxes. States and provinces collected about one-quarter, most of it from income and sales taxes. Localities—including cities, counties, and regional districts—collected the remainder, mostly from property taxes.

Taxation in the Pacific Northwest is now characterized by complexity. The single largest tax affecting the region, for example, is the U.S. federal income tax. Like its federal counterparts in Canada and its provincial and state counterparts in British Columbia, California, Idaho, Montana, and Oregon, it is widely regarded as progressive because the tax rate increases on additional increments of income. The rationale for this progressivity is that higher incomes increase people's ability to pay.

The fairness of the tax is flawed from the outset by its focus on current cash income, or what is earned, rather than on wealth, or what is owned. The latter ultimately determines ability to pay. But even disregarding this basic flaw, the tax's progressivity is frittered away in its fine print: the U.S. tax code is so full of perverse incentives, loopholes, and special exceptions that the tax is hardly progressive at all in practice. The mortgage interest deduction gives more housing assistance to the rich each year than low-income housing programs give to the poor. Tax breaks for employee parking give more transportation assistance to the upper classes than mass-transit subsidies give to the lower classes. People with high incomes can find countless ways to reduce their taxes, while poor people have few options. Income tax avoidance is among the biggest service industries catering to the wealthy.

Furthermore, amid the complexity of the law are provisions of accounting that make the tax fall more heavily on income from labor—wages and salaries—than on income from land and capital, such as income from real estate rentals and sales, investments, and inheritance. The federal income tax, in combination with federal and state payroll taxes such as Social Security, unemployment insurance, and workers compensation, increases the price of labor to businesses by one-third or more of take-home pay. This dead weight on hiring is a monumental incentive to practice unemployment.

State and local taxes are similarly rife with counterproductive provisions, as the example of taxation in Washington State—the region's most populous jurisdiction—illustrates. Washington has no state income tax. It uses a state sales tax and a state property tax to collect most of its revenue.

The state sales tax is levied on retail sales, but this is not a tax on all consumer expenditures. It is a tax on expenditures at retail establishments, and like all such taxes, it is strongly regressive. It hits the poor and lower middle class far harder than the rich. It excludes things that people with greater wealth buy disproportionately, such as private education, travel, second houses, land, and better medical care.

The sales tax is antiecological, too. Because it excludes wholesale transactions, it leaves high-impact commodities such as chemicals, minerals, and timber untaxed. And at the retail level, it exempts gasoline, electricity, and natural gas but not goods used for their conservation such as bicycles, insulation, and efficient appliances.

Washington's state and local property taxes fall on the value of physical assets as estimated by local tax assessors. As such, they are taxes on wealth rather than income, which suggests they might be progressive. Wealth is more concentrated than income, and ownership of land—the most valuable physical asset—is more concentrated still.

Unfortunately, the property value assessments performed by most local tax authorities are skewed; they overstate the value of buildings and understate the value of land. Because the wealth of middle-class owners of homes and businesses tends to be in buildings rather than land, the effect of skewed assessments is to shift the property tax from the rich toward the middle class. This reduces or nullifies the tax's progressivity. Underassessing land values also encourages land speculation, which speeds sprawl.

A comprehensive tax shift would gradually reduce or eliminate many taxes on income, sales, property, and enterprise. In their place would be a greatly expanded and tightened land-value tax, divorced from existing property taxes' levy on buildings, along with an array of new or expanded taxes on pollution, resource consumption, and other uses of the gifts of nature.

In a tax shift, some of the region's existing minor levies would simply be expanded. The State of Washington and its localities, for example, already collect a fifth or more of revenue from an assortment of imposts that are, in effect, taxes on the gifts of nature. The largest of these are the neglected land-value portion of the property tax and the tax on motor fuels. Others include a utility tax, a motor vehicle excise tax, and health-oriented taxes on alcohol, tobacco, and soft-drink syrup. The state has small hazardous materials fees, oil spill prevention fees, timber severance taxes, commercial fishing taxes, and a used car–tire recovery fee. Like all jurisdictions in the region, the state also generates revenue through sales of timber, grazing permits, and other natural resources it manages on behalf of its citizens.

New taxes on air pollution from smokestacks, chimneys, and tailpipes, taxes on fuels based on their emissions of greenhouse gases, and mileage-based charges on motor vehicles to cover other hidden costs of driving could contribute billions of dollars to Northwest governments. In a proposal for a tax shift for the state of California, Cliff Cobb of the research group Redefining Progress in San Francisco estimates that these types of taxes alone could generate one-third of current tax revenue in that state.

Other taxes with substantial revenue potential need little explanation. Northwest governments could shift the tax base onto high-impact raw or virgin materials such as chemicals, minerals, plastics, and timber, and onto fresh water impounded behind dams or withdrawn from rivers and aquifers.

The tax with the largest revenue potential and the greatest need for explanation is the revised property tax. A property tax is actually two conflicting taxes rolled into one. It is a tax on the value of buildings and a tax on the value of the land under those buildings. As experience in Australia, New Zealand, Taiwan, and Pennsylvania shows, shifting the tax from the former to the latter aids compact development while suppressing land speculation, promoting productive investment, and tempering housing costs, especially for the poor. It does these things because of the unique nature of land values.

In land values, location counts for everything. Land in a crime-infested, run-down neighborhood is worth a fraction as much as an identical lot in a safe, popular neighborhood. Paradoxically, property owners can increase their building values by improving their buildings, but nothing they can do to the property will change their land values. Only their neighbors, government, and society at large can do that. Government actions are especially important, and they usually increase land values. If a city builds a park, a province expands transportation infrastructure, or a nation restores a historic landmark near a parcel, the land's value will rise. Curiously, property-rights defenders decry the reductions of land values caused by government actions, which they call "takings," and they demand compensation for them. But they do not call for landowners to repay public coffers for the more common "givings"—in which government actions increase land values.

Location matters a great deal to people. In King County, for example, the assessed value of real property exceeded $100 billion in 1993; of that $61 billion was the value of private buildings, approximately what it would cost to reconstruct these structures. The remaining $46 billion was the value of land—what people were willing to pay purely for location.

And location matters more to people as time goes by. As incomes rise, people spend an increasing share of their earnings on location. Historically, urban land values have increased faster than population, the consumer price index, or income. In economic terms, rising wealth is capitalized in land values; in common parlance, to quote comedian Will Rogers, "Buy land, because they ain't makin' any more of it."

These peculiarities of land values make land speculation possible. Most successful investments—whether in businesses or buildings—create salable products not otherwise available. The investor makes money, and consumers have more of what they want. But successful land speculation—the purchase of land for the purpose of holding it until its value increases—fails the public. It does not create any salable goods or service; it prevents full utilization of premium sites. The investor makes money, and society has less of what its members want. Land speculation explains why roughly 5 percent of private urban land in Pacific Northwest cities is vacant, while perhaps three times as much is underused.

Land speculation is parasitic, not productive. Its antidote is to shift the property tax off buildings and onto land. Where this has been done—in dozens of North American jurisdictions such as Pittsburgh and thousands of localities in Australia and New Zealand—it has resulted in aggressive development of the most valuable sites, almost all of which were in cities rather than suburbs. When land is taxed, density increases. Apartment and office-space supplies increase. Rents fall. Parking supply declines, as parking lots—a standard holding pattern for land speculators— are developed. Finally, shifting the property tax onto land is highly progressive, because land ownership is extremely concentrated in the hands of the rich. Those who own no land benefit enormously, and even middle-class homeowners benefit, because their houses are usually worth more than their land.

Redefining Progress's proposal for a tax shift in California estimates that a land-value tax could generate as much revenue as all existing state taxes and still have positive effects on the state economy and environment. State and local land-value taxes in the Pacific Northwest could fill all government revenue needs not covered by other resource taxes.

Administering and enforcing a new arrangement of taxes on the gifts of nature would be easier than administering and enforcing current taxes. Land-value taxes, for example, are easier to administer than property taxes. Land-value taxes are easier to collect than income taxes, because all title deeds to land—unlike all income payments to individuals—must be recorded in government offices to be valid. Land-tax evaders, unlike income-tax evaders, need not be tracked down and prosecuted; governments can simply condemn property for back taxes.

Of course, people cheat on any tax; some would cheat on the new taxes. The question is whether they would cheat more than they do on existing taxes. The answer is no. Physical activities such as driving and polluting are much harder to hide than are the money transactions at the base of income, sales, and enterprise taxes.

A tax shift is not a sufficient condition for creating a way of life that can persist in the Northwest, but it is a necessary one. Nothing else would make prices tell the truth as effectively; nothing else would as decisively harness economic means to ecological ends.

What could stop an idea that makes so much sense? Those who profit most from the existing tax system will no doubt try to stop it. These include, in the short term, land speculators, heavy polluters, resource extractors and processors, and despoilers of human health and wild places. But their resistance would be nothing against the short-term winners, were those winners informed and organized. Service-sector businesses—which generate by far the largest share of income and jobs in the Northwest—would benefit enormously from the tax shift. Their largest expense is usually salaries and wages, and the tax shift would cut that cost by a third or more, without reducing workers' take-home pay.

In the long term, everyone would win. Taxes on the gifts of nature fall on actions, not people; and everyone could reduce their high-tax actions. Besides, in the long run, everyone loses from a dead landscape and a divided society. The price of the status quo, though familiar, is exorbitant. The price of a tax shift, though unfamiliar, is a bargain.

And a tax shift—combined with measures to slow population—is the only hope for reining in an economy that is galloping toward the brink.


# January

As a practical matter, it made sense for me to delay my vasectomy until after Peter's birth. Amy, pregnant for the second straight year, could not afford for me to be unable to lift heavy objects, like children, for two weeks.

And after Peter was born late last summer, it made sense for me to delay my vasectomy for two months while Amy recovered. After that, there were at least four good reasons to get on with it: First, fairness. Women have to endure pregnancy and labor; men ought to take responsibility for contraception. Second, conscience. World population grows by about a hundred million a year, and my kids will gobble up dozens of times as many resources as children in poor places like India or Africa. Third, compassion. Even without a vasectomy, we would adopt if we ever wanted more children. There are so many children who need adopting. Fourth, lust—so Amy would stop whispering, "When are you going to get that vasectomy, honey?"

Still, for three long months, I did not call Matt's office. I turned my mind away from the medical clinic in the old grocery. And I did not know why I was avoiding the issue.

In mid-January, Amy and I took the children on a cross-country ski trip on the flanks of Mount Rainier. We were moving along slowly but enjoyably atop the fathom-deep snowpack. Amy had Peter on her back, I had Kathryn on mine, and Gary was skiing between us when the wind wheeled and lanced polar blasts into our faces. Kathryn and Peter wailed hysterically as shards of icy snow bit their exposed cheeks, and Gary, quickly losing sensation in his fingers and toes, was falling into the drifts. We turned back and made it to shelter without great trouble, but the experience shook me.

Driving home that night, I had a lump in my throat. I was overwhelmed by an unspeakable fear, and I realized that this fear was now a constant facet of my consciousness: the fear of losing my children, the fear that their lives might end. No. Wait. Let me say it baldly: I live in fear that Gary, Kathryn, or Peter will die; that despite all our precautions, the wind will turn; that despite all our vigilance, their helpless tears might someday be beyond our powers to cure. It is a possibility so terrifying that I can scarcely face it.

That night, I carried each of the sleeping children from the car to their beds; then Amy and I held each other and watched Peter and Kathryn in their cribs. As we had done so many times before, we lowered our ears over them just to be sure they were breathing. This fear is unlike any I have felt before. It is worse than the fear I felt as a teenager when a bear sniffed around my tent. It is worse than the fear I felt at gunpoint on a Guatemalan highway. This fear grips me inside my spine and permeates my cells. Perhaps it is the expression of a biological imperative: my evolutionary function is to allow my genes to outlast me—to reproduce and then to keep my children alive until they too can reproduce.

In any event, this fear was, I realized, the cause of my inaction about a vasectomy.

The unspeakable possibility of losing my children was keeping me from calling Matt's office. It was not because I wanted to have the choice of conceiving different children if any of these should perish. Amy and I had discussed that terrible prospect and were in agreement that adoption would be the way we parented any children besides Gary, Kathryn, and Peter. No, somewhere inside me— in a place beyond reason and logic but not beyond the reach of the deathly wind on the mountain—was the idea that if my children died, I could make them over again. They would be born again as infants and would grow again as they had, again bestowing on us their blessedness. Perhaps intensity had burned the memories of how each arrived so deeply into my consciousness that somehow the events had escaped from chronology. The experiences seemed not part of the past, but a continuous, living fixture of the present. The arrivals of my children seemed to be perpetually occurring, and—somehow—they seemed repeatable.

When, watching over the children in their beds, this became clear to me, I was no longer hesitant to call the doctor's office.

Keeping two convoluted foot-long sperm ducts intact in my scrotum would not guarantee the safety of my children. Nothing could.

The morning of my vasectomy, Matt was in top form. He prompted Amy to breathe with me, "Huh, whew, huh, ththth. Huh, whew, huh, ththth." The procedure itself went off without a stitch—I mean, hitch. And he told me about his own vasectomy, which, as it turned out, he had just had done. It seems he didn't follow doctor's orders. Instead of taking it easy, he played racquetball the next day, ruptured something, and landed in bed for a week. He told his story slowly, with great humor, and by the time I stopped laughing, I had been cut out of the reproductive population. No shrinkage. No queasiness. Nothing.

Amy and I were packing up to go home before Matt told us the stinger. "Oh, by the way, guys, that won't work for two or three months. System's got to be flushed clean. So be careful, all right?"

All right, Doc. All right.

*chapter six*

# POLITICS

*April*

**TODAY IS THE TWENTY-FIFTH** Earth Day, and what am I doing? I am taking Gary shopping. Yep, we're heading out to engage in acts of wanton consumption. But it's not what you think, really. It's just, well, it's just the neighborhood. It has proved hard to sink tendrils into. Folks mostly keep to themselves and don't stop to chat or borrow a cup of sugar. This has left us puzzled and empty. We have a strong attachment to the Northwest, but still only shallow roots on our street.

And roots were the whole point. They were why Amy and I abandoned Washington, D.C., traversed the continent, and plunked ourselves down in Seattle, a place I had not lived in for more than a decade, and a place she had only visited. We did not come for the scenery, although we do not complain about it. From our house, tucked in a valley so deep that our television set picks up only two stations, we cannot see any of the vistas for which the Northwest is famous. But on the rare clear day, when we crest the hills in any direction, our eyes are assaulted by orchestral fanfares of water-forest-mountain.

We came here because of memories and hopes. We came because, in some inscrutable way, we had no other choice. The Philippine priestess had pitied me. She had appalled me with the realization that I was—for all my good intentions—a global vagabond. I was dis-placed. Indeed, by background, education, and taste I was a member of the shifting class of rootless professionals who efficiently oversee the juggernaut of business-as-usual. That my professional role was to be a critic hardly seemed to matter.

The only way out was to re-place myself, to install myself in the mundane particulars of a locale to which I had a bond—a bond that superseded, or preceded, all the abstract, cosmopolitan rationality trained into me in school and sharpened in the circus of international affairs. Coming home, I was racked with doubts about whether my decision made me a deserter; now I believe the decision was the most *radical* I have ever made. After all, radical comes from the Latin word for "root."

Still, here we are, swamped with the chores of childrearing and in a neighborhood that offers precious little by way of community togetherness. At times, it seems downright tough: we have heard gunfire on two occasions and belligerent domestic quarrels on a dozen. Gary found hypodermic needles in a nearby vacant lot, and once, when he was putting his bicycle away, he startled a cokehead thief who had snuck into our garage. I worry about Amy and the kids when I am away overnight.

Besides, despite our house's location right in town, we still have to get in the car too much. Our neighborhood, like many in Seattle, is residential monoculture. To get to Gary's school, the grocery store, the playground, or the library requires that we strap Peter and Kathryn into their car seats.

In one way we are deeply fortunate: we have kin. My sister's house is five blocks north of ours. My parents live a mile east. My mother's mother lives two miles west. And my father's mother lives five miles south. Amy's folks are so taken with their grandchildren that they keep coming back for longer and longer stays. And, amazingly, all these people get along. We visit each other several times a week.

But we want more. We want our children to grow up not only enveloped in extended family but also supported by a thick weave of relationships with diverse neighbors and friends. And, despite our decision to become endemic to this place, this weave is not weaving. The urge to flee is strong.

About a month ago, Amy found a three-bedroom apartment near my folks' place that seemed much better. She called me at the office. "Gary could bike to school. I could put the kids in the stroller and go to the grocery store, the beach, a great co-op preschool, or the playground. And you wouldn't have to worry because it's on the third floor of a locked building." When we looked at the money, though, these thoughts were crushed. If we sold the house, we would not have enough left after settling with the bank to pay the realtors, insurers, and tax collectors. And we were too strapped to chip in the difference from savings.

It was hard to accept. We spent three weeks in a mist of regret over the decision we had made to buy our current home. Motivated by the urge to nest, Amy said, we had uncritically accepted the images that permeate our culture, images of upstanding parents raising beaming children in spacious old houses on spacious green lots. "The whole white picket fence thing," she called it. "We got taken, and it just makes me crazy. We wanted a home, and instead we got a headache. Now look at us! We're spending our weekends cleaning gutters. *I just want to play with my children.*"

Last week, she called me at work again. "I can't stand talking about it anymore," she said. "Let's agree that we won't even discuss moving for a year. Then we'll be able to afford a move. And let's make the best of it in the meantime. We'll make it through and maybe things will get better. This neighborhood has potential. We've just gotta try harder."

I grudgingly conceded the wisdom of her plan. After all, I was the one who was always mouthing off about how we all had to learn to endure—meaning, according to the dictionary, to remain firm under hardship.

So today, the twenty-second of the month, Earth Day, I am attempting to follow her injunction. I am going to invest in a loom of community. We are going to buy a basketball hoop.

**THE PACIFIC NORTHWEST IS ALREADY** a global leader in reconciling people and nature. The region has wholeheartedly adopted recycling and spent millions of dollars on public transit, waste reduction, streambank protection, energy conservation, and the cleanup of polluted sites. Other hopeful examples of ingenuity, innovation, and positive change are abundant.

Yet things are still going the wrong way. Population is on a course toward quadrupling in a century. Energy consumption per capita and carbon dioxide emissions per capita are rising again, after dropping in the decade after 1973. In Canada and the United States overall—no figures are kept for the Northwest alone—rates of per capita consumption are high and either stable or rising for aluminum, fresh water, paper, plastic, steel, synthetic chemicals, and most other high-impact commodities.

Ecologist William Rees and a team of researchers at the University of British Columbia recently estimated that the typical North American—and Northwesterners hew to the norm—consumes each year resources equivalent to the annual yield from twelve acres of productive farm- and forestland. For all the world's people to consume at that rate, Rees and his colleagues calculated, three extra planets would be needed.

Thirty years ago, the things that the region is doing today might have been sufficient. Minor course corrections could once have produced a stable population, cities shaped to foster community rather than throughput, landscapes able to support both native species and human demands, and economic incentives designed to integrate ecological values. Now the region needs to slam on the brakes and turn around. Looked at without flinching, the current Northwest economy must be pronounced wildly, screamingly unsustainable. It cannot last. It will not last. If people do not recast it by choice, natural forces will likely dismantle it with pitiless disregard.

Compounding the gravity of the situation, the region's body politic is ill. Political discourse in much of the bioregion has devolved into fearmongering and scapegoating. Highly paid media consultants manipulate people's anxieties and prejudices—racism, sexism, homophobia, xenophobia—to keep them from perceiving common interests. Political parties have diminishing grass roots presence; they bring fewer voters into public life, groom fewer leaders, and do not hold those leaders accountable to an organized constituent base. Voter turnout is low in the U.S. Northwest: 20 percent of eligible voters was all it took to win a congressional seat in an off-year election in 1990. More Northwesterners now recycle than vote; indeed, more Northwesterners play the lottery than vote.

The face-to-face institutions of democracy are in disrepair. The latticework of voluntary organizations that once gave form and ballast to civil society is atrophying. Pressed for time, inundated with electronic entertainment, and separated from one another by rising distance and distrust, individuals are increasingly alone. They join fewer book groups, bowling leagues, churches, labor unions, mutual support societies, PTAs, YWCAs, and sewing circles. They identify themselves less with neighborhoods, workplaces, or communities of faith.

## April

I came to my belief in the power of basketball hoops early. When I was ten, my folks put up a backboard on the side of the house. It wasn't much of a court. It sloped, and the garage interfered with lay-ups on the left side. But overnight it became the neighborhood gathering place. Though I was bookish and shy, once that court went in, I was rarely at a loss for companionship. So perhaps it was inevitable that when Gary started coming home from school with nothing but playground games of hoops on his tongue, I began wandering outside in spare moments, scratching my head and looking for a ten-foot perch.

The best I have been able to come up with is the decorative green garden trellis over our puny driveway. It is two feet shy of regulation, and it puts the free throw line about a yard into the street. But it is high enough for the time being—Gary is not much over four feet—and it will allow lay-ups on either side. So this Earth Day morning, Gary and I have cracked the yellow pages in search of a cheap backboard and hoop that we can bolt to the parallel two-by-twelves overlooking the sidewalk.

"Dad, let's call Eagle," Gary suggests. "They have everything." Indeed. "More of Everything" is, I believe, the motto that beckons from the battlements of Eagle Hardware's concrete-and-steel bunker down in the ganglands of the Rainier Valley. It is not exactly my philosophy. But I'm curious. I dial.

"Hello! Eagle. How may I direct your call?" Chirpy voice.

"I'm looking for a basketball hoop."

"Just a moment, sir." Eagle Radio comes on the line, playing nonstop promotions.

"Hello. Eagle. How can I help?" Chirpy voice number two.

"I'm looking for a basketball hoop."

"Just a moment, sir." More Eagle Radio: New chemicals available for slug control. Get ready for barbecue season.

"Eagle. Were you looking for a basketball hoop?" Chirpy voice number three.

"Uh-huh."

"Sorry, sir. We don't stock them in the off-season."

I gloat, "Gary, Eagle doesn't have any." We try some sports shops and discover that new hoops with backboards start at $160.

Gary is getting despondent. He knows I don't have that kind of dough. "Maybe we could get a hoop without a backboard, Dad. I'm a pretty good shot."

"No, buddy, don't worry, what we need is a used one. Hey, what's the name of that place we took Mom's old karate gear?"

"Oh yeah! That Second Base place. Let's call them!"

We call them up. "Second Base." Normal human voice.

"Hi. I'm looking for a basketball hoop and backboard. Do you have any?"

"I think there's a few up in the attic. I dunno. Hey, the owner is across the street at the bathroom. Can you call back in five minutes?"

We call back. Yes, there are some hoops. Gary and I drive over the hill to the store, which is beside a soccer field where my team once won the city championship for ten-year-olds. We clamber up to the top floor. There, as Gary exclaims over the wooden snow-shoes, three-speed bicycles, and mildewed boxing gloves ("What's this, Dad? What's that for? Look, there's a life jacket!"), I turn the backboards over one at a time and compare their rears to the trellis in my head. At first, it doesn't look good. These hoops are arrayed for sloping roofs, vertical poles, and gymnasium walls.

"Will they work, Dad?"

"I'm not sure. We might have to make a lot of changes."

But Gary is not listening. He is crawling under a long table by the rear wall. "Look, Dad. What about this one?"

He has apparently found another one back under the lace-up ski boots. "Oh, buddy. It's probably broken or something. They probably put it under there for a reason."

"But would it work, Dad?"

I stoop and squint. Gary's got his head inside the black steel hoop. He's studying the board. "Check this out. PowerSlam! It's really cool." I hesitate for a moment, then crawl in after him, inadvertently crushing a boxed badminton set and overturning a rack of croquet mallets.

"Will it work, Dad? Will it work?"

"Maybe. I need to measure it." It looks good, but I don't want him to get his hopes up until I am sure. The previous owner had mounted the board on a pair of vertical two-by-fours. Bolts through these might attach perfectly to the trellis.

"Will it work, Dad? Will it work?"

I am manipulating the tape measure as quickly as I can, but have only one free hand. The other is propping the backboard up over my head.

"Will it work, Dad? Will it work?"

I sneeze. It's dusty under here. "I think so, buddy. I think we've got ourselves a basketball hoop." Gary pounces on me with one of his full-contact hugs. "Whoa, Gare. Easy!" I sneeze again.

**THERE IS A YAWNING CHASM** between what is politically possible and what is achingly necessary. Ecological pricing, population stabilization, and other requisites of sustainability are, politically speaking, preposterous idealism. The short-term likelihood that any government in the region will shift from income, sales, or property taxes to resource and land-value taxes is nil. Nor is there hope of swift progress against the anti-ecological subsidies that riddle tax and spending codes, such as fire-sale prices on publicly owned timber and grass, deeply discounted hydropower rates for aluminum smelters and irrigators, and the billion-dollar giveaways under U.S. hard-rock mining law.

This is true because advocates for the long-term future are up against something devilishly difficult to fight: they are up against a worldview.

Everyone operates from a worldview. It is a set of simplifying assumptions, an informal theory, a picture of how the world works. Worldviews are rarely brought out into the light of day, so people are not usually aware of them. They sit down deep in human consciousness, quietly shaping reactions to new ideas and information, guiding decisions, and ordering expectations for the future. Often worldviews are internally inconsistent; in fact, they usually contain parts that are just plain false. Still, their historical and psychological roots are deep enough to prevent easy uprooting.

In the Pacific Northwest, as elsewhere in North America, the commonly held worldview is an old one from the frontier. It comes from the rearview mirror, reflecting times when the world was big and people were few. Through this lens, the world looks empty and indestructible. The environment and human community appear subordinate to the economy, as things worth protecting if you can afford to after paying the bills. In this worldview, production looks like the creation of tangible objects that meet basic human needs. Resource industries—logging, farming, mining, energy production—seem to be the locomotive that drags the entire economy along. This view is familiar and comforting, and demonstrably false.

The emerging worldview, held as yet by a minority of citizens, is grounded in the reality of the present: a time when the world is small and people are many. Through this lens, the world looks full and fragile. The economy and human community are subsets of the broader ecosystem. Production is the provision of desired amenities, services, and qualities, physical and nonphysical, to people enmeshed in communities. The pursuit of quality of life— through the application of human ingenuity—is the locomotive of the economy. This set of assumptions is new, unfamiliar, and accurate. Because few people yet see the world in its terms, the majority of citizens misconstrue their interests. They do not see their interests as tied up with those of forested watersheds or as threatened by climate change.

Worldviews are parts of culture and change over time. They are influenced by what parents teach their children, by what young people learn in school, by what adults learn from peers, books, and social institutions such as churches. They are also influenced by mass media. The politics of sustainability, therefore, is about changing not only laws and habits but also—even primarily— worldviews. The challenge is to change them quickly enough.

Much of what needs doing is plain old grass-roots organizing. But other methods of social change have their place as well, including everything from big-stakes lawsuits to consensus-based community dialogues. The main thing is to root politics in place. The affinity for home permits a broad reach in the process of coalition building. It allows strange bedfellows to find one another. It allows worldviews to surface and change. It allows politics to remain an exercise in hope. And it allows the unthinkable to happen sometimes. This, after all, is the Northwest, a place with a history of audacious undertakings fueled by little more than idealism, ingenuity, and determination.

## April

Back home, we take the hoop from the trunk of the car and attract a swarm of children. From the yellow house four doors over come Marcus and his half-brother Jerry. From the corner come Daron and his brother Devon. From across the street come Sam and his half-sister Sara. From some place farther off come Larissa and half a dozen others whose names Gary, and therefore I, do not know.

"Whachew doin' wiff dat basku'baw hoop?" Marcus asks. When we first moved to the neighborhood, Marcus, then three, greeted Gary with a barrage of rocks. Now he comes and knocks on the door, asking Gary to come out and play. He is four and, to Amy's and my minds, gets far too little supervision. We worry about him.

"We're gonna put it up," Gary says. Unlike me, he has never been shy. "You can play here, but you have to ask my permission. Dad, doesn't he have to ask my permission?"

"If you're playing here, he should ask and you should usually say yes. If no one's around, he can play."

"When I'm here, you have to ask my permission. We're going to put it up right away. Right, Dad?"

"Soon as we can. I hope we have some bolts."

"Hey, Jerry, don't you guys have a ladder at your house?" I know that they do. I've seen it lying in the side yard. But I'm hesitant to knock on the door and ask for it. You see, Tyrone, the mayor of our block, has put ideas in my head about the folks in the yellow house.

Tyrone, who lives across the street from us, told us a few days after we moved in, "Oh, you all are nice folks. It's a blessing!" He lowered his voice conspiratorially. "You want to watch yourself with those folks. That's a drug house." He was looking at the yellow house where Jerry and Marcus live—the one where I know a ladder lies in disuse. "They're all on dope. You don't want to get mixed up with 'em. Nothin' but trouble. Stay away."

We didn't know if we should believe him. The large clan in the house did seem scragglier and less communicative than average and they kept odd hours, but they kept their yard in good shape, and Marcus and Jerry and the other kids who congregated there seemed well enough fed and clothed. We did not want to prejudge them, and who knew about Tyrone? At the time, we thanked him for the advice and filed it away for further investigation.

Since then, enough police cars have stopped at the house, and we've noticed enough strange occurrences, to make us think Tyrone may be right. But we aren't sure. Be that as it may: while the whole house may have a monkey on its back, it also has a ladder in the side yard. And I need one.

"Gary, why don't you watch the hoop while I go fetch a ladder?" I walk over to the house with ten-year-old Jerry, who is reveling in being needed by a grown-up. He goes inside, emerges in a moment, and leads me along the side of the house to the extension ladder. There he exchanges quick words with a man in work clothes whom I've never seen before: "Grandpa says he can take the ladder." "It's not his ladder," the man says, eyeing me suspiciously. I realize that there are two rental apartments down here, tucked out of view of the street. No wonder so many people come and go from this address. Maybe they're not coming to shoot up drugs. Maybe they're just visiting.

I am not sure what is going on between Jerry and this man, so I play dumb. "Hey, how ya doin'? I'm putting up a backboard over at my place so the kids on this street can shoot hoops. Trouble is, I don't have a ladder. Do you suppose I could borrow this one?" For some reason, my palms are sweating. Damn that Tyrone.

He looks at me, smiling cockeyed, and says, "You're puttin' up a hoop?! Yeah, take the ladder."

I press my advantage. "My name's Alan," I say, extending my hand. "I'm Michael," he says, shaking it. "Nice to meet you. Let me know if you need anything else." In later weeks, Michael and I begin to wave to each other. I often see him working on the house. He is industrious. Who knows if he or anybody else in the house has a drug habit? That's none of my affair.

I have my ladder. I have met my neighbor. Gary calls, "Yay! We can do it!" as I approach.

TEN GANGLY MEN, THEIR EYES lined from constant squinting, fold themselves onto benches on a cramped Fraser River dock on the edge of Vancouver. Paul Kandt is speaking from a notebook that has lost its cover. He is a heavy plug of a man, his long hair back in a ponytail. The men at the ends of the benches must lean forward to hear his halting words. He is giving an obligatory reading of the minutes of the previous dock meeting of the United Fishermen and Allied Workers Union, Local Five.

Mae Burrows, the only woman on the float, is fingering a beaded Indian bracelet and studying the weathered faces around her, awaiting her turn to speak. She has come a long way with these men, keeping them engaged in one of the Northwest's most successful coalition-building efforts—a campaign so successful that it serves as a model of organizing for sustainability. But she still cannot predict their reactions. And today she has bad news.

Mae glances upstream toward a looming pulp mill and downstream toward a gravel pit. The river is even heavier with sediment today than usual, and it's littered with debris from the log booms and mills farther inland. Since her childhood, spent floating in inner tubes and plunging off bridges, Mae has never tired of watching the river's daily moods. It feels strong underfoot, under the floating dock section that is Local Five's union hall. In a matter of weeks, she knows, the early Stuarts will begin passing—sockeye salmon bound for the Stuart River. To get there, they will travel five hundred miles up the winding Fraser and another fifty up its third largest tributary, the Nechako. The Stuarts are one breeding run among the dozens that make the Fraser the greatest salmon stream on Earth.

Onshore, things look about the same as the last time she was here, a few weeks ago. The union's sheds still look like a hobo camp—bare wood and tar paper set among the blackberry brambles. Beyond them, four lanes of traffic bulge toward the dock to avoid a housing subdivision.

Paul Kandt, the man with the ponytail, has led the group through several agenda items.

"Now, everybody here knows Mae." He nods in her direction. "She wanted to give us an update."

Mae gets to her feet. Her sleeveless top and polka-dot leggings stand out among the coveralls and visored caps. "I'm afraid there's bad news on the Nechako." Some of the men cross their arms. Most of them are studying the sun-bleached planks of the dock.

Mae does political work for the union. She advocates for healthy fish habitat—for rivers that are clean, cold, and wet. In the process, she comes up against some of the most powerful industries in the province. The fishermen are used to bad news from Mae.

A few of them appear to be keeping their heads down, bracing for a gale.

But Mae starts slowly, hooking them before she touches the reel. "In January, all of us in the fishing community were all happy and everything when Harcourt [the premier of British Columbia] went on TV and announced that government was canceling the Kemano Completion Project." Heads nod slightly. Paul is watching her.

The Kemano Completion Project is a water diversion project spearheaded by Alcan Aluminum Ltd. In 1950, Alcan dammed the Nechako at a site about halfway up the province—some three hundred miles from Vancouver. The river pooled westward behind the dam, flooding 170 square miles of river valley and rising above the mouth of a ten-mile-long tunnel Alcan was boring westward through the Coast Range. Roughly half of the river's water was soon flushing through the tunnel to the Pacific rather than running down the length of the Fraser to its delta near Vancouver. At the outlet of the tunnel, a place named Kemano, Alcan installed hydro-electric turbines. From Kemano, it strung high-tension wires north over a mountain pass to Kitimat, on an inlet of the Pacific. And at Kitimat, Alcan built a smelter where it could turn alumina barged from Jamaica or Australia into aluminum to sell in Japan and other Pacific nations. The entire complex, commonly known as Kemano I, was among the most ambitious engineering feats ever accomplished in British Columbia. It was a monument to Northwestern idealism, as informed by the old worldview. Unfortunately, it also jeopardized the salmon that spawned in or passed through the Nechako, drowned the territory of the Cheslatta Indians, and constituted a massive resource grab. The special legislative act that enabled the venture stipulated that whatever share of Nechako water Alcan was diverting in 1999 would be Alcan's forever.

In 1979, Alcan proposed a second tunnel, more turbines, and other earthworks that would send much of the remaining Nechako water through the Kemano cutoff. This endeavor is called the Kemano Completion Project, or just Kemano II.

"And maybe some of you were at the union convention when Harcourt got a standing ovation and he was going on about the Fraser River being the heart and soul of the province." Three men meet Mae's hard brown eyes.

"Well, it's five months later—three, maybe five weeks 'til the end of the legislative session—and there's been no legislation. All we've got is a press release! They haven't done their paperwork." They are hooked. Mae gives a tug on the line.

"Well, I'm sorry. That just won't do." Mae speaks in Canadian brogue. Sorry comes out "soar-ee"; do erupts from the dome of her palate.

"I'm just shitting, guys. I'm starting to worry that we got duped. There's been no legislation, and what's become clear to me is that they don't *have* any legislation."

She pauses, then hauls hard on the pole. "If they don't get it done this session, it'll go 'til after the elections.

"Then we could be starting over again with a new government." They all know what that means: a return to outsider status. The ruling New Democratic Party has labor roots. The Liberal Party, the official opposition, called for canceling the Kemano Completion Project before the NDP announced its own plans to cancel the project, but the Liberals' roots are in the business community and their commitment is untested. The third-ranked Reform Party, meanwhile, speaks for resource extraction industries at every opportunity.

"Aw, it's *politics*," fisherman Mark Pretunia says, spitting the word as if he has swallowed one of the mosquitoes buzzing the dock. "We're already dead."

"I thought we were dead before on this thing," Paul disagrees. "Maybe we're not." Paul fished for months with a "Stop Kemano II" sign on his prow.

Mae is encouraging the men to get on the phone. Referring to members of the legislative assembly, she urges, "If anybody knows an MLA, now's the time to call. Or just call up the radio and the TV. Why aren't they covering this?"

"They'll say we need the aluminum jobs, but Kemano II isn't about aluminum. Alcan has cut its smelter payroll from two thousand to fourteen hundred by changing technology. It's about electricity. Alcan makes a million dollars a month selling power to BC Hydro." BC Hydro is the provincially owned electric utility.

"It's feeding power into the grid. With Kemano II, they'll be making seven to eight million a month. And they're taking it out of the fish," Mae says. "They'll be taking 87 percent of the water out of the Nechako, and they'll have rights to do so in perpetuity. The scientific report is very clear: the Fraser is going to heat up to where the salmon get sick, go crazy, or just cook."

A young Asian fisherman is getting angry. "They're making a million a month and, when they're done, we're going to get the hoop."

The conversation continues, the fishers growing steadily more angry. Their statements suggest they have come to see the world as full and fragile. As Mae takes her leave, she makes a final plea. "We've come so far for this river of ours, guys. We've just got to get in their faces and make them do the paperwork."

After the dock meeting, Mae tells the story of the fight against Kemano II, a long and convoluted tale of jab and parry, feint and counterfeint.

Organized opposition began almost immediately after Alcan announced its plans for the Completion Project in 1978. The Cheslatta Nation—displaced by Kemano I—and the Carrier Sekani Tribal Council to which it belongs were among the early opponents. Non-native residents of the Nechako Valley also picked up the banner early on. Lawsuits flew. In 1987, Alcan, the province, and the federal government—which has jurisdiction over oceanic fisheries including salmon—signed an agreement behind closed doors. It allowed the project to proceed without further environmental review. Construction began. More lawsuits ensued. By 1991, aluminum prices had plunged, and Alcan—a Canadian-based corporation with operations in more than a dozen countries—was suddenly drowning in red ink. Losses ran into the hundreds of millions of dollars. Alcan halted construction.

In 1993, under the NDP government, a provincial commission undertook a review of Kemano II. The mandate was narrowly circumscribed, but the commission's eighty-seven days of public hearings heated up opposition like a pressure cooker. Most British Columbians learned for the first time where the Nechako River was, how aluminum was made, and what the 1987 settlement said. The more they learned, the less they liked the Completion Project. It became the stuff of talk radio. In late 1994 the Liberals, sniffing political pay dirt, called for cancellation. In January 1995, Premier Mike Harcourt did an about-face and announced that the Kemano Completion Project was rotten to the core. If he could not find a way to nullify the 1987 agreement, he declared, he would ask the legislative assembly to simply outlaw the project.

In 1991, around the time construction ground to a halt, the fishers union hired Mae to fight Kemano II. She became the only full-time campaigner on the issue outside the Nechako River valley, and the principal campaigner working in the part of the province where most of the population was. By default, that put a trade union in a leadership role in dealing with one of the most important environmental conflicts in the Pacific Northwest. Why did fishermen care?

"The Nechako is hundreds of miles from anywhere. Up there, there are lots of fish and no fishermen. But fishermen in Sointula, on Vancouver Island, catch Nechako-bound salmon. Twenty percent of the fish canned in Prince Rupert, on the mainland coast, is Nechako-bound salmon. There are thirty thousand jobs in the fishing industry in B.C. And every fifth salmon in the Fraser River swims up the Nechako—to say nothing of the sturgeon and oolichans. This is a big fish issue," says Mae.

For Mae, the Nechako quickly became a matter of pride in place. It was by appealing to pride that she and others helped to turn the tide. The thing that most rankled her about the deal was the thought of a multinational corporation—or anyone else—owning a river in her province.

Growing up poor in the small town of Haney, she would wait impatiently on summer evenings for her dad to get home from whatever work he had at the time—he tried his hand at everything from carpentry to mail delivery. When he came, she would plead for a picnic on the nearby Alouette River, a tributary of the Fraser west of Vancouver. "Dad would say, 'The only thing that's free is the river!' And off we would go."

How did the Kemano opponents elevate the Nechako to a matter of provincial significance? Mae says she and her cohorts had no special knowledge or skills, just persistence. And that is good news for advocates all over the Northwest.

"Organizing is like composting. At first, you have slimy scraps of this and that, and you just keep putting 'em in and mixing 'em around, and putting 'em in and mixing 'em around. Sooner or later, like magic, it gets hot. You keep mixing it and the next thing you know you've got this rich, beautiful, fertile soil."

"That's what we did: we mixed it up. When we started this we had nothing—I mean nothing. The elected people wouldn't talk to us. The media wouldn't give us the time of day. So we talked to ourselves, and we talked to anybody who would listen. We went anywhere. I spoke at dock meetings of fishermen up and down the coast and on Vancouver Island. I spoke at rod and gun clubs, fly clubs, trappers organizations, environmental groups, native groups, schools. Others did the same. Anywhere you could go to be in anybody's face, we did it. That was the theory. We called in to talk radio shows. Later, we got the province's biggest talk show host exercised about the issue. We worked the unions, from the locals up to the district labor councils and on to the provincial labor council. We got a resolution calling for cancellation, and we got it over the objections of the union that represents the smelter workers. We went to the municipal councils. These guys are at your swimming pool or your day care center. They can't ignore you. We got them to take municipal positions for cancellation, which we took to the provincial body of the municipal councils. We worked the NDP constituency meetings and the NDP convention and got the same. So the party was saying, 'Kill it,' while the folks in office were talking about 'difficult choices' and 'the investment climate.'"

She and the others found, in the tangle of issues surrounding Kemano II, "something for everybody." For outdoors lovers, there were the effects on angling. For environmentalists, there were the ecological impacts. For the Left, there was the corporate control angle. For the Right, there was the issue of huge government subsidies—property tax holidays, corporate tax deferrals, and water-use rates one-tenth of the provincial average. For labor unions, there were the jobs: more in fishing than in aluminum and electricity. For farmers and ranchers, there was the precedent: because Alcan had first call on the water, there sometimes was not a drop left for irrigation. For scientists and academics, there was the politicization of research: federal officials muzzled the fisheries scientists who had been studying the Nechako before the 1987 settlement. And for everybody, there was the back-room deal making and subversion of legally required environmental reviews. Not only was Alcan getting a river, it was not subject to the same rules as everybody else.

The grassroots campaign against the Kemano Completion Project is a textbook example of how to organize for sustainability. Across the Northwest, hundreds of other grass-roots campaigns are going on. Those that succeed usually develop according to Mae's composting theory. They start with scraps, and then just keep gathering and mixing until the heap heats up.

That has been the key for Peter Cervantes-Gautschi of the Workers Organizing Committee (WOC) in Portland, Oregon, which has been organizing the janitorial and housekeeping staffs of Portland's hotels. Among the chief concerns of this labor organization is its workers' heavy exposure to hazardous industrial cleaners.

WOC is a leader in the Northwest's nascent environmental justice movement, which springs from poor and minority communities that have suffered the most from pollution. In the Pacific Northwest, as across North America, "low-wage workers are disproportionately exposed to toxics in their lives," says Peter. The darker your skin and the lower your income, the more likely you are to breathe unhealthy air, drink contaminated water, and work with toxic substances. You are also more likely to live near a hazardous waste site but far from a park or beach. And you are more likely to have lead paint on your windowsills and loud, dangerous traffic outside your window. "For us," says Peter, "environmental protection is about protecting our bodies from poison."

But poor and minority communities are just beginning to organize themselves to demand justice in these arenas. So Peter spends much of his time, as Mae Burrows does, talking to whoever will listen, going anywhere, doing whatever is necessary to deliver the message. "Regardless of who is in public office," Peter says, "if we can bring the facts and the issues to the public, we'll get enough support to win."

Up and down the rainy coast, and inland to timberline in the Rockies, dozens of other Northwesterners are organizing for ends that, whether explicitly or not, line up with sustainability. Along the way, the worldviews of those touched by the campaigns shift. All of these people know that persistence pays, that boldness brings its own support. They feel the power of place lurking beneath the surface of normal political discourse. Darlene Madenwald, veteran campaign leader for the Washington Environmental Council, speaks for them all when she says, "If you think you're too small to be effective, you have never been in bed with a mosquito."

In the fight against Kemano II, no final resolution is in sight, yet the outcome is all but determined. The province, the national government, and Alcan are wrangling over who owes what to whom, but the political will is against Kemano II. And that is the result of sheer tenacity on the part of its opponents. "The movement's success consisted of just picking away for fourteen years," says Louise Burgener, a resident of the town of Vanderhoof and member of the Nechako Neyenkut Society, a local conservation group.

Pat Moss, chair of the Rivers Defense Coalition, which coordinated opposition groups, contends that victory came because Kemano became more than an "environmental" issue. It became a people issue, a British Columbian issue—an issue of home. At different times, the critical actions came from a trade union, an Indian band, a trapper, local business owners, a conservative talk show host, and government scientists. And it was the coalition of these and others that heated up the compost.

Most twists and turns of the plot are ultimately unimportant. What matters is the two lessons about politics that Mae learned in the process: First, politicians aren't like other people. They are more like weather vanes. You cannot talk a weather vane into changing directions. You just have to make a lot of wind.

"Lobbying was one insult after another," she says. "You talk to the political people and they don't care. Mike Harcourt didn't wake up one morning and realize that the Fraser was the heart and soul of the province. That's bullshit. He read the polls. We got the public will. When Harcourt announced cancellation, it was the best polling week he ever had."

Second, in politics, savvy and persistence sometimes count more than money does. "The most delicious irony," Mae says, "is that Alcan's got platoons of slick P.R. people and big budgets for TV and all that. All we have is our telephones and fax machines. A lot of this is me and my cronies padding around our kitchens in our pajamas feeding our fax machines."

## April

While I am up the ladder working a bit and brace to prepare the trellis for the backboards, Tyrone crosses the street to see what I am up to. Gary, who is holding the ladder and continuing to lord it over the other children, tells him, "We got a basketball hoop!"

"It's a blessing!" says Tyrone. This is what he has said to me on most occasions. I always agree with him from my side of the street, and that is about the extent of our conversations. I am surprised that he has crossed the street. I find myself explaining, defensive about the ladder, "Gary and the other kids oughta have a place to play ball."

He nods and smiles, "It's a blessing!"

"Yes, it is," I say. He is silent. I assume our conversation is over. I don't want him to start in on the yellow house right now, so I turn back to the task and again press my forehead on the base of the brace. I have discovered no other way to keep the worn bit true. I grind away, feeling each rotation in my spine, wondering if I should call around for a power drill.

Suddenly, I hear Tyrone again. He has been watching me. "You know? I been here forty years. Got here in 1955. And we've never had a basketball hoop." This is strange. At least he's not bad-mouthing anybody. "This street's been through some bad times. Crime, drugs, you name it. But times were better before." I keep puffing and straining, trying to keep the bit chewing on wood fiber, and not sure what to say.

"I bought my house for four thousand dollars, and interest was only 4 percent. But I still had a hard time making the payments. Fifty dollars a month. In those days, I was only making a dollar-fifty an hour. I was washing cars at Cadillac Lane. I'd go out after work and rake leaves in Broadmoor to pay the bills."

Why, I wonder, is he telling me this? The old guy is talking more than he has all year. I had written him off. What has inspired his sudden bout of neighborly recollections? I pause to let the blood back into my forehead and try to keep up my end of the neighborliness. Tyrone is standing with his sandals planted just inside the key. He is squinting up at me, his ebony skin setting off the brass medallion at his neck. Across the street, his old green Lincoln Continental and his old red Escort are both running. As on most mornings, Tyrone has come out to wash and tune them. While he is out, I realize, he must be keeping an eye on the block.

"But I enjoyed those days. I enjoyed them all. My wife and I would take all the kids on the block down to Madison Beach." The only times I have seen his wife were when an ambulance came to take her to the hospital and when it brought her back. Before the ambulance came, I did not even know he was married. "We had picnics and barbecues. We were always going to the park, taking our kids. Just like you folks. It's a blessing!" I had not known he was a father.

Dizzied by the flood of socializing, I inquire tentatively, "How many kids you got?"

"Two. Girls. They're both out of college now. They went to college in Louisiana, where I come from." I had no idea. My father, who is approximately Tyrone's age, also grew up in Louisiana, although on the other side of the color bar. Feeling awkward about all the eye contact, I start drilling another hole.

"You know my dad's from New Orleans?"

"Is that right? It's a blessing! Your father drives the, uh, white Horizon, right?" Tyrone obviously knows more about us than we do about him.

"Yeah, that's him. I'll introduce you. You old guys can talk gumbo."

He laughs softly.

"It's gonna be good for these kids to have a hoop. Maybe bring things back a bit. It's a blessing! It's a blessing!" He still has the faraway sound in his voice. We fall quiet and listen to the dull grind of the bit. Gary charges off down the sidewalk with the other children, tired of watching me play ram with my cranium.

"You know?" His voice is closer, hushed and tense now. "They had a raid." He is, I presume, speaking of the yellow house. Amy saw police cars there a week or two ago. I drill harder. "That old woman, she broke parole. She's back in penitentiary." How does Tyrone know so much just from washing his cars each morning? I am pondering this and pressing hard when the drill bites air through the last hole. With an embarrassing thud, the brace bottoms out against the trellis. I rub my forehead and try to act nonchalant. "Is that right?" I ask as I back down Michael's ladder.

My work being done for the moment, I hurry inside to gather bolts for the next stage. When I come back out, I look down the street at little Gary playing on the parking strip with six or eight other children. And I look across the street at Tyrone, who has returned to his morning automotive rituals, and the world shifts a few degrees. Is our neighborhood unfriendly, or am I unfriendly?

Maybe I have been the one who has failed to weave community. I have never crossed the street to inquire about Tyrone's cars, or his family, or whether he could lend us a cup of sugar. I am always in too much of a rush—to the park, to the bus stop, to the airport— to just stand near him and watch him work. I never even warned him about the hypodermic needle in the vacant lot or the burglar in the garage. I do not know his last name or his wife's name or his phone number. I have never invited him in for a glass of iced tea or to take a tour of our house—a new house that faces his on the street where he has lived since before I was born.

Community, I am beginning to understand, is made through a skill I have never learned or valued: the ability to pass time with people you do not and will not know well, talking about nothing in particular, with no end in mind, just to build trust, just to be sure of each other, just to be neighborly. A community is not something that you *have*, like a camcorder or a breakfast nook. No, it is something you *do*. And you have to do it all the time.

**BY THE TIME THE SUN** reaches its zenith on the last Tuesday in June, two hundred cars are already awaiting their drivers on the desolate asphalt plain encircling the Wild Horse Gaming Resort. The drivers are inside, beyond the decorative tomahawks and war-painted caricatures, feeding their paychecks into three hundred slot machines. When they emerge again, walking out past the clichéd Indian motifs, most of them will be poorer. When they return to their homes scattered among the oversized fields of wheat and wool or nestled in the nearby town of Pendleton, Oregon, they will leave behind them an Indian war chest fortified for a wild-eyed bid at sustainability—and one that might just work.

The Wild Horse Gaming Resort belongs to the Confederated Tribes of the Umatilla Reservation. "We're using the casino to raise money to sue the government," says Donald G. Sampson, the resolute thirty-four-year-old tribal chairman.

"We've tried to work with the federal government and state agencies for the past 150 years. They've been responsible for all the regulation and all the management" of the tribe's cultural mainstay, the salmon. And they have regulated and managed the salmon almost into extinction. In the Columbia Basin, only one-fortieth of the original wild salmon still return.

"If it requires us to drop the big one, we're going to. We have so much at stake." Donald's sad brown eyes do not waver as he gazes across his desk in the plywood-walled tribal offices a few miles from the casino. He has turned off his lights to reduce his dependence on the Bonneville Power Administration and the U.S. Army Corps of Engineers.

"To drop the big one" means to file a suit in U.S. District Court. It is to charge that, by shepherding the Columbia's mighty aquatic herds toward the same precipice over which the buffalo tumbled a century ago, the federal government has violated the treaty it signed with Donald's people in 1855. It is the big one because legal precedents suggest that such a suit might succeed. It is the big one because it would put the tribes in the driver's seat. They could dictate terms for the management of the Columbia Basin's dams, diversions, spillways, and fish ladders—the multibillion-dollar infrastructure that, in these parts, is referred to simply as "the hydrosystem." Federal judges, unlike all other makers of public policy, are not limited by political palatability.

Of course, to drop the big one would also be to incur the wrath of every farmer, rancher, smelter hand, barge pilot, and ratepayer from Yellowstone to the deep blue sea. Indians, Donald included, might get shot at. So he is none too anxious to do it. He and his people, and their fellow Columbia Basin treaty tribes, have preferred to work through the labyrinth of federal, state, and local agencies that collectively supervise the hydrosystem.

The Umatilla tribes have, over the decades, looked optimistically to each white generation's answer to dwindling salmon numbers: the New Dealers' Bonneville Power Administration, the early seventies' Endangered Species Act, the early eighties' Northwest Power Planning Council, and, overlapping with these, the bewildering array of commissions, task forces, consultative groups, blue ribbon panels, and regional compacts that have swirled through the Northwest states in response to the disappearance of the watery migrants.

The tribes have used the federal support guaranteed them in their treaties to hire lawyers to keep track of these gyrating institutional dances. They have spent years in meetings and hearings. They have commented on hundreds of draft plans and watershed blueprints, each the size of a telephone book. (Indeed, down the hall from Donald's office, staff attorney Carl Merkle is hauling columns of these phone books from his cubicle; the fire marshal has cited him for stockpiling combustibles.)

In desperation, Donald even appealed directly to the president, urgently requesting that Bill Clinton "declare a STATE OF EMERGENCY in the Columbia River Basin to prevent the extinction of additional salmon runs. . . . In a few weeks, juvenile Snake River spring/chinook, listed as endangered under the Endangered Species Act, will begin their journey to the sea." For them, it was to be the last good year. From more than seven million outmigrants, the number of juveniles will likely drop to half a million two years from now. *Tell the Corps of Engineers to throw open the floodgates*, the young chairman pleaded of the young president. Let the river run like a river to carry the young fish to sea. Don't let the corps continue putting them in barges. The president did not respond.

And so, having tried everything else in defense of his place's totemic creature, Donald Sampson is about to meet with the tribal board of trustees to "see how much money we can get out of the casino for treaty rights litigation."

"According to our ancestors, the salmon were put here to help us live." Donald is explaining why salmon running up the river matter to the sixteen hundred Cayuse, Umatilla, and Walla Walla Indians who share the Umatilla Reservation. In the beginning of the world, tribal culture teaches, the salmon "were like us, but they were selected to become the salmon people. We lived together for a long time: seven hundred generations." Donald's neck is collared by symmetrical obsidian-dark braids that meet at his solar plexus. So do his palms, which he is pressing together unconsciously as he searches for words to express this interspecies kinship.

"Salmon was the central part of our economy, central part of our religion, central part of our culture." He speaks with a restrained, dignified passion that he may have absorbed at his father's knee; his father is traditional chief of the Walla Walla.

"I fished on these rivers. I fished on the Columbia with a couple of grandpas. I fished with my father, my uncles, in all these tributaries." He, like his father before him, passed his manhood rite on the river: weaving a net, forming a gaff hook, catching his first great chinook, and presenting it as an offering to the community. He thus became "a provider" and knew where he "fit in our community." Now his own sons and daughter may never have this opportunity. The fish are almost gone. This spring, the Umatilla tribes and their counterparts on three other reservations—the Yakama, Nez Percé, and Warm Springs—agreed, for the sake of the fish, to limit themselves to six hundred spring chinook: six hundred swimmers for seventeen thousand people. It was not even enough to give everybody a taste at the first salmon ceremonies, sacrosanct rituals of thanksgiving that indigenous Northwesterners have performed for hundreds, perhaps thousands, of years.

"What if we said to the Catholic Church, 'You can't give out bread or wine because we don't have it for you anymore?' It's the same thing for us. We can't practice our religion."

In the end, wild-spawning salmon matter so much because they define identity. As an Indian, Donald says, "Sure, you can go to the store, you can get a hamburger, a pizza, but you lose that connection to where it comes from. You lose [the understanding] that salmon comes from a river . . . you lose that connection to this earth. That's what a lot of people in this country have already lost. . . . There's no connection between the food you get on your table and where it comes from." Lacking their distinctive communion with the salmon people, Indian people become half people.

Fifteen years ago, he remembers being on the banks of the Umatilla with an assembly of officials, discussing the possibility of restoring wild salmon to the river, which is the main watercourse on the reservation. "All the biologists from all the agencies said, 'It can't be done.' We said, 'No, we can do it. We have to do it.'

"In the Lewis and Clark journals, there were records of our tribes sitting at the mouth of the Umatilla waiting for the salmon to return. There were thousands upon thousands of salmon coming up the Umatilla. You could walk across their backs."

But between 1914 and 1960, the Umatilla was, as it is delicately phrased, "dewatered"—irrigators sucked it dry. The spring chinook, fall chinook, and coho salmon died. Only their cousins, the steelhead trout, survived; they travel in winter, when the Umatilla still runs.

The tribe began working aggressively to restore the salmon population in the Umatilla. It cut deals for water, pressed for policy reforms, mended degraded habitat, and studied fishing regulations. But, most important, "we started putting fish in the river before all the problems were fixed. We knew when they came back it would continue the pressure on everybody. The first year there were only a few salmon. Now a couple hundred have come back to spawn, next year a couple thousand."

And so, having tasted success on the little Umatilla, the Confederated Tribes are ready to take on the Big River.

It sounds ludicrous: three shrunken, tattered tribes on a federally funded Indian reservation setting terms for the operation of what are arguably the largest waterworks anywhere. But look backward.

Three of the most dramatic, fundamental shifts toward the sustainable management of natural resources in the history of the Northwest were the actions not of elected officials but of U.S. District Court judges. Legal challenges, even ones that defy credulity, sometimes succeed. Political winds don't affect them. Only precedents do.

In March 1994, district court judge Malcolm Marsh rejected the analysis of the National Marine Fisheries Service (NMFS)—called a "biological opinion"—of the effects of hydrosystem operations on endangered salmon. Marsh concluded that NMFS's decision-making process was "too heavily geared towards a status quo that has allowed all forms of river activity to proceed in a deficit situation—that is, relatively small steps, minor improvements and adjustments—when the situation literally cries out for a major overhaul."

Look further back. In the spring of 1991, district court judge Bill Dwyer cut off four-fifths of proposed timber sales on federal land west of the Cascades and decried "a deliberate and systematic refusal by the Forest Service and the Fish and Wildlife Service to comply with the laws protecting wildlife." Again, a fundamental shift. The galloping auction of centuries-old groves was slowed to a walk, and government foresters began to put habitat integrity and species diversity before board feet.

To really see the implications, look even further back. In the midseventies, Judge George Boldt redistributed half of the fish catch and half of the fish management authority to treaty tribes around Puget Sound, redistributing wealth and realigning power with the stroke of a pen. That action partly explains why Puget Sound salmon runs are in better shape than those elsewhere in California, Idaho, Oregon, or Washington. In the wake of Boldt's decision, there was nearly a revolution among white fishermen. State Attorney General Slade Gorton, now a U.S. senator, howled all the way to the Supreme Court. But he lost. The highest court affirmed that Indians get half the fish. They share authority over fisheries management with the state. None of the more recent legal challenges to these principles made any headway either. In fact, the principles have been further entrenched, and even extended beyond salmon to shellfish on private tidelands.

Here is the stinger. The Umatilla tribes, like all the Columbia Basin tribes, signed treaties just months after the Puget Sound tribes did. They signed treaties with the same U.S. emissary as did the Puget Sound tribes, a punctilious army general named Isaac I. Stevens, who signed up almost every band between the Olympic coast and the Rocky Mountains in the space of eight months. And they signed treaties almost identical to those of the Puget Sound tribes, in which they renounced their claims to most of their land but reserved for themselves smaller areas of land—"reservations"—and undiminished rights to continue fishing forever where and how they always had. If the Puget Sound tribes are entitled to share management authority over the fisheries to which they have reserved their rights, should not the Columbia Basin tribes share such authority, too? If the tribes reserved their rights to fish as they always had, are they not entitled to a fishery undiminished by federal action?

In the long run, Donald Sampson believes his tribe is entitled, as he wrote in a letter to the National Marine Fisheries Service, not merely to salmon populations that are off the endangered species list, but to "healthy, viable populations sufficient for sustainable Indian harvest." And not just for existing runs but for those presently extirpated.

It sounds like a pipe dream. Restore all the salmon runs that used to exist? Return them to a condition that would allow Indians to harvest large numbers? Why not just call for tearing down all the dams in the Columbia River Basin, starting with Grand Coulee?

"I don't believe the dams will be there forever," Donald says without hesitation. He thinks about the future differently than most people, reflecting an ancient but ecologically founded worldview. "We're not going away. We're always going to be here. It might not be in my lifetime, but as long as I am here I will fight for the salmon and as long as my children are here they will fight for the salmon. And as long as their children are here—as long as there is a breath of life in any of us—we will fight for the salmon. And the salmon will come back." His gaze, both humble and confident, does not waver.

"Seven generations ago our grandfathers reserved for us the fish, the game, and land in our treaty of 1855. Seven generations from now our grandchildren will say to each other, your grandfathers and grandmothers stood up for the salmon and they came back."

"They will come back."

## April

As the last nut goes into place, a balding white man I've seen next door to Tyrone's house comes over. He introduces himself as Andy. "I've been meaning to have you folks over to pop a bottle of something for months. I see your kid out on his bike all the time. His name's Gary, right?" I climb down the ladder and stand with him looking up at the hoop, talking about this and that.

Andy helps me pull the ladder off the trellis, which sets off a stampede from down the block. Gary and the others charge toward us, veering off course only to scoop up basketballs, kickballs, and dog-chewed tennis balls from the front stoops and shrub-skirted hideaways of neighboring houses. When the herd is about thirty feet out, the balls start to fly. And the music of basketball begins, to continue uninterrupted for weeks on end: the dark clap of balls striking fiberglass, the vibrating ring of the steel rim.

The noise brings Amy outside with Kathryn and Peter. We stand around, holding the little ones and watching the play. Other adults stop to watch, too, replacing each other slowly on the sidewalk. The hoop makes it easy to be neighborly. You just watch the kids play. You don't have to think of what to say. There is Hanna, our next-door neighbor; Gerri, who lives beyond her, and Gina, whose driveway circles behind our place.

Over the days ahead we meet more neighbors: George, who has just moved in between us and the yellow house; Ray, who is Daron and Devon's father; Junior, who is—we think—Marcus's father; and Hillary, who lives up a block but has a kid the same age as Kathryn. Other folks stop too, folks who walk this way to the bus or the minimart. Amy and I find we are spending more time out front, visiting there when our parents drop by, rather than going inside right away. When we were looking for housing, we had wanted a front porch big enough to sit on. We did not find one, but the basketball court performed some of the same function.

The hoop starts to pay off in tangible ways, too. My work ethic has always made me regard sidewalk chatter as idle and unproductive; in fact, it is highly productive. It is like putting money in the bank. When we need curry powder, we know from courtside conversations that George is a bit of a cook, and, sure enough, he has a little stash. When we need garden tools to beat down the weeds behind the house, we know that Hanna has a good collection. And when Hanna needs somebody to walk her dog, she knows it will make Gary's day. Daron's dad, Ray, invites Gary to play on a basketball team he is going to coach in the winter. Eleven-year-old Sara proves so good with Peter and Kathryn that Amy invites her to come over after school to help out. Petty con artists sometimes knock on our door, saying they live just across the way and need ten bucks to take a sick relative to the hospital by cab. Before we knew our neighbors, we did not know what to believe. Now we can't be fooled.

After the hoop has been up for a couple of months, Tyrone comes over to stand with me as Gary practices three-pointers and Peter crawls on the pavement. "It's a blessing!"

"Yes, it is!" I agree. He compliments Gary on his shooting. I ask how his wife is doing. We discuss the weather. He and I have talked a fair bit since the hoop went up. I am no longer uncomfortable.

After a quiet spell, he lowers his voice. I can tell he's going to give me an update on the yellow house. "You know, they've been doin' better, 'specially the kids. The whole family is doin' better. It's a blessing!"

"Yes, it is!" I still have no idea how he knows what he knows, nor whether to believe him. But it is nice to hear that he thinks matters are improving on our troubled block. I think they are too.

AT THE VFW HALL IN REXBURG, IDAHO, out by the county fairgrounds, Dale Swensen is calling to order what must be the most cockamamie meeting this eastern corner of the Pacific Northwest has ever seen. "We sit in a circle to try to find community in the betterment of the Henry's Fork Basin," he begins, speaking deliberately and with a twinge of a drawl. Through tinted, oversized glasses, he is scanning the seventy men and women seated in folding chairs around him. He sounds more like a group therapist than the director of one of the Northwest's powerful resource interests, the Fremont-Madison Irrigation District, which distributes water from Bureau of Reclamation dams to seventeen hundred farms.

He passes his gaze slowly around the circle again. Looking back at him are old-time farmers and ranchers, fly fishermen, chamber of commerce members, county commissioners, forest rangers, game wardens, environmental activists, and bearded adherents of deep ecology. He has known most of these people for years, some of them for decades. He has crossed swords with many of them, too.

"All of us," he says, pausing to swallow, "share the goal of a healthy and productive watershed." Until two years ago, the only things these people shared were lawsuits. Then the Fremont-Madison Irrigation District teamed up with its environmentalist nemesis, the Henry's Fork Foundation, to convene this Henry's Fork Watershed Council. Several dozen such bodies now pepper the organizational map of the Pacific Northwest. They aim to resolve local controversies locally, and, where even the meagerest compromise has been impossible, they are sufficiently audacious—some would say foolhardy—to seek consensus.

Place is the glue in all of these groups; here in southeastern Idaho, the glue seems to hold. At the center of the place is the Henry's Fork River. Rising in the Centennial Range, where Idaho nuzzles up between Montana and Wyoming, the Henry's Fork makes a beeline for the Snake, gathering reinforcement from streams pouring out of Yellowstone and Grand Teton National Parks. Together, the Henry's Fork, its tributaries, and their extensions—irrigation canals—run to three thousand miles. Scattered along that length are eddies and pools famous enough for their trout to draw anglers from California and the eastern seaboard. The land drained through that dendritic structure yields some famous potatoes too, and the highlands are home to grizzly bears and trophy elk.

The signature of the Henry's Fork, however, is probably its view. From outside the VFW hall, as from much of the basin, the horizon is interrupted by the glistening massif of the Grand Teton, rising from the high plain and stabbing the heavens like an unsheathed stiletto. It is a disorienting sight, looming over this landscape of well-tilled farms and meandering creeks. It suggests that the order of things is occasionally broken by radical discontinuities.

Dale is reviewing the ground rules for the meeting: use I-statements and speak for yourself, not your organization. This is bedrock irrigation country, a place that praises God but damns government, and half of the basin is public lands. For there to be any talking at all, institutional politics have to be checked at the door.

There is an irony here. In the Northwest, there is a direct relationship between the rancor with which a state's elected officials berate Big Government and that state's financial dependence on Big Government. Alaska and Idaho—the archconservative jurisdictions that bray their self-reliance at the slightest provocation—get more federal dollars per capita than other Northwest jurisdictions. Indeed, Alaska gets more federal dollars per citizen than any other state in the union, and Idaho ranks not far behind.

"We come with strong feelings." Dale is intentionally understating things. For decades, conservationists and proponents of development have battled in this basin, just as they have contested in most other parts of the Northwest. Here, their struggles came to a head in 1993, in the process of formulating a watershed plan. Local residents lost all equanimity. Environmentalists painted irrigators as welfare cowboys slopping at the public trough. Resource developers painted conservationists as citified misanthropes bent on socialism. Dave Rydalch, vice chair of the Idaho Water Resources Board and operator of a reservoir at the top of the Henry's Fork watershed, explained the fight. "The old Mormon brethren in the valley didn't want the state telling 'em what to do." Tempers flared, insults flew, threats circulated, and tires got slashed.

Finally, the state legislature adopted the Henry's Fork Basin Plan, banning water development on 195 miles of stream in the basin and allowing it elsewhere. Few were happy with the outcome, but worse, the fight destroyed all sense of community among the valley's forty thousand residents. That was when Dale Swensen, the voice of irrigation, and Jan Brown of the Henry's Fork Foundation, the voice of conservation, decided, in Dale's words, "to bury the hatchet. If we could work together, anyone could." They gambled that making peace might be more productive than making war. And to make peace, they figured, they would have to ban voting. Voting just gets people into their trenches.

As Jan says, "We're trying to model good behavior. The whole idea is being inclusive. We don't vote; everything is by consensus. I didn't say unanimity, I said consensus. The idea is that we operate in community. It's a thorny, long process. It takes all day. Only the desire for community gets people out of themselves and allows us to move forward together." Talking face to face can be far more radical than hurling invective on talk radio.

In the big ring at the VFW hall, Dale is still reviewing the ground rules. "Listen to your inner voice. Become aware of when you are moved to speak and when you are not," he intones. "Consider what others are saying with respect." There are, he knows, scores of grudges in this room. "Be aware of your barriers, stereotypes, prejudices, expectations, preconceptions." He is trying to do this himself.

Things are getting more cockamamie all the time. "Understand the value of silence," Dale suggests, and to underline it, he calls for three minutes of complete quiet. Here in the Mormon heartland, in what is arguably the most traditional, conservative part of the entire Pacific Northwest, this watershed council is acting like a Quaker meeting. It is sitting together in a peace that is disturbed only by squeaking chairs and humming lights.

On the agenda, what comes next is called Community Building. It runs from nine o'clock to nine-thirty and again from four-thirty to five. It too is more like a Quaker meeting. People speak, in no particular order, stating their first names and whatever they are moved to share. "I'm Ruth. I'm wondering how to start this kind of process down at Bear Lake. We need it. Things are getting tense." Heads nod. Jan and Dale glance at each other across the ring and scribble in their notebooks.

"My name is Rod. There's sixty people around this circle. I'm not much good at math, but I'd guess there are two hundred years of college education, twenty-four hundred years of life experience, a thousand years of job experience. You know, we founded the United States with less than that!" There is laughter.

On it goes, with silences interrupted by one, two, sometimes three voices. Many express reverence for the Henry's Fork, attributing to it much that is right with their lives. "My name is Stan. I spend days and days traveling to meetings for the senator." Stan Clark is the local representative for U.S. Senator Dirk Kempthorne, who is on record as intending to roll back many environmental regulations. "As the sun came over the Tetons this morning, I was out on my horse. There isn't anything that teaches me who I am better than that horse between my legs, and good cows and calves in front of it, and looking at those things [the mountains]." He is leaning forward in his chair and clasping his hands together. "We have a way of life that should be preserved, and I think it can be preserved with the diversity of people here."

Others reflect on how much things have changed.

Dale himself is a bit incredulous. "I don't know of any other group that does this, except maybe in church."

"My name is Ed. This is born of controversy." Ed Clark is chairman of the board of the Fremont-Madison Irrigation District, a representative of the Idaho Water Users Association, and a man with a large presence in the room. He looks up. The others know what he means. "But I've made a lot of new friends from among former adversaries." He looks up again. "Especially with the militant attitude in the United States right now. . . ." Again, the others know what he means. Armed militias are all over the news.

Jan Brown is standing on a chair, struggling to get people reassembled from the coffee and doughnut break. "The community level in here is out of hand!" At last, the hordes subdued, she introduces Jerry Reese, supervisor of the Targhee National Forest, which includes most of the headwaters of the Henry's Fork, to kick off the day's topic of discussion: roads.

Stationed in front of six maps of the forest, each of them decorated in different colors, the poker-faced Jerry explains that the Targhee is in the midst of forest plan revisions and has mapped six alternatives for management. Each alternative prescribes logging levels and road closures for each section of forest. The alternatives range from wide-open driving and logging to little logging or driving.

Jerry, two forest planners on his staff, and Mike Donahoo of the U.S. Fish and Wildlife Service each go over some details of the alternatives. The way they talk, everything is rational, orderly, passionless: the Targhee is analyzing these alternatives with advice from the Fish and Wildlife Service. In a few months, the Targhee will choose one, and prepare a draft environmental impact statement and draft forest plan. A year later, it will finalize both.

As the day progresses and others speak, a different picture emerges. Years of logging, replanting, brush clearing, and fire fighting have made the Targhee forest an insect's paradise. According to the teachings of orthodox forestry, logging bug-infested lodgepole pine prevents the further spread of insects. Recent research suggests, however, that logging does not control bugs well and often causes worse damage in the process. The Targhee National Forest, whether for motives pure or expedient, was "logged hard and fast," says Theo Chu, elk specialist for the Idaho Department of Fish and Game.

To get to the timber, logging roads were built in a hurry. All-terrain vehicles (ATVs) with two wheels, three wheels, four wheels, or snow-treads followed the roads. Some of the people mounted on these ATVs were out for game; others were out for the ride. Adena Cook, a snowmobiler and president of the ATVer's Blue Ribbon Commission, argues that the leading form of recreation in national forests nationwide is "driving for pleasure." Many ATVers found cross-country travel enticing, so they left the logging roads and wore down unmapped tracks between them. The logging boom quickly dispatched available timber, but the driving was still good.

By 1993, the Targhee had an estimated thirty-eight hundred miles of official and unofficial roads and motorized trails— "spaghetti," in one forest ranger's words. The same crazy-quilt growth of the road network was going on throughout the Northwest: almost three-quarters of a million miles of roads crisscrossed the bioregion in 1994, enough to loop around the equator twenty-eight times.

Unfortunately, roads are tough on fish, elk, and grizzly bears. "Of all the activities in mountain areas," says Ronna Monte, a hydrologist for the Targhee National Forest who speaks later in the day, "road construction is the biggest threat to water." In the Targhee, new logging roads send between 40 and 150 tons of soil downhill from each acre they cross. Much of this dirt lands in creeks, choking fish habitat and clogging downstream irrigation works. The farmers and fly fishers are listening carefully.

During a road's first year, the rate of soil loss is commonly a hundred times greater than the rate of soil formation. From a hydrological perspective, Ronna says, the more roads closed, the better. And they must be not only gated off but "ripped out deep, recontoured, and reseeded." As another forest worker says, "you gotta maintain them forever or lay them to bed."

Art Talsma of the Boise-based Rocky Mountain Elk Foundation says elk herds become "larger but also less balanced" in heavily roaded areas. "There aren't as many big, mature bulls. There are lots more cows per bull." That leads to later breeding and sicklier young. The question, Art concludes, is whether people are willing to hunt on foot again, as they did before the logging roads fanned out through the lodgepole. The reward would be healthier elk herds. Art is warmly received. Among outdoor pursuits, only fishing has more adherents in Idaho than hunting. Many in this room do both.

Less openly embraced is Dave Mattson. "Wherever bears have been studied, they underuse habitat near roads," says Dave, an earnest young professor at the University of Idaho in Moscow, Idaho, and a leading expert on grizzly bears in this greater Yellowstone region. The group is paying close attention, but many jaws seem set.

Dave has brought a pile of transparencies to illustrate the conclusions of bear science. They show, for example, that in the contiguous American states, "Grizzly bears now inhabit 2 percent of their 1850 range." Almost all of the remaining grizzly range is in the Pacific Northwest.

More than 80 percent of grizzly bear deaths are caused by people, and "more than any other measurable factor, roads determine the prospects for bears," Dave says. Where roads go, people follow. Where people go, conflicts with bears ensue, and—headlines of the occasional mauling notwithstanding—bears end up dead. Hunters kill most of them, wildlife managers the others. There is little choice when bears are no longer wary of humans.

Grizzlies need large habitats to survive. If half of the Targhee is to be secure bear habitat, Dave's transparencies demonstrate, the length of roads through it must not exceed a quarter mile for each square mile of area. At present, there is six times that much road in the Targhee National Forest.

Dave speaks affably and sticks to the data. He finds several opportunities to thank the group for the chance to share in its deliberations. He knows he is treading on thin ice. Every time Dave says "bear mortality," there are a few audible snickers. He means bears that die, but everyone is thinking about bears that kill, too. Overriding this sense, however, is something strangely akin to pride. At lunch, tree huggers and tree luggers swap bear stories, finding a primordial commonality. And most of the Henry's Fork Watershed Council seems to consider a pinch of fear a small price to pay for the privilege of neighboring with *Ursus arctos horribilis*, one of the continent's most magnificent predators.

No, the reserve on many faces does not come from wishing ill on bears; rather, it is political. Local and regional environmental advocates, notably the Greater Yellowstone Coalition, unsuccessfully contested the heavy logging and roading of the Targhee for years. Logging and driving interests always prevailed. Then, in 1993, the conservation camp found a more powerful weapon: the Endangered Species Act. Relying on the research of Dave Mattson and other biologists, they sued the Targhee National Forest for harming grizzly bears, a protected endangered species. Logging and roading, by eliminating secure habitat, were effectively killing bears.

The suit set in motion most of what the Targhee National Forest has since done about logging and road closures: it has shut down all logging and is considering closing up to two-thirds of the roads. The environmental advocates have, to the minds of the old-guard loggers, farmers, and ATVers, upset the apple cart. That explains the diffidence toward Dave Mattson.

Yet Dave's message is solid, clear, and nonpartisan. The conclusion is hard to resist: bears or roads, you choose. As that thought sinks in, the Henry's Fork Watershed Council becomes a case study in how worldviews change.

Many in the group accept the premise but desperately seek an escape from the conclusion. They spin out questions by the yard: Is it the roads themselves or the people on them? Might not the problem be camping, not road access? Can you close roads temporarily and provide secure bear habitat? Can you close them at night? Might not hiking trails be worse for bears, since hikers surprise bears?

They are good questions, but they are asked pointedly. They are asked more to inflict political harm than to seek new knowledge. Dave nevertheless answers each question carefully and factually, relating the results of his fifteen years of testing hypotheses like these. People in the room are uncomfortable because their worldviews are changing; they are learning that the world is full and fragile.

There is a lot of this kind of talking going on. In British Columbia, the B.C. Round Table on the Economy and the Environment, composed of representatives of many sectors of society, made consensus-based recommendations on environmental, energy, transportation, land use, and economic development policy from its founding in 1987 to its dissolution in 1994. Its reports remain among the best sources of data on sustainability in the bioregion.

Also in British Columbia, the Commission on Resources and the Environment (CORE) convened consensus-based land management planning groups on Vancouver Island, in the East and West Kootenays, and in the Cariboo/Chilcotin district. Conflict was heated both at the CORE tables and away from them. The net result was the designation of areas for parks and conservation areas, timber cutting, and a variety of other categories of resource use.

In the Northwest states, citizen-initiated round tables are robust in, among other places, Washington's Willapa Bay, the Applegate watershed that spans the Oregon-California border, and the Clark Fork watershed of western Montana. The state of Oregon has started consensus-based councils in each of its watersheds, and some of them are vibrant and effective.

Talk is cheap, of course, and few of these consensus sessions have shifted the tide. The recommendations of B.C.'s CORE were ultimately just advice to the government. Some environmentalists decried CORE's activities as "talk and log," because resource development continued unabated during the planning process. As important as CORE in protecting ecosystems in British Columbia were pressure tactics such as grass-roots blockades of logging roads in Vancouver's Clayoquot Sound, which nationalized the issue, and consumer boycotts in Europe, which internationalized it.

But that is the short-term view—the view that measures progress by battles won rather than new coalitions fostered. If there is hope for the dramatic changes sustainability demands, watershed organizations are indispensable. Devotion to place and hope for the future are the only passions sufficiently widespread in the Pacific Northwest to serve as antidotes to blinkered self-interest. If forward-looking Northwesterners are going to effect substantial change in institutions, both public and private, they will need much broader coalitions than they currently have. They will have to mix things up and find strange bedfellows. And they will have to do the slow, tedious, even boring work of establishing trust in fractured communities. So what is going on at Rexburg is necessarily a long-term proposition.

In the Rexburg VFW hall, as time elapses and the chances of finding an escape hatch from the logic of grizzly bear science diminish, a vocal minority of the council members simply deny the evidence before them. They reassert old beliefs.

Fremont County Commissioner Neil Christiansen, a scrappy old logger with a shock of dark curls, tells Dave Mattson, the bear biologist, "I have been on the Targhee since 1944. Back then, there was little wildlife." The bears have come since, he contends, some of them at the same time as the logging and the roads. To Neil this is fact, and none of Dave's evidence to the contrary matters. Among the old-timers in the room, Neil's voice resonates. He speaks from their worldview.

Neil denies data on the proliferation of roads and trails as well. "They're already closed. You can go up and drive around and you'll see it. You'll see it. They're all closed." He insists that ripping out roads is shortsighted. "We need to be able to use those roads if there's a fire or something of that nature." And he denies forest ecology when he contends that logging is crucial to the health of forests. "Fire is not being used to manage the forest. Logging is the only management tool. You have to log it before it gets decadent." To Neil, mature forest ecosystems—those with the richest diversity and fullest cycling of nutrients—are just dying wood. They are moribund and wasteful; leaving them alone is perilously close to immoral.

But it is late in the day when Neil finally expresses what is, to his mind, the nut of the problem—the raw, offensive, soft-headed, nefarious crux of everything that is wrong with environmentalism. The council has divided into small groups for closer consideration of the roads issue, and he is sitting across from Marv Hoyt, field representative of the Greater Yellowstone Coalition, the group that initiated the lawsuit for road closures.

Neil asks for a turn to speak but is, for once, slow to get started. He gnashes his teeth for a long moment before declaiming, "The missing word is *economics*." He leans his head down and lowers his voice to an incredulous, agonizing whisper. "We're closing the roads for that bear. People don't matter a bit." Gasps ripple around the room; some are gasps of dismay, others gasps of recognition. That is what bothers them. It seems as if bears are getting more attention in this forest-planning exercise than people.

Marv Hoyt raises his voice. "Neil, we *are* talking about economics. We *are* talking about people. Neil, the economy has changed." Marv says this with a bit of "touché" in his voice—the two of them have been sparring much of the day—but he says it with genuine warmth as well. Marv understands what Neil means and gives him the deference befitting an elder. He steps lightly across the circle and offers Neil an inch-thick manuscript. It is, he says, a study of the economy of the greater Yellowstone region. It covers the Henry's Fork. It covers Neil's Fremont County.

The study, Marv says, shows the shape of the emerging economy—an economy that depends on ecological health, strong communities, sustainable resource extraction, clean water, good hunting, good fishing, and great bears in the woods. It documents for the Henry's Fork the same decline in traditional resource industries and the same economic diversification that have transformed the Pacific Northwest overall.

"The issue," Marv argues, "isn't about grizzly bears versus roads. It's about this big chunk of land and water, and all the critters that are tied to this place. It's about ecological and economic diversity that makes living and working here like no place else on Earth."

Neil is publicly unmoved; he eyes Marv cautiously, as if on guard. But others in the room are paying heed. And Neil accepts the document, setting it down on his lap and resting his elbow on it, as if to say, "It cannot hurt to page through it."

All around him worldviews bend an inch or two. The dialogue has hit pay dirt. Two distinct and opposed descriptions of how the world works—each with radically different implications for public policy and individual behavior—have surfaced in this room.

Neil sees the world the old, familiar way: physical production drives the economy; the world is empty and indestructible; environmental quality is a luxury. Marv sees the world the new, unfamiliar way: quality of life drives the economy; the world is full and fragile; environmental quality is a necessity.

Without the Henry's Fork Watershed Council and its well-nurtured devotion to togetherness—all the Community Building and I-statements and listening to inner voices and understanding of silence—it is hard to see how this fleeting exposure of worldviews could have taken place.

And that may be the greatest strength of the council and its counterparts scattered across the Pacific Northwest. They may resolve few issues in the short term. They may reach agreements that are watered down to the point of insignificance. But watershed councils lay the cultural foundations for a lasting way of life. They establish the traditions of responsible speech, of civil democracy, and of making decisions based on factual information and well-articulated values. They embody the long-term perspective of sustainability, seeking not quick fixes but deeper understanding and new alternatives. They manifest the profoundly Jeffersonian idea that citizens, meeting face to face, rooted in place, are the best form of governance. They echo, most of a century later, the stirring ideal for the West first articulated by the explorer and geographer John Wesley Powell: watershed-bounded commonwealths in which most governance is decentralized self-governance. And, more practically and perhaps most importantly, they are, in themselves, expressions of profound optimism, declarations of citizens' continued faith in each other and in the possibility of progress. Without this belief, sustainability is reduced to unalloyed defeatism.

# *May*

Amy is out front by the hoop when Julie stops by, her stroller loaded with her two kids. She lives in the next block in a walk-up duplex. She and Amy get to talking about traffic. "It just goes too fast, doesn't it? I'm afraid to let the kids play outside. I'm afraid to cross the street." Amy agrees. While I have been attempting to weave community with a basketball hoop, Amy has been doing it with a baby stroller. She has been walking places: she has become the best customer of a new produce stand that opened three blocks away, and she visits a nearby children's consignment store almost every week.

"A friend of mine passed a petition around among her neighbors to request a traffic island from the city," says Julie. The city measured traffic speed and found it was over the speed limit. It built a planting circle in the middle of the intersection. Cars slowed down. People felt safer.

"Maybe we could get one on our street, too," says Amy. "Let's do a petition."

Amy has begun pointing out to me the traffic circles and diverters that are going in all over the city's neighborhoods. We watch them sprout from the blacktop like alder in a clear-cut. First come the spray-painted shapes on the pavement, then the Engineering Department's orange cones, then holes in the ground, then fresh concrete, and then soil and shrubs. The pace at each calms down.

When we are walking in our neighborhood nowadays, Amy points to the intersections where she wants bumps, bends, bubbles, and circles. She points to the sidewalks that are too narrow and the corners where the curb is impassable with a stroller. She points to empty lots that could become playgrounds or corner stores. A new landscape is taking shape in her head: what our community could be.

The petition, cooked up beside the basketball court, goes up and down the street quickly, and Julie mails it downtown. We are waiting for a response.

**THE PACIFIC NORTHWEST.** No part of the industrial world has as large a share of its ecosystems intact. And no other place on the continent matches its depth and breadth of sustainability initiatives, efforts undertaken by businesses, citizens, communities, and governments. A single biological region stretching from Prince William Sound to the Redwood Coast of California and from the Pacific Ocean to the crest of the Rockies, an economic region encompassing fourteen million people and $300 billion of annual production, the Pacific Northwest can be the test case for sustainability.

Drawing on its tradition of turning outlandish dreams into practical realities, the Northwest may be the place that demonstrates how to trade the old worldview for the new, and in the process exchange sprawl and malls for compact, vibrant cities; clear-cuts and monoculture for enduring farms, forests, and fisheries; throwaways, overpackaging, and rapid obsolescence for durability, reuse, and repair; volume for value; and consumerism for community.

The Northwest could model a way of life comprising less stuff and more time, fewer toys and more fun. Above all, it could become a place whose civility, whose culture—whose humanity—are as stunning as its scenery.

The politics of place is a politics of hope. It is sustained by a faith—somewhat mystical perhaps—in *place* itself. Whether they are descendants of Asian hunters who crossed the Bering land bridge during the Ice Age or mongrels with New England Puritan–Irish-Polish-Jewish blood, all people who put down roots are shaped by their home ground. Over time it seeps into them, and they become natives. In the Northwest this means they look up at twilight and draw strength from the mountains. They seek renewal at the rivers and the shores. They taste communion in the pink flesh of the salmon. The rains cease to annoy.

Here is the hope: That this generation becomes the next wave of natives, first in this place on Earth and then in others. That new-found permanence allows the quiet murmur of localities to become audible again. And that not long thereafter, perhaps very soon, the places of this Earth will be healed and whole again.

From Port Arthur in British Columbia, maverick timber boss A. J. Auden of the Abitibi Power and Paper Company had it right fifty years ago when he said, "We have spent these past two hundred and fifty years . . . in restless movement, recklessly skimming off the cream of superabundant resources, but we have not used the land in the true sense of the word, nor have we done ourselves much permanent good. It's high time that we . . . settled down, not for a hundred years, but for a thousand, forever."

## August

The hoop came down. It came down rudely. One Sunday morning in June we discovered it. The rim was severed from the board and dangling by a strand of fiberglass. Somebody—a teenager, I suppose—had probably hung from the rim in the night. It wasn't anybody on our street. On our street, everybody knew it wasn't strong enough to swing from. Ray, Andy, Tyrone, and the kids all suspected a group of boys who often came through on their bicycles acting tough.

Amy and I were incensed. Kathryn just stared, her usually active young vocabulary silenced for once. Gary was crushed. His play space had been invaded and its centerpiece snapped in two. That afternoon, he started playing in our scrawny backyard, and over the weeks that followed, he practically withdrew from street life. We, too, stopped spending time out front. We didn't notice the change at first. It was just a hoop, after all. We would fix it when we could, but at the moment we could not. My work was crazy. There was no time for repairs. It took me most of a month just to get the wreckage down.

In late July, I started thinking about mending the hoop, standing out front with a measuring tape. Peter was sleeping in a child carrier on my back. The more I studied the problem, the madder I got. Tyrone and other neighbors stopped to watch me, and I realized that I missed them. I realized that the damned kid who broke this hoop had spoiled my fun as much as Gary's. Well, I'd show him. Not only would I put the hoop back up, I'd make it stronger. As many times as they ripped it down, I'd put it back up. Not only that, I would raise it to regulation height, out of reach of most teenagers and better for the kids on this street anyway. This hoop would stand.

Trouble was, I did not have the first idea of how to fix the thing. And so, lacking all shame, I appealed to a higher authority, my father-in-law. Peter Thein could, as far as I knew, fix anything. As it turned out, he was already contemplating the problem and was just waiting for an invitation to lend a hand. With his plans in place, we set to work. I shuffled over to the lot where Gary had found the hypodermic needle and begged for some scrap lumber from the carpenters who were framing a new house there. Meanwhile, my father-in-law gathered the new hardware he said we would need—a few bags of bolts and wood screws and two thin plates of steel. With these, and Gary's help, he reassembled the hoop on weekdays while I was away. At night, I would admire his handiwork. The backboard was sturdier than ever, and heavier too.

This weekend, in late August, I finally did my part of the job. Climbing the ladder that I had borrowed again, I reinforced the trellis everywhere I could. It would need to be stronger to support an elevated hoop. Then I called over to Andy, and he helped me lift the goal into place. We bolted it on, and Gary brought out the measuring tape. Sure enough, Peter had built it perfectly. It was ten feet on the nose. We lowered the ladder, and Gary threw the first ball. A dozen other kids sent their balls up in its wake. Andy and I stood to the side and watched with satisfaction. Amy came home with young Peter, and I went inside to pick Kathryn up from her nap.

As we came outside, she rubbed her eyes, surveyed the scene, and asked to get down. Then she started to dance in a circle and sing, "Dah kids is back! Dah kids is back! Daddy fix oh backetball!" Amy and I felt like dancing right along with her. It is amazing what a basketball hoop will do.

# DEBTS

*This Place on Earth* is a bundle of debts, and its creditors are numerous. Each page is not only my work but also that of dozens of others. Naming these people and the contributions they made is a pleasure.

The largest debt is owed to my wife, Amy, and to our children, parents, and friends. The book exists thanks to the support I received from them.

I wrote *This Place on Earth* under the auspices of Northwest Environment Watch (NEW), a private, nonprofit research center in Seattle. Much is owed to the scores of people who gave time, money, and love to NEW between 1993 and early 1996. Still, the views expressed are my own and do not necessarily represent those of NEW or its directors, officers, staff, or contributors.

An enormous debt is owed to the twelve interns who devoted months of their lives to NEW during this project, volunteering up to full time even while they held down night jobs to support themselves. They are Michael Aaron, Aaron Best, Sara Jo Breslow, Beth Callister, Peter Carlin, Christopher Crowther, Angela Haws, Amy Mayfield, Chandra Shah, Aaron Tinker, Christina Tonitto, Lisa Valdez, and Michael Wewer. The debt to Chris Crowther is especially large: he labored on the book unpaid for more than eighteen months.

Other NEW volunteers contributed greatly as well. They did everything from stuffing envelopes to auditing NEW's accounts. Here is a partial list: Bill Berg, Monica Bertucci, Mick Braddick, Alycia Braga, Ian Burke, Ed Chadd, Jeff Clark, Susan Clark, Sacha Crittenden, Randy Dill, Jean and Marvin Durning, Sandra Blair Hernshaw, Kevin Klipstein, Norman Kunkel, Wendy Lawrence,

Rob Linehan, Flo Lipton, Hollie Lund, Lyn McCollum, Maura McLaughlin, Maria Miller, Emi Nagata, Albert Paulding, Loretta Pickerell, Don Read, Marilyn Roy, Julene Schlack, Brian Skinner, Stephanie Smith, Alyson Stage, Scott Stevens, Steve Swope, and Janet Wilson.

A debt is owed to NEW's all-volunteer board of directors, who oversaw the organization deftly and conscientiously, offering guidance, support, and trust: Spencer Beebe, Lester Brown, Sandi Chamberlain, Jane Lubchenco, Tyree Scott, and Rosita Worl.

NEW's Canadian and American staff shaped the book from the outset. Day in and day out, office manager Rhea Connors, communications director Donna Morton, and research director John Ryan applied rare insight, vision, and determination to the mission of NEW, as did office manager Agi Kim during her term.

A somewhat more literal debt is owed to NEW's financial supporters. These include approximately a thousand individual contributors and ten private foundations: the Bullitt Foundation, Nathan Cummings Foundation (which provided a project grant for the research and writing of the book), Ford Foundation, Global Environment Project Institute, William and Flora Hewlett Foundation, Henry P. Kendall Foundation, Merck Family Fund, Surdna Foundation, Tortuga Foundation, and an anonymous Canadian foundation. I thank them for their confidence.

Critical readers of various sections and drafts kept the project from jumping the track. Research director John Ryan effectively backstopped the research and writing of the entire book and read each part of it repeatedly for accuracy, logic, and clarity. Others who contributed by reviewing most or all of the manuscript include Amy Thein Durning, Marvin and Jean Durning, Neva Goodwin, Martin Teitel, Ted Wolf, and most of the NEW staff and intern corps. Drafts of some chapters were improved by suggestions from Cliff Cobb, Nick Lenssen, Todd Litman, Norine

MacDonald, Vicki Robin, Richard White, and John Young. The book was ably edited by my bus stop-mate Gary Luke of Sasquatch Books.

The final debt I owe is fundamental. The book came into being, ultimately, because of two traits I have never been able to shake: a consuming need to learn about what ails my society and an equally powerful passion to do something about it. Sometimes I am dismayed by these traits; they can be tyrannical. Still, in the end, they also give life focus.

I have belatedly recognized that these twin fuels—curiosity and activism—were supplied in abundance by my parents, Marvin and Jean Durning. A father myself now, I look back and am humbled. Somehow, without my noticing, they inculcated in me a hunger for knowledge and a faith in truth. They imparted the instinct to put knowledge into action: they fed me on the speeches of back-to-back political campaigns and tucked me into bed where I could hear the next campaign cooked up around the kitchen table.

They taught me one other lesson as well: each challenge may be a blessing in disguise. When their basement leaked, for example, they diverted the rainwater by building a basketball court. To them, I dedicate this book.

# SOURCES

The research for this book was conducted in four ways. First, I read reams of articles from newspapers, journals, magazines, and newsletters. These sources are collected for NEW's research files by volunteers across the region. Among the sources regularly monitored by NEW are the *Christian Science Monitor*, *Globe and Mail*, *High Country News*, *Idaho Statesman*, *New York Times*, *Oregonian*, *Seattle Post-Intelligencer*, *Seattle Times*, *Spokesman-Review*, *Vancouver Sun*, and *Victoria Times Colonist*. Second, I reviewed the technical literature from academic and government sources on specific topics. Third, I conducted interviews with practitioners and analysts in particular fields; some of these interviews are described in the text. Fourth, I gathered data from government sources on selected questions and provided fresh analysis of it. Below, I provide a partial accounting of the sources I relied on. For most readers, these will likely be more than sufficient; for readers using the book for scholarly purposes, I apologize for the lack of detailed documentation. I have voluminous notes and data sets, which I am happy to share with others as time permits.

Throughout the book I rely most heavily on other NEW publications, including John C. Ryan, *State of the Northwest* (1994) and *Hazardous Handouts* (1995), my own *The Car and the City* (1996), and four *NEW Indicators*: "Northwest Jobs Depend Less on Timber and Mining" (November 1994), "Vehicles Outnumber Drivers in Pacific Northwest" (January 1995), "Greenhouse Gases on the Rise in Pacific Northwest" (August 1995), and "Roads Take Toll on Salmon, Grizzlies, Taxpayers" (December 1995). These documented publications are natural follow-up reading. Portions of them are available on the World Wide Web (http://www.speakeasy.org/new).

For regional population and economic trends, I rely on databases kept by NEW, which are assembled from official sources. For population, NEW draws primarily on the U.S Bureau of the Census's Current Population Reports series and data from the Canadian Socio-Economic Information Management System Time Series Data Base. For income and employment data, NEW relies on official statistics gathered for the national income accounting system and other purposes, and obtained from the U.S. Department of Commerce, Bureau of Economic Analysis, Regional Economic Information on CD-ROM (Washington, D.C.: 1994); and unpublished data from B.C. Stats, Ministry of Government, Victoria; Statistics Canada, Ottawa; and state employment departments in Alaska, California, Idaho, Montana, Oregon, and Washington.

Several books on the region provided both information and inspiration: William Dietrich, *The Final Forest* (New York: Penguin, 1992); Ivan Doig, *Winter Brothers* (San Diego: Harcourt Brace Jovanovich, 1980); Timothy Egan, *The Good Rain* (New York: Vintage, 1990); Sallie Tisdale, *Stepping Westward* (San Francisco: HarperPerennial, 1991); and Richard Manning, *A Good House* (New York: Grove, 1993) and *Last Stand* (New York: Penguin, 1991). Finally, Philip L. Jackson and A. Jon Kimmerling, eds., *Atlas of the Pacific Northwest* (Corvallis: Oregon State University Press, 1993) was a useful reference.

## Chapter One: Place

**Personal sections:** The article I wrote from my research in the Philippines is "Last Sanctuary," *World Watch*, November/December 1992. My previous book is Alan Thein Durning, *How Much Is Enough?* (New York: W. W. Norton & Co., 1992). Leopold quote from *A Sand County Almanac* (New York: Oxford University Press, 1966).

**Northwest sections:** Human protoplasm from Edward O. Wilson, "Is Humanity Suicidal?" *New York Times Magazine*, May 30, 1993. Human appropriation of terrestrial plant matter from Peter M. Vitousek et al., "Human Appropriation of the Products of Photosynthesis." *Bioscience*, June 1986.

Congress quoted in David Lavender, *Land of Giants: The Drive to the Pacific Northwest, 1750–1950* (Garden City, New York: Doubleday, 1958). Political boundaries from histories cited in sources for Chapter 2, and from Richard White, professor of history, University of Washington, Seattle, private communications, 1995.

Indigenous Northwest cultures from various articles in Wayne Suttles, ed., *Handbook of North American Indians, Vol. 7, Northwest Coast* (Washington, D.C.: Smithsonian Institution, 1990); and Carl Waldman, *Atlas of the North American Indian* (New York: Facts on File Publications, 1985).

Egan quote from *The Good Rain* (New York: Vintage, 1990).

Vancouver quoted in Dorothy O. Johansen and Charles M. Gates, *Empire of the Columbia* (New York: Harper and Brothers, 1957). Haswell quoted in Lavender, *Land of Giants*. Ludlow quoted in Bruce Barcott, ed., *Northwest Passages* (Seattle: Sasquatch Books, 1994). Share of Northwest population consisting of first-generation residents from various reports of the U.S Bureau of the Census, based on its decennial censuses beginning in 1850.

Ecological uniqueness of region from John C. Ryan, *State of the Northwest* (Seattle: NEW, 1994).

## Chapter Two: Past

**Personal sections:** Levertov's poem "Settling In" is reprinted in Bruce Barcott, ed., *Northwest Passages* (Seattle: Sasquatch Books, 1994). Prehistoric flood from David D. Alt and Donald W. Hyndman's *Roadside Geology* series, including volumes on Oregon (1978), Washington (1984), and Montana (1986) (Missoula:

Mountain Press Publishing), and Bates McKee, *Cascadia: The Geologic Evolution of the Pacific Northwest* (New York: McGraw-Hill, 1972).

**Northwest sections:** Northwest resource industries' histories are well documented, although their ecological consequences are not. NEW's *State of the Northwest* is the single best source on the latter question.

For general and industrial histories, all sections rely on Dorothy O. Johansen and Charles M. Gates, *Empire of the Columbia* (New York: Harper and Brothers, 1957); David Lavender, *Land of Giants: The Drive to the Pacific Northwest, 1750–1950* (Garden City, New York: Doubleday, 1958); Carlos A. Schwantes, *The Pacific Northwest: An Interpretive History* (Lincoln, Nebraska: University of Nebraska Press, 1989); and Richard White, *Land Use, Environment, and Change: The Shaping of Island County, Washington* (Seattle: University of Washington Press, 1980) and *Organic Machine: The Remaking of the Columbia River* (New York: Hill and Wang, 1995). Also, Rondo Cameron, *A Concise Economic History of the World* (New York: Oxford University Press, 1989); Alfred W Crosby, *Ecological Imperialism* (New York: Cambridge University Press, 1986); and Angus Maddison, *The World Economy in the 20th Century* (Paris: Development Center of the Organization for Economic Cooperation and Development, 1989).

The effects of disease on Northwest cultures from, among others, Robert T. Boyd, "Demographic History, 1774–1874," in Wayne Suttles, ed., *Handbook of North American Indians, Vol. 7, Northwest Coast* (Washington, D.C.: Smithsonian Institution, 1990).

Nineteenth-century trapper quoted in Sallie Tisdale, *Stepping Westward* (San Francisco: HarperPerennial, 1991).

Fur trade's ecological consequences from, among others, G. R. VanBlaricom and J. A. Estes, *Community Ecology of Sea Otters* (New York: Springer-Verlag, 1988); Edward C. Bowlby et al., *Sea Otters* in *Washington: Distribution, Abundance, and Activity Patterns* (Olympia: Washington Department of Wildlife, 1988); and Robert J. Naiman et al., "Alteration of North American Streams by Beaver," *BioScience*, December 1988.

Mining's environmental effects from, among others, James S. Lyon et al., *Burden of Gilt* (Washington, D.C.: Mineral Policy Center, 1993); various articles in *Wilderness*, Summer 1992; and Arthur J. Horowitz et al., *The Effect of Mining and Related Activities on the Sediment-Trace Element Geochemistry of Lake Coeur d'Alene, Idaho, Part II: Subsurface Sediments* (Atlanta: U.S. Geological Survey, 1993).

Current status of salmon from, among others, *Pacific Salmon and Federal Lands: A Regional Analysis* (Washington, D.C.: The Wilderness Society, 1993) and Carolyn Alkire, *The Living Landscape: Wild Salmon as Natural Capital* (Washington, D.C.: The Wilderness Society, 1993).

The environmental effects of agriculture—specifically livestock—from, among others, Reed F. Noss et al., *Endangered Ecosystems of the United States: A Preliminary Assessment of Loss and Degradation* (Washington, D.C.: U.S. Department of the Interior, National Biological Service, 1995). Livestock numbers from U.S. Department of Agriculture, National Agricultural Statistics, online database maintained by Cornell University, Ithaca, New York, and from National Agricultural Statistics, *Agricultural Statistics* (Washington, D.C.: U.S. Department of Agriculture, various years).

Crop production's environmental effects from Frederick Steiner, *The Productive and Erosive Palouse Environment* (Pullman, Washington: Washington State University Cooperative Extension, 1987); U.S. Department of Agriculture (USDA), *America's Soil and Water: Conditions and Trends* (Washington, D.C.: 1987); and USDA reports on Oregon and Washington soil conditions. Also from S. Stewart et al., *The State of Our Groundwater: A Report on Documented Contamination in Washington* (Seattle: Washington Toxics Coalition and

Washington State University Cooperative Extension, 1994). Agricultural employment in the inland Northwest from Ray Rasker, *A New Home on the Range: Economic Realities in the Columbia River Basin* (Washington, D.C.: The Wilderness Society, 1995).

Water power and irrigation from, among others, Tim Palmer, *The Snake River* (Washington, D.C.: Island Press, 1991) and Marc Reisner, *Cadillac Desert: The American West and Its Disappearing Water*, Revised and Updated (New York: Penguin, 1993).

Timber from, among others, Ken Drushka et al., *Touch Wood: B.C. Forests at the Crossroads* (Madeira Park, B.C.: Harbour Publishing, 1993); Patricia Marchak, *Green Gold: The Forest Industry in British Columbia* (Vancouver: University of British Columbia Press, 1983); and John Osborn, M.D., *Railroads and Clearcuts: Legacy of Congress's 1864 Northern Pacific Railroad Land Grant, a Photographic Essay* (Spokane, Washington: Inland Empire Public Lands Council, 1995). Timber harvest trends from database assembled by NEW from publications of U.S. Forest Service and B.C. Ministry of Forests. Dietrich quote from William Dietrich, *The Final Forest* (New York: Penguin, 1992).

In concluding section, Morgan quote from Dietrich, *The Final Forest*. True sources of wealth from, among others, World Bank, *Monitoring Environmental Progress: A Report on Work in Progress* (Washington, D.C.: 1995). Decoupling of economy from resource and manufacturing industries, and the characteristics of labor and income from different sectors, from Thomas Michael Power, *Lost Landscapes and Failed Economies: The Search for a Value of Place* (Washington, D.C.: Island Press, 1996); and Thomas Power, professor of economics, University of Montana, Missoula, private communications, June 1995. The declining significance of timber and mining, and the relative roles of extraction, manufacturing, government, and services from John C. Ryan, "Northwest Jobs Depend Less on Timber, Mining," *NEW Indicator*, November

1994. Quality of life as economic engine also from various studies by Ed Whitelaw and Ernest Niemi, ECO Northwest, Eugene, such as *Evaluation of No-Growth and Slow-Growth Policies for the Portland Region* (Eugene, Oregon: 1994); and from Rasker, *A New Home on the Range*.

Employment benefits of environmental regulation from E. B. Goodstein, *Jobs and the Environment: The Myth of a National Trade-Off* (Washington, D.C.: Economic Policy Institute, 1994) and Robert Repetto, *Jobs, Competitiveness, and Environmental Regulation: What Are the Real Issues?* (Washington, D.C.: World Resources Institute, 1995).

## Chapter Three: Cars

**Personal sections:** The history of Madison Street and Madison Valley is told in Terry McDermott, "A Neighborhood Left Behind," *Seattle Times*, special section, December 13, 1992.

**Northwest sections:** Much of the material in this chapter also appears in an endnoted format either in my book *The Car and the City* (Seattle: NEW, 1996) or in "Vehicles Outnumber Drivers in Pacific Northwest," *NEW Indicator*, January 1995.

The chapter is informed by the analyses of James Howard Kunstler, *The Geography of Nowhere* (New York: Simon & Schuster, 1993); Marcia D. Lowe, *Shaping Cities: Environmental and Human Dimensions* (Washington, D.C.: Worldwatch Institute, 1991); Peter W. G. Newman and Jeffrey R. Kenworthy, *Cities and Automobile Dependence: A Sourcebook* (Brookfield, Vermont: Gower Technical, 1989); Gordon Price, "Tale of Three Cities," *New Pacific* (Vancouver), Autumn 1992; and B.C. Round Table on the Economy and the Environment, *State of Sustainability* (Victoria: Crown Publications, 1994).

Traffic fatalities from "Vehicles Outnumber Drivers in Pacific Northwest," *NEW Indicator*, January 1995, and National Safety

Council, *Accident Facts 1995* (Itasca, Illinois: 1995). Typical car's pollution emissions from City of Vancouver, *Clouds of Change, Final Report of the City of Vancouver Task Force on Atmospheric Change, June 1990*. Car emits own weight in carbon dioxide from Christopher Flavin and Alan Durning, *Building on Success: The Age of Efficiency* (Washington, D.C.: Worldwatch Institute, 1988); regional carbon dioxide emissions from John C. Ryan, "Greenhouse Gases on the Rise," *NEW Indicator*, August 1995.

Driving, sprawl, and auto ownership trends from "Vehicles Outnumber Drivers in Pacific Northwest," *NEW Indicator*, January 1995.

Role of density in auto use—and role of sprawl in causing environmental, economic, and social problems—from the major sources listed above, and from David B. Goldstein, "Making Housing More Affordable: Correcting Misplaced Incentives in the Lending System," Natural Resources Defense Council (NRDC), San Francisco, 1994; John Holtzclaw, "Using Residential Patterns and Transit to Decrease Auto Dependence and Costs," NRDC, San Francisco, 1994; Doug Kelbaugh (professor, School of Architecture and Urban Planning, University of Washington), presentation at "Building with Values '93" conference, Seattle, November 13, 1993; Todd Litman, *Transportation Cost Analysis: Techniques, Estimates and Implications* (Victoria: Victoria Transport Policy Institute, 1994); the many excellent "LUTRAQ" reports published by 1000 Friends of Oregon in Portland; Henry Richmond and Saunders C. Hillyer, "Need Assessment for a Metropolitan and Rural Land Institute, Summary," 1000 Friends of Oregon, Portland, April 30, 1993; Preston Schiller, "Car-rying Capacity," *Moving Lightly, Living Lightly* (Sierra Club, San Francisco), December 1993; the now-defunct newsletter *Gridlock Gazette* (Institute for Transportation and the Environment, Seattle); and Washington State Energy

Office, *Municipal Strategies to Increase Pedestrian Travel* (Olympia, Washington: 1994).

Shares of Northwest households with children from unpublished data from U.S. Bureau of the Census and Statistics Canada; shares of housing in single-family and multifamily buildings from B.C. Round Table, *State of Sustainability, and King County, 1994 King County Annual Growth Report* (Seattle: 1994).

Transportation and land-use history from sources already mentioned, including those listed as sources for Chapter 2, and from Graeme Wynn and Timothy Oke, eds., *Vancouver and Its Region* (Vancouver: University of British Columbia Press, 1992). Differences between U.S. and Canadian urban planning from Jeanne W. Wolfe, "Canada's Liveable Cities," *Social Policy*, Summer 1992. History of rail transit initiatives in Seattle from Danny Westneat, "Late for the Train: Why Seattle Has Always Let Commuter Rail Pass It By," *Seattle Times*, March 5, 1995, and Walt Crowley, "Track to the Future," *Seattle Post-Intelligencer*, March 5, 1995.

Downtown Portland's planning success from sources already cited and Philip Langdon, "How Portland Does It," *Atlantic Monthly*, November 1992.

Opposition to land-use planning in rural Northwest from, for example, Paul Larmer and Ray Ring, "Can Planning Rein in a Stampede?" *High Country News*, September 5, 1994.

## Chapter Four: Stuff

**Personal sections:** The production history of a cup of coffee from my paper, "Ecological Wakes," Northwest Environment Watch, Seattle, February 1994. At press time, NEW planned to expand this paper into a short book in its *NEW Report* series.

**Northwest sections:** The conceptual frame of this chapter is drawn from two primary sources: John E. Young and Aaron Sachs, *The Next Efficiency Revolution: Creating a Sustainable Materials*

*Economy* (Washington, D.C.: Worldwatch Institute, 1994), and Herman E. Daly and John B. Cobb, Jr., *For the Common Good* (Boston: Beacon Press, 1989). The chapter's local content is informed by three excellent newsletters: *Pollution Prevention Northwest* (Pacific Northwest Pollution Prevention Research Center, Seattle), *Reiterate* (Recycling Council of British Columbia, Vancouver), and *Remarketable News* (Clean Washington Center, Seattle). Much of the data in the chapter is drawn from the voluminous technical studies and surveys of the Clean Washington Center (Seattle), Metro Solid Waste Department (Portland), Seattle Solid Waste Utility, Washington Department of Ecology Solid Waste Services Program (Olympia), Statistics Canada (Ottawa), and the Oregon Department of Environmental Quality (Salem). Another helpful source was Kitty Weisman et al., "Taming the Toxic Threat: The Hazardous Waste Dilemma in the Northwest," *Northwest Report* (Northwest Area Foundation, St. Paul, Minnesota), April 1991.

Daily per capita resource consumption from my *How Much Is Enough?* (New York: W. W. Norton & Co., 1992). The Wuppertal Institute's concept of a "factor-ten economy" cited in Young and Sachs, *The Next Efficiency Revolution*.

The material on agriculture, food, and sewerage from, among others, Palmer, *The Snake River*, and various editions of *Journal of Pesticide Reform* (Northwest Coalition for Alternatives to Pesticides, Eugene, Oregon).

Water conservation potential from Bureau of Reclamation, Pacific Northwest Region, *Upper Deschutes River Basin Water Conservation Project* (Boise: 1993) and subsequent reports on the project by the bureau. Farming trends in the Palouse from Curtis E. Beus et al., eds., *Prospects for Sustainable Agriculture in the Palouse: Farmer Experiences and Viewpoints* (Pullman, Washington: Washington State University, 1990); David Granatstein, *Amber Waves:*

*A Sourcebook for Sustainable Dryland Farming in the Northwestern United States* (Pullman, Washington: Washington State University, 1992); and Robert Howell, "What Is Sustainable Agriculture: An Empirical Examination of Faculty and Farmer," *Journal of Sustainable Agriculture*, Vol. 3, No. 1, 1992. Northwest Coalition for Alternatives to Pesticides' survey is from Gwendolyn Bane, "Pesticide Use Reduction in Washington and Oregon," Eugene, Oregon, September 16, 1994. Sustainable agriculture trends generally from Northwest Area Foundation, *Which Row to Hoe: The Economic, Environmental, and Social Impact of Sustainable Agriculture* (St. Paul: 1994). Arcata sewerage from William Thomas, "From Waste to Wetlands," *Ecodecision* (Montreal), Fall 1994, and David Riggle, "Creating Markets Close to Home," *Biocycle*, July 1994.

Repair, rental, and reuse employment from state and provincial employment offices, and from U.S. Department of Commerce, and Statistics Canada. These agencies all keep employment data according to the uniform Standard Industrial Classification (SIC) system, allowing comparisons across time and space. NEW identified relevant categories and collected data on each. Unfortunately, the SIC system does not allow thorough measurement of many industries involved in reduction, reuse, and repair.

GreenDisk from Jim Erickson, "Local Company is World Leader in Recycling Used Diskettes into New Ones," *Seattle Post-Intelligencer*, October 26, 1995. Library use rates from the *American Library Directory*, 1994–95. Appliance durability trends from Gopal Ahluwalia and Angela Shackford (National Association of Homebuilders), "Life Expectancy of Housing Components," *Housing Economics*, August 1993.

Buildings section relies partly on Steve Loken and Walter Spurling, *ReCraft 90: Construction of a Resource Efficient House* (Missoula: Center for Resourceful Building Technology, 1993). Additional information from David Malin Roodman and Nicholas

Lenssen, *A Building Revolution: How Ecology and Health Concerns Are Transforming Construction* (Washington, D.C.: Worldwatch Institute, 1995); Michael O'Brien and Debbi Palermini, *Guide to Resource Efficient Building* (Portland: Sustainable Building Collaborative, 1993); and presentations at "Building with Values '93" conference (sponsored in part by the Sustainable Building Collaborative), Seattle, November 12–13, 1993.

In the discussion of paper, I used Atossa Soltani and Penelope Whitney, eds., *Cut Waste, Not Trees: How to Save Forests, Cut Pollution and Create Jobs* (San Francisco: Rainforest Action Network, 1995), along with technical reports from the Clean Washington Center and the Northwest Pulp and Paper Association. Resource savings from paper recycling from Robert Cowles Letcher and Mary T. Sheil, "Source Separation and Citizen Recycling," in William D. Robinson, ed., *The Solid Waste Handbook* (New York: John Wiley and Sons, 1986).

## Chapter Five: People and Prices

**Northwest sections:** Population, migration, and natural increase data in this chapter, as elsewhere in the book, is from a database maintained by NEW. This database is compiled from state, provincial, and federal sources. At press time, NEW planned a fully documented publication devoted to regional population issues; it would provide readers with specific documentation of some of the material in this chapter. Among the sources used to compile the NEW population database are the Current Population Reports of the U.S. Bureau of the Census (specifically, series P-25, nos. 139, 304, 460, 957, 1106, and 1111) and published and unpublished information from the Canadian Socio-Economic Information Management System Time Series Data Base provided by the B.C. Ministry of Government Services's B.C. Stats in Victoria. Also among the sources are annual reports on migration published by the Center for Population Research of Portland State University, by the Idaho Secretary of State, and by the Washington State Office of Financial Management; and annual publications on vital statistics from the Center for Health Statistics of the Oregon Department of Human Resources, Center for Health Statistics of the Washington State Department of Health, Center for Vital Statistics and Health Policy of the Idaho Department of Health and Welfare, Division of Vital Statistics of the B.C. Ministry of Health, and the National Center for Health Statistics of the U.S. Public Health Service.

Additional sources on natural increase include Carnegie Council on Adolescent Development, *Great Transitions: Preparing Adolescents for a New Century* (New York: Carnegie Corporation, 1995); Laurie Cawthon, "First Steps Database: Family Planning," Office of Research and Data Analysis, Department of Social and Health Services, Olympia, September 1995; and Institute of Medicine, *The Best Intentions: Unintended Pregnancy and the Well-Being of Children and Families* (Washington, D.C.: National Academy Press, 1995).

Additional sources on migration include Virginia Abernathy, *Population Politics* (New York: Insight Books, 1993); Center for Immigration Studies, "Backgrounder: Immigration-Related Statistics—1995," Washington, D.C., July 1995; ECO Northwest, *Evaluation of No-Growth and Slow-Growth Policies for the Portland Region* (Eugene, Oregon: 1994).

The prices sections of this chapter draw on the work of the subjects interviewed, and of Clifford Cobb, "Fiscal Policy for a Sustainable California Economy," draft, Redefining Progress, San Francisco, 1995. They also draw on research on ecological taxation done by the Worldwatch Institute and the World Resources Institute over the past half decade.

Salmon cost and price from Carolyn Alkire, *The Living Landscape: Wild Salmon as Natural Capital* (Washington D.C.: The Wilderness Society, 1993). Status of Yakima River salmon from, among others, Northwest Water Law and Policy Project, *Water Sustainability in the Columbia River Basin* (Portland: Lewis and Clark College, Northwestern School of Law, 1995). Full costs of gasoline and driving from Todd Litman, *Transportation Cost Analysis: Techniques, Estimates and Implications* (Victoria: Victoria Transport Policy Institute, 1994). Full cost of road map is my own estimate, based on existing price premiums for commercially available high-recycled-content paper. The rent premium Carolyn Alkire pays is estimated by Cliff Cobb, private communication, December 28, 1995.

Failure of progressivity in U.S. federal tax code from, among others, Neil Howe and Phillip Longman, "The Next New Deal," *Atlantic Monthly*, April 1992.

Material on full cost of driving from, among others, Litman, *Transportation Cost Analysis*; Todd Litman, "Marginalizing Insurance Costs as a Transportation Demand Management Measure," Victoria Transport Policy Institute, Victoria, October 12, 1995; and Todd Litman, "Marginalizing and Internalizing Parking Costs as a Transportation Demand Management Measure," Victoria Transport Policy Institute, Victoria, October 12, 1995.

Material on tax shift draws heavily on Cobb, "Fiscal Policy for a Sustainable California Economy." Revenue and rates in existing tax structure from information provided by state, federal, and provincial tax authorities. King County property values from Thomas A. Gihring, "Converting from a Single Rate to a Differential Rate Property Tax," paper presented at Pacific Northwest Regional Economic Conference, Seattle, April 28-30, 1994. Land-value taxation also from Eugene Levin, "Let the State of Washington . . . Look to the Land," Common Ground U.S.A., Seattle, March 1994.

## Chapter Six: Politics

**Personal sections:** I changed some of the names in this chapter.

**Northwest sections:** Regional environmental trends from NEW publications. Mathis Wackernagel and William Rees, *Our Ecological Footprint: Reducing Human Impact on the Earth* (Gabriola Island, B.C.: New Society Publishers, 1995). Political vitality from, among others, publications of Western States Center, Portland; Frances Fox Piven and Richard A. Cloward, *Why Americans Don't Vote* (New York: Pantheon Books, 1988); and Robert D. Putnam, "The Prosperous Community," *American Prospect*, Spring 1993. Voting and recycling rates from "More Northwesterners Recycle Than Vote," *NEW Indicator*, June 1996.

The campaign against Kemano II from, among others, Bev Christensen, *Too Good To Be True: Alcan's Kemano Completion Project* (Vancouver: Talonbooks, 1995), and news articles such as John Goddard, "Sold Down the River," *Harrowsmith*, December 1993.

Environmental justice movement from, among others, Robert D. Bullard, *People of Color Environmental Groups 1994–1995 Directory* (Flint, Michigan: Charles Stewart Mott Foundation, 1994).

Discussion of Henry's Fork Watershed Council draws on Northwest Policy Center, "An Evaluation of the Henry's Fork Watershed Council," Seattle, 1995. Trends in consensus-based watershed dialogues from, among others, William deBuys, "Elements of an Answer," and other articles in *Northern Lights*, Spring 1995; Kirk Johnson, "Forest Partnerships: Seeking Peace in the Woods," *Community and the Environment* (Northwest Policy Center, Seattle), December 1993; and Commission on Resources and the Environment, *A Report on Community-Based Multi-Stakeholder Sustainability Groups in British Columbia* (Victoria: 1995).

Auden quoted in Ken Drushka et al., *Touch Wood: B.C. Forests at the Crossroads* (Madeira Park, B.C.: Harbour Publishing, 1993).

# INDEX

papermaking chemi-
cals, 172, 175
radioactivity, 48
sulfur emissions, 214,
215. *See also* Environ-
mental pollution
Traffic control methods,
78, 105. *See also*
Automobiles
Transportation
all-terrain vehicle use,
280
bicycles, 73, 80,
154–55
by automobile. *See*
Automobiles
by bus, 73, 81, 109
cost/price ratios, 202
modes, comparison, 73
railroads, 41–44, 52,
55
rivers as thoroughfares,
13–14
streets, urban design,
77–78, 109
urban systems, 20. *See
also* Access, High-
ways, Public trans-
portation, Sprawl
Tualatin, OR, Commons,
community center,
109

## U–V

U.S. Government agencies
Bureau of Land Man-
agement, 43, 200
Bureau of Reclamation,
40–41, 46–48, 274
Corps of Engineers, 40,
265
Department of Agricul-
ture, 141, 143
Department of Energy,
169
Federal Housing
Authority, 96
Fish and Wildlife Ser-
vice, 279

Forest Service, 54, 200
National Marine Fish-
eries Service, 270,
271
Soil Conservation Ser-
vice, 138, 141
Umatilla Indians, 267,
271
Umatilla Reservation,
Confederated Tribes.
*See* Confederated
Tribes
Umatilla River, 269
Urban design
desired features, 78–80,
91, 104, 110, 116
pedestrian safety,
amenities, 78–80,
117
photos and public
design awareness,
110
street grids, 78, 109
street trees, land-
scaping, 78. *See also*
Community, Planned
land use, Sprawl
Vancouver Island, B.C.,
38–39, 283
Vancouver, B.C., 6, 20,
34, 42, 65, 101, 123
high–density neighbor-
hoods, 85
West End neighbor-
hood, 70, 72,
77–81, 85–87,
89–90, 103, 106,
123
Yaletown neighbor-
hood, 90. *See also*
Pacific Northwest
Vancouver, Captain
George, 17–18

## W

Walla Walla Indians, 267,
268
Warm Springs Reserva-
tion, 268

Washington County, OR,
Thousand Friends
group activities, 102,
106, 108. *See also*
LUTRAQ
Washington Environ-
mental Council, 260
Washington Public Power
Supply System. *See*
WPPSS
Washington State
air pollution statistics,
208
Department of Social,
Health Services, 190
energy conservation
policies, 211–13
population, 186
Washington Environ-
mental Council, 260
Waste material
as useful "digested"
resources, 130
from housing construc-
tion, 159–60
generated in Wash-
ington, statistics, 180
paper manufacture,
reuse, 175
reduction in food pro-
cessing, shipping,
145, 147. *See also*
Solid waste disposal
Wasted resources
as lost value, 130
auto–related expenses,
219
disposable items, 130,
148, 156
excessive packaging,
130
irrigation–ditch evapo-
ration, 141
planned obsolescence,
151, 155–56
soil erosion, 42, 141,
146, 280, 285.
*See also* Recycling